For Ciro Paoletti

Contents

Introduction

A man who has not been in Italy is always conscious
of an inferiority, from his not having seen what it
is expected a man should see. The grand object of
travelling is to see the shores of the Mediterranean.

> Samuel Johnson, who did not in fact visit Italy,
> in James Boswell's *Life of Johnson*, 11 April 1776

In our way to Milan we stopped at a pretty large town
called Novara . . . here we had a true Italian breakfast
consisting of the large Italian pigeons and tripe
dressed with oil and Parmesan cheese, grapes, figs,
and an excellent polenta which is a kind of pudding
made of the flower of Indian wheat mixed with oil and
cheese.

> Margaret, Viscountess Spencer, 1763

Travel occurs in space and time. This brief history is primarily for
visitors who would like more than the potted history found in most
travel guides. But to do so faces a particular problem for Italy, which is
a country that has not had the long-term unified history of many other
states such as France. Divided for much of its history, Italy, moreover, had major parts that were territories of bigger, often competing,
empires, notably those of Spain and Austria. In addition, modern
tourists rarely 'do' Italy, a country that in fact has too much to offer to
be covered in any one trip. Instead, there is generally a focus for tourists on particular cities and regions. This matches a history much of
which was indeed regional, or, at least, experienced as regional.

To tackle the history of Italy for visitors thus faces the problem
that the regions can get lost if the sole approach is chronological, but
taking a regional approach leads to repetition. The solution here is,

1

first, a history of Italy covering the main developments and organised in a chronological fashion and, second, a brief coverage of the regions where relevant. Within the text, there are also boxes on particular topics.

It is a great pleasure to record over half a century of visiting Italy, beginning in the early 1960s when my parents took me there four times. Most pleasantly this has been from 1979 with Sarah, and we have together visited the Abruzzi, Bologna, the Lipari Islands, Lucca, Modena, Naples, Parma, Rome, Sardinia, Sicily, Turin, Tuscany, Umbria, Venice and Verona. I have benefited from opportunities to lecture in Lombardy, Naples and Tuscany, which introduced me to such pleasures as the superb condiments used in the Adda valley, calm cloisters in Prato and Italian 'new cuisine' restaurants in Naples, and to carry out archival research in Florence, Genoa, Lucca, Modena, Naples, Parma, Turin and Venice.

I am very grateful to Paolo Bernardini, Mike Broers, Luigi Loreto, Ciro Paoletti, Gabriella Poma, Luisa Quartermaine, Guglieo Sanna, Peter Wiseman and Patrick Zutshi for their comments on all or part of an earlier draft. They are not responsible for any errors but, instead, have helped greatly. Duncan Proudfoot has proved an exemplary publisher. This book is dedicated to Ciro Paoletti, a good friend and fellow academic, to mark over fourteen years of friendship and scholarly cooperation.

CHAPTER ONE

Classical Glory: To 476

GEOGRAPHY

Italy's history first becomes different and important with the rise of Rome to imperial power. Prior to then, it had been a case of the general sequences of prehistory and early man, with hunter-gatherers being increasingly replaced by farmers across a future country that was then divided into tribal homelands. This division owed much to the range of tribal groups and to the lack of physical, economic and political agglomeration.

In the case of Italy, the geography was highly unfavourable for cohesion, a situation that remains the case. In particular, there were many mountains, and relatively few plains and river valleys. The most significant was the Po valley, with its sub-Mediterranean climate and cold winter mists, and the relatively flat Lombard plain. There were other plains further south, notably near Rome, the Campagna, now mainly submerged in the urban sprawl; Campania, the plain inland of the Bay of Naples; and in Apulia (Puglia to Italians); but none on that scale.

The plains and river valleys that did exist were divided by the mountains, which were generally forbidding. The Alps, the dramatic geological result of Italy's 'recent' crashing, thanks to continental drift in the Tertiary era, into the rest of Europe, divided Italy from the Continent. The first Roman road to cross the Alps, the Via Claudia Augusta, completed in 46–47 CE (Common Era, AD), crossed the Reschen Pass en route from Verona to modern Augsburg. Another Roman road crossed the Brenner Pass from Austria to Italy from the second century CE and, in 1777, a carriage road was laid out through the pass. No pass across the western Alps was open to wheeled traffic until the Col di Tenda, connecting Nice with Cuneo in Piedmont, in the 1780s, and most until much later. At the order of Napoleon, a road was constructed between 1801 and 1805 over the Simplon Pass between Switzerland and Domodossola in Piedmont. Even then, the pass was closed to traffic each winter from October to late April. The Simplon Tunnel opened for rail travel in 1906.

Further south, the lengthy Apennine chain divided Italy from within. Moreover, this chain in practice was a complex series of mountainous areas. Thanks to this geography, the realisation of Italy to its peoples was that of specific areas, often sharply separated from each other, a situation also seen in Spain. However, in Italy, because there was not the unification seen from the fifteenth century in Spain, there was not the tension between centre and periphery that was to be apparent, notably in rivalry between Castile and both Catalonia and the Basque Provinces. Instead, that tension essentially awaited the period after Italian unification in 1860–70.

Linked to the geography, soil erosion was a major problem, one that led to the depletion of mountain soils that were deposited, instead, in valleys, plains and the sea. This process was to be encouraged when much of the tree cover was cut down, as it was in Italy relatively early in historic time because of the long period of human settlement. As a result, much of upland Italy today is barren, as it has long been, and therefore often badly eroded.

In addition, many valleys are very steep, and the combination of generally relatively short rivers and water produced by snowmelt and/or heavy rain made them difficult to cross prior to modern bridge-building. The situation in river valleys therefore varied greatly by season. There could be major floods, as with those on the River Arno that hit Florence hard in 1740 and 1966. That of Rome in 1870, as well as the malaria that had been responsible for the death of his wife, Anita, in 1849, led Giuseppe Garibaldi to plan in 1875 to divert the River Tiber from Rome and to transform it into a navigable waterway, a plan that was not implemented. Flooding also affected transport, both along and across rivers, disrupted industries, such as milling, that were dependent on water power, damaged the most fertile agricultural areas, and helped lead to malaria.

The difficult terrain greatly accentuated the impact of distance, which itself was considerable by the standards of early man and, indeed, remains so today, although the journey is now far, far faster. Speed was not achieved until the nineteenth century. To travel from the Alps to the Calabrian tip of mainland Italy is to go a very long way, even ignoring the distance added by having to go up and down or round mountain chains, and the many and persistent difficulties involved. To then add the problems posed by a crossing of the Strait of Messina so as to reach Sicily, the largest island in the Mediterranean, was even more serious. In an age before steam, travel by sea was difficult due to contrary winds or no winds. The latter encouraged a reliance on rowing as well as sails. The Strait of Messina between the eastern tip of Sicily and the western of Calabria was probably the source of the legend, first seen in Homer's *Odyssey*, of Scylla, a six-headed monster, and Charybdis, a whirlpool, wrecking ships. There is indeed a natural whirlpool in the Strait. This legend testified to the fear they created and also to the way in which this geography was fixed by legend. So also with the *Isole dei Ciclopi*, the Islands of the Cyclopes, north-east of Catania in Sicily, which were supposedly the rocks thrown at Odysseus' escaping boats by Polyphemus, the newly blinded giant.

Distance and terrain hampered communications, a problem the Romans sought to overcome by means of building roads, the precursors of the *autostrade* built from the mid-1920s when the first was completed connecting Milan to Varese (now the A8). The situation was easier if the terrain was flat. Thus, in the early sixteenth century, special couriers could speed messages from Milan to Venice in twenty-four hours, and even from Rome to Venice across the Apennines in fifty, but these were exceptional timings. Until the major nineteenth-century improvements that arose from railways, steamships, telegraphs and more potent explosives to create tunnels, journeys and messages were generally slow and unreliable. This was particularly so in the winter. Periods of political instability made the situation much worse.

The Apennines were not only an obstacle, a classic view of city-dwellers. They were also a place where many people lived. Indeed, peasants and shepherds lived and worked on the slopes. Long a tension in Italian society, one seen in politics as well as religion, was that of attempts by town-based authorities to control upland areas that they judged marginal and posing problems. This was seen, for example, with the persecution of the Waldensian religious minority in the western Alps, with, more generally, the Counter-Reformation Church in the sixteenth and seventeenth centuries, with 'Enlightenment' government in the eighteenth century, with the Napoleonic regime, and with the new kingdom of Italy from 1861. Although they provided loyal and reliable troops to rulers, including of Piedmont, Naples, Modena and Italy, the mountainous areas of the Alps and the northern Apennines were the major bases of the resistance to Germany and Mussolini in 1943–5. This geographically based cultural tension is still a major factor today.

As a separate issue, on a very different timetable, and as a consequence of geological novelty, notably of the Apennines, Italy also faces the problems created by significant geological instability. Volcanic explosions can enrich the soil, but lava can also produce much devastation. This is especially true of the volcanoes of Etna (Europe's highest volcano, supposedly the consequence of the goddess Athena throwing Sicily at the giant Enkelados) and Vesuvius. Each of them are near major inhabited areas, unlike volcanic islands such as Stromboli. Pompeii and Herculaneum famously fell victim to Vesuvius in 79 CE, while the 1669 eruption of Etna engulfed the city of Catania, ensuring that it was rebuilt in the Baroque style that still makes it distinctive.

Earthquakes have been devastating, as in Friuli in 1511 and 1976, Sicily in 1693 and 1968, Umbria in 1979 and 1997, Naples in 1980, Mantua in 2012 and central Italy in 2016, a list that could be readily extended. In 1908, however, Messina and Reggio di Calabria were destroyed in an earthquake in which 80,000–100,000 people were killed, with 77,000 a reliable lowest estimate. The devastation was greater than that of war and the government did not respond well. In

1915, 30,500 people died when another earthquake devastated central Italy east of Rome.

Personal and collective experiences were moulded by such experiences and threats, as was Italian culture: fatalism and religious devotion were both strengthened. In 1756, Charles Emmanuel III, King of Sardinia and ruler of Piedmont, and his family participated in the celebrations in the cathedral of Turin to give thanks that the city had survived a recent earthquake relatively unscathed. The prediction that Naples would be entirely destroyed by an earthquake in March 1769 threw some of its population into confusion. The churches were full.

For much of Italy's history, disease was also crippling. The first *lazzaretto*, a permanent plague hospital, was opened by Venice in 1423 on the island of Santa Maria di Nazareth (now called *Lazzaretto Vecchio*) opposite the Lido. It later became a shelter for the poor when the plague ceased being a problem. The second *lazzaretto* in Venice followed in 1468. The Venetian system was quickly adopted by Genoa and elsewhere. Plague went on hitting until 1743 when the last epidemic in Italy killed about 47,000 people in Sicily and Calabria. That year, Venice sent warships into the Adriatic to prevent the arrival of ships from infected areas and that winter prohibited trade with the rest of Italy. Her regulations did not respect rank and Duke Francesco III of Modena was forced into quarantine. In 1781, major precautions were taken in Italy in order to prevent the spread of plague from the Balkans.

EARLY HUMANS

There were early sites in Italy, with finds of Neanderthals, a separate branch of the *Homo* genus, in Circeo and Saccopastore in west-central Italy. Sites of early humans have also been found, notably in Grimaldi in Calabria and Romanelli in Apulia. The earliest evidence for human habitation in Sicily dates to about 13,000 BCE. During the last ice age, Italy was well south of the main ice sheet. As the ice receded further north in about 8300 BCE, the improved climate ensured deciduous woodland and plentiful game. This was a benign environment for early humans.

Farming spread from the Middle East into southern Italy by about 6200 BCE, when the first farming villages appeared there and in Sicily, and into the rest of Italy and Sardinia by 5000 BCE. Pigs, cattle and other animals were domesticated, staple crops, including barley, put under cultivation, and pottery developed. However, in the third and second millennia BCE, the lack of intensive, irrigated agriculture kept population density in Italy relatively low, while the distance and difficulties of travel further ensured that there was no early consolidation of political control, as, in contrast, there was in Egypt, Mesopotamia (Iraq) and China.

Nevertheless, Italy was part of the trading world of Copper Age Europe (c. 4500–2500 BCE). There was copper-working in central Italy, where ceramic remains have also been discovered. In Early Bronze Age Europe (c. 2500–1500 BCE), there was trading from Italy with Greece, transalpine Europe and Spain. Sardinian copper was exported to Greece, notably Mycenaean Greece, from which pottery was imported, as it also was to Sicily, which was already a major agricultural region. Within Italy, fortified settlements developed, followed by towns. Iron technology followed, making weapons and tools more effective.

Italy was affected by other wider developments, notably an influx of Indo-European groups migrating over a long period of time, at least as far back as 2000 BCE, such as the groups who produced what has been described in archaeological terms as the Villanovan culture of Emilia-Romagna and Umbria. Such archaeological descriptions are very difficult to identify with any specific ethnic or linguistic group. Having spread to Greece, variants of the Phoenician alphabet were introduced to mainland Italy. The first example of Greek script comes from a site less than 15 miles east of Rome, at Osteria dell' Osa in an archaeological context dateable to between 950 and 770 BCE. The Phoenicians themselves established trading posts in western Sicily in the period 900 to 700 BCE. Italian numerical systems were also heavily influenced by Greece.

ETRURIA

Of the tribes, the Etruscans became important by 800 BCE. Living in what was in effect a confederation of city-states, they became dominant in the centre of the peninsula by the seventh century, and expanded north into the Po Valley and south to Campania round Naples. Etruscan power peaked in possibly about 530, with the repulse from the Greek city of Cumae in 524 a blow. Over the following two centuries, the Etruscans were affected by Gallic (or Gaulish) expansion from the north and by the opposition of local Italian peoples, notably the Romans to the south who expanded to control southern Etruria by 350.

Etruscan civilisation has since always been overshadowed by that of Rome, although the latter initially drew heavily on the Etruscans, who were impressive. They could certainly cast iron, construct arches and produce portraits. A lack of most literary records leaves the Etruscans obscure and contributes to their fascination. Their tombs remain impressive and can be readily visited, as at Tarquinia and Cerveteri, as well as the early Etruscan complex of Poggio Civitate near Siena. Museums with Etruscan remains are well worth a visit, although there can be a failure by visitors to connect compared to the response to the Romans, about whom far more is known.

The Italian tribes were affected, sometimes challenged, by the independent city-states of *Magna Graecia* that were established along the coasts of Sicily (from 734 BCE) and southern Italy by Greek settlers. These settlers were possibly affected by overpopulation in Greece and/or were seeking new opportunities. The ruins of several of the cities, notably of Agrigento, Segesta and Syracuse in Sicily, of Paestum on the Gulf of Salerno, and of Metaponto and Policoro in Basilicata, remain most impressive. The last are the less well known, in large part because Basilicata is not a classic destination. Pythagoras founded a school at Metaponto. Indeed, compared to these settlements, Rome and those of Etruria must have seemed rather primitive, rather as Macedon and Epirus to the north were seen from Greece.

Rome was not the only expanding power. Peoples north of the

Alps, known as Gauls or Celts, moved south, indeed sacking Rome in 390 BCE. Under Dionysius I (r. 405–367 BCE), the city of Syracuse conquered most of Sicily in the 390s, expanding into southern Italy in the 380s.

THE RISE OF ROME

Etruria was to succumb to the rise of Rome, initially a small settlement in the lower Tiber valley. Allegedly founded in 753 BCE by Romulus and Remus, descendants of Aeneas, a royal refugee from the fall of Troy, there is evidence of a village on the Palatine Hill by 850 BCE and suggestions of earlier settlements. Rome was ruled by the Tarquins, kings who were Corinthian by origin, until the last, Tarquin, was driven out by Latin nobles who created a republic. The conventional date, 509 BCE, is less reliable than 507, which was given by the historian Polybius on the strength of well-informed earlier Greek sources.

As was the case with cities elsewhere in the Ancient World, this republic was ruled in practice by an oligarchy. Thereafter, tensions between oligarchy and more popular politics interacted with rivalries within the oligarchic élite, although the ends, as well as means, of power were at issue.

Crucially, the Romans proved formidable warriors, and much of the history of Italy indeed reflects its repeated moulding, and remoulding, through war and its consequences. The Romans were particularly impressive not only for the training and discipline that enabled them to march at a formidable rate, to deploy in a variety of planned formations, including the *testudo*, the means to conduct sieges, and to perform complex and effective manoeuvres on the battlefield, but also for the ability to deploy and operate in a range of physical and military environments, in part by fort and road-building. Gnaeus Domitius Corbulo (d. 67 CE), a general who fought in Germany and conquered Armenia, observed that the pick was the weapon with which to beat the enemy. Trajan's Column in Rome shows Roman soldiers digging. Roman forces were trained and adept at building marching camps every time they stopped.

These generally occurred at 15-mile intervals, the average daily rate of march expected of a legion. The camps followed a standardised pattern and, in what would today be referred to as a standard operational procedure, each element of the marching group understood its role in the construction process. The camps provided security and good communications on their line of advance. Many camps became the bases of settlements.

In 396 BCE, the Romans captured Veii, one of the Etruscan League of Twelve Cities. Having subjugated other peoples who were made to become allies, Rome unified Italy in campaigning that also entailed resistance to Celtic attacks from the north and to invasion, on behalf of the Greek settlements, in 280 BCE by Pyrrhus, King of Epirus in Greece, an effective general whose army included elephants. This sentence covers several hundred years of history and presents, as a smooth process, what was in practice quite a difficult one. Rome encountered considerable resistance. Rome's major opponent in the interior, the Samnites of southern Italy, proved a formidable foe, with wars in 343–341, 328–304 and 298–290 BCE, and a key Roman victory at Sentinum in 295. As a consequence, the Samnites were forced to become allies. Rome cemented its position by establishing colonies (settlements) of Latin citizens at key places, and by building roads, notably the Via Appia from Rome across the Apennines to Capua in 312 BCE, and the Via Flaminia from Rome to Rimini on the Adriatic in 220.

Roman victory over the Samnites permitted pressure on the Greek cities of southern Italy, especially Tarentum (Taranto). Although victorious at Heraclea (280) and Ausculum (279), Pyrrhus was defeated in 275 BCE at Maleventum (which changed its name to Beneventum after this victory). He then returned to Epirus. This led to the Roman capture of Tarentum (272), to the other Greek cities coming to terms with Rome, to the establishment of more Latin colonies, and to the extension of the Via Appia, so that most of Italy was under Roman control by 250 BCE. The speed was far slower than in the Piedmontese conquest/unification of Italy between 1859 and 1870 CE, but the

Romans did not benefit from external intervention and support as the Piedmontese did, respectively, from France and Prussia. Nor was technology at the same pitch.

Incessant warfare helped ensure that Rome's culture, public memory, public spaces, religious cults, society and political system were militaristic. Indeed, in many respects, Rome was Italy's Sparta. It praised martial values, and promoted and honoured politicians accordingly.

Roman success against the Greeks brought them into rivalry with Carthage, a Phoenician settlement founded near modern Tunis that had become, by the third century BCE, the major maritime and imperial power in the western Mediterranean. Already, in 410–405 BCE, the Carthaginians had invaded western Sicily, seizing most Greek cities including Agrigento, while, in 409, they established a permanent presence at Palermo. There were also Phoenician settlements in southern Sardinia, notably at Caralis and Tharros.

The Romans eventually triumphed in the three Punic Wars with Carthage. These were wide-ranging struggles that involved conflict in mainland Italy, Sicily, Spain and North Africa. In the First Punic War (264–241 BCE), Rome's struggle with Carthage focused on the control of Sicily, which then, and repeatedly, suffered from being a meeting place of civilisations. In this struggle, the Romans were hit hard initially by their lack of naval power and this led them to develop a navy that proved able to defeat Carthaginian fleets off Sicily. In battle, the Romans rammed their opponents and then used the plank-like *corvus*, which had a spike that attached it to the enemy ship, to form a bridge between ships, and thus enable rapid boarding of the enemy vessel. War at sea was thereby transformed into land battle afloat to the benefit of Rome. However, the *corvus* appears to have been a one-war wonder. Used to advantage in battles in the First Punic War, the *corvus* was not employed thereafter, possibly because it had been linked to the loss of many Roman ships in storms.

Naval strength provided Rome with a crucial margin of advantage that allowed it to conquer Sicily and, more tangentially, to project power to North Africa, although the expeditionary force sent there was defeated, in part by the Carthaginian use of war-elephants. Having lost that war and ceded Sicily, which became Rome's first province, Carthage faced a rebellion by its mercenaries. As an instance of the serendipitous way in which the Roman Empire expanded as opportunities were exploited, this rebellion gave the Romans the opportunity to annex Corsica and Sardinia in 227 BCE. In his *Histories*, Polybius recorded, 'The Romans, from the moment they concerned themselves with the sea, began to entertain designs on Sardinia.' Their horizons literally expanded.

Subsequently Carthage and Rome came to compete over southern and eastern Spain. This competition, which touched off the Second Punic War (218–201 BCE), reflected the extent to which Rome's ambition increasingly extended over the Mediterranean. This extension indeed proved more significant to Rome than expansion north over the Alps. Hannibal (247–183 BCE), the key Carthaginian general, having done well in Spain, decided to attack the base of Roman power in Italy itself, and thus to secure the Carthaginian achievements. To do so, he marched across southern France, crossed the Alps, a formidable undertaking, in 218 BCE, and attacked the Romans in Italy. Hannibal bringing his elephants across the Alps helped posterity to see this as an epic struggle, although only one survived the crossing and it died soon after.

Hannibal's arrival created an acute crisis for Rome. His highly professional force was ably led and gained control of the dynamic of campaigning. Major Roman armies were defeated at the River Trebia (218), Lake Trasimene (217), Cannae (216), and Herdonea (210). Cannae proved one of the biggest defeats of antiquity, with a Roman army having its flanks driven in, and then, the victims crushed together, being slowly and systematically slaughtered. There were about 50,000 Roman casualties. The sites of these battles were long and eagerly sought by travellers with an interest, from childhood education, in the Classical world. Defeat led some of Rome's allies, including the city of Capua, to desert. In Sicily, Syracuse, which had maintained a semi-autonomous status after the First Punic War, backed the Carthaginians, which led to an eventually successful Roman siege of the city from 213 to 211.

Defeat also created acute political pressures within Rome. Different commanders and strategies were pushed to the fore in a desperate search for solutions. Deciding whether or not to engage in battle was a key choice, the avoidance of battle being given the name Fabian with reference to the commander Quintus Fabius Maximus, known as Cunctator, 'the Delayer', who advocated it. Brought to the fore after Hannibal's victory at Lake Trasimene, Fabius avoided battle on the plains, preferring to rely on attritional conflict in the hills where Rome's infantry was particularly valuable as opposed to Carthaginian cavalry. Popular impatience led to the abandonment of his strategy and then to disaster at Cannae, after which Fabius was reappointed.

In the event, Hannibal failed not because of defeat in battle in Italy but as a result of his inability to translate victory in battle into his intended outcome: the collapse of Rome and its territorial system. Hannibal's army was small and lacked a siege train. Advancing from Spain, Hasdrubal's army was defeated by the Romans at the Metaurus (207) and was thus unable to join Hannibal in Italy, and naval supply to Hannibal's army was effectively blocked by the Romans. Moreover, the Romans quickly freed a great number of slaves so that they could join the Roman army. The city of Rome proved too strong to storm and most of Rome's allies remained firm.

The Carthaginian system was brought down, first by Roman successes in Spain, where Scipio won the decisive battle of Ilipa (206), and then because of a transfer of the war to North Africa in 204. There, in 202, Scipio won a crucial victory over Hannibal at Zama. The Romans had learned how to thwart Carthaginian elephants. Hannibal had needed to return there in order to address the threat posed by Scipio who proved more successful than the Roman force that invaded North Africa during the First Punic War. Scipio was thereafter called Africanus. Rome's victory in the Second Punic War left Rome dominant in the western Mediterranean, including in east and south Spain. It was not thenceforth to face so wide-ranging an opponent, and was therefore better able to direct resources against opponents.

The large size of the army of republican Rome derived from the organisation of the peoples of Italy into various citizen and allied statuses, all of which were required to serve in the Roman army. Like the Han rulers of China, the Romans believed in a mass army based on the adult males of the farming population, which provided huge reserves of manpower for use against Carthage. Maybe up to a quarter of a million Italians were in the Roman army in 31 BCE, nearly a quarter of the men of military age.

Having defeated Hannibal, the Roman legionaries, with their short stabbing iron sword, heavy javelin and shield, fighting together shoulder to shoulder, were involved in conflict further afield. Benefiting from superior manpower, resources, willpower and organisation, they had taken control of the eastern Mediterranean, Egypt, Gaul (France) and Spain by 30 CE, following up with most of Britain and the Balkans by 100 CE. Julius Caesar was the key figure in the conquest of Gaul, most dramatically by overcoming Vercingetorix, his major opponent, in 52 BCE.

Caesar also launched expeditions against Britain in 55 and 54 BCE. In 55 BCE, Caesar did not move from his precarious beachhead in Kent. The Romans were victorious in hard fighting, but the damage done to their ships by equinoctial gales, and the scale of the resistance, led Caesar to come to terms with the local tribes. In 54 BCE, he invaded anew with a larger force, benefiting from his opponents' naval weakness, which meant that they could not contest the passage of the English Channel. Moving from the beachhead, Caesar defeated the local tribal leader and imposed a settlement. In 43 CE, approximately 40,000 troops landed unopposed and the Britons were defeated, the Emperor Claudius coming along to take the credit.

However, defeat in Germany in 9 CE, and the lack of staying power east of the River Euphrates in modern Iraq, demonstrated in the 110s CE, led, eventually, to a shift to a policy of consolidation and fixed, defensive frontiers. Formidable systems of walls and fortresses were designed to provide both sites for defence and bases for attack.

Meanwhile, the word *Italia* was applied to what is now Italy. This was a major shift from the earlier period when the Romans had referred to northern Italy as Cisalpine Gaul, i.e. Gaul on the Italian side of the Alps, as opposed to Transalpine Gaul, i.e. modern France. The defeat of the Cimbri at the battle of Vercellae at the confluence of the Po and Sesia rivers in 101 BCE meant that northern Italy was no longer Celtic.

THE END OF THE REPUBLIC

While the process of conquest continued, the Roman republic had collapsed, as competing military commanders, first Marius and Sulla, and then Pompey and Caesar, pushed force to the fore as the means to settle political issues within Rome. As later with France and Napoleon in the 1790s, the intertwining of politics and the military proved a key problem. Ambitious politicians sought military command on the frontiers, and then tried to have resources directed to their campaigning. They also pushed forward the empire, often taking an aggressive stance on their own account. Indeed, in the nineteenth century, British imperial figures who acted in this fashion, such as Sir Charles Napier, were to be referred to as proconsular in a direct reference to the Romans.

The victories of Gaius Marius (157–86 BCE) in Spain, North Africa and Gaul led to his being repeatedly elected Consul and supreme commander (104–101 BCE). He changed the army from a duty of citizenship to a semi-professional body, which encouraged the willingness of the troops to identify with the army and to follow generals. Marius played a major role in politics, notably from 100 BCE until his death. Lucius Cornelius Sulla (138–78 BCE) was another general-turned-politician. The historian Plutarch noted that Sulla was regarded, when Proconsul of the province of Cilicia, as displaying 'a vulgar and ill-timed display of arrogance' in his treatment of neighbouring Parthia. Such conduct was not atypical for Roman officials and generals. A rival of Marius,

Sulla captured Rome when the latter sought to thwart his career and defeated his opponents in civil wars in the 80s BCE, although Spain remained under the control of Marius's protégés. Dictator from 81 to 79 BCE, the somewhat grim Sulla tried to control power for the benefit of a senatorial oligarchy, and thereby limit the power of the people and the tribunes.

There were major divisions in Roman politics, notably tensions within the oligarchy and between the oligarchs and the bulk of the population. These were not, however, the same divisions as those of civil conflict several centuries earlier. At the same time, alongside a tendency to see politics in the structural terms of social divisions, it is necessary to note important differences over policy within each social group, a point that is also valid for later periods of Italian history.

Gaining success, as Julius Caesar very much did in Gaul and sought to do in Britain, as Gnaeus Pompey (the Great) did in Spain and against Mediterranean piracy, and as M. Licinius Crassus sought to do in Syria, commanders then used their resulting reputation to pursue their ambitions in Rome. Inherently, this was an unstable process. The military was factionalised, and the factionalisation very much focused on the ambitions of men who were not interested in compromise which, indeed, they understood as likely to cause a loss of face. Competition cascaded down the decades, as military factionalism sustained enmities. Pompey (106–48 BCE) had backed Sulla and was sent by him to overcome Marius's supporters in Sicily and Africa. Pompey and M. Licinius Crassus joined Julius Caesar in the First Triumvirate (55 BCE), an agreement to share power, notably over Rome's areas of military activity and in support of the Roman people, an agreement that pushed the Senate (oligarchs) aside.

This pact, however, did not last. Defeated at Carrhae by the Parthians in 53 BCE, Crassus was killed. In turn, Pompey, who presented himself as the champion of the Senate, and Caesar went to war with each other in 49 BCE, Caesar leading his troops across the River Rubicon (near Rimini) from Cisalpine Gaul into Italy. He won a key victory over Pompey at Pharsalus (48 BCE) in Greece. The civil war continued even after Pompey was killed, as his sons' supporters fought on, notably in Spain and North Africa, only to be defeated.

The new situation, however, proved unstable ('however', as so often, serving the historian as an appropriate word). Caesar, the leading *popularis*, although himself a patrician, very much associated with the plebeians, while his opponents, most prominently Brutus and Cassius, the leading *optimates*, sought an emphasis on a republic directed by the aristocracy. This division led to Caesar's assassination in Rome on the Ides of March (15 March) in 44 BCE, and then to a civil war in which a triumvirate of Caesar's supporters totally defeated the conspirators at Philippi (42 BCE) in Greece.

In turn, the triumvirate fell out. Its weakest member, Lepidus, was pushed aside, while Mark Antony allied with Cleopatra, ruler of Egypt, only to be defeated in a great naval battle at Actium on the west coast of Greece in 31 BCE by the forces of the third triumvir, Caesar's heir and adopted son, Gaius Octavius, also called Caesar. The last was the eventual winner of the struggle and became Augustus. This is a term that is difficult to define. It is best to translate as 'the Implementer' or 'the Increaser' because the word comes from the Latin verb *augeo*, meaning to implement, to increase and to render greater, while 'Eminence' is employed to define something already greater or more important than surrounding people or things. Augustus was the most powerful general. He pursued Mark Antony to Egypt where Mark Antony and Cleopatra both committed suicide. Egypt was to be a key possession, notably as a major source of grain for Rome. Octavian had already defeated Sextus Pompey, a son of Pompey the Great, in Sicily in 36 BCE.

AUGUSTUS AND THE COMING OF THE EMPIRE
The conqueror of Egypt and the Balkans, Augustus boasted of bringing peace to Rome and Italy itself, and certainly his period in power was far more stable than the preceding half-century. He brought reform and sought to beautify Rome. The governmental system was complex. Augustus had neither palace, nor court, nor regalia. The machinery of the republic continued to operate, and his military command was

formally limited in both space and time. His personal position, like his personal popularity, was unique, but that did not make him an emperor in any meaningful sense. To refer to Augustus as emperor is to anticipate what his successors turned the system into.

Lasting stability eluded them. In part, this was due to divisions within the ruling family and to the inadequacies of his successors, notably Caligula (r. 37–41 CE), who was either mad or behaved in a way that critics could present as mad. Under Caligula, Hellenistic court practices were introduced. He was assassinated. The divisions interacted with tensions within the ruling élite, tensions that brought together ideological differences, kinship rivalries, links within and into the ruling family, and particular political issues.

These inadequacies hit hard at Augustus's creation of a position that was associated with the continuation of republican traditions, institutions and rhetoric, an association that required effective leadership. In his *Pharsalia*, an epic on the civil war between Caesar and Pompey, Lucan (39–65 CE), a favourite of Nero (r. 54–68 CE) from a wealthy background, who took part in the failed conspiracy of Piso against the Emperor and was made to commit suicide, blamed this civil war for Rome not being even more successful. Lucan added, 'if now in Italian cities the houses are half-demolished and the walls tottering, and the mighty stones of mouldering dwellings cumber the ground', that was also the responsibility of internal strife. Rebels, such as Lucius Clodius Macer, who, in 68 CE, launched an unsuccessful attempt to replace Nero, argued that they were opposed to a particular ruler and not to the Roman constitution.

There was the long-standing problem of military control. The government's desire to monopolise force and to insist on strict central control faced the problem of autonomous frontier units whose commanders could launch bids for power. This was very clearly shown in 68–9 CE when the unpopularity of Nero, and then his death, led four commanders to seize their opportunity. Vespasian (r. 69–79), originally backed by the legions in Syria and subsequently also by those on the Danube, was the eventual victor, creating the new and effective Flavian imperial dynasty (r. 69–96). However, the practice of the army making and unmaking emperors was now entrenched.

The capital of a far-flung empire, Rome became multi-ethnic, as did its army. In the first century CE, much of the recruiting in Italy occurred among the population of northern Italy, especially in the Po river valley region. After then, the bulk of the legionaries (regulars) ceased to be Italian.

In Italy, as elsewhere, the Romans produced an identikit infra-structure of solidly built roads and aqueducts, as well as theatres, tombs, baths and other public buildings. Much is still visible to tourists, albeit as stone husks and fragments that do not capture the life, energy and rituals centred on these buildings, nor their splendour when new and decorated. Tourists will have their favourite Roman sites, both in Rome and elsewhere, for example the imposing amphi-theatre in Verona, which is the (hot) setting for opera, that in Caserta, the frescoes in the Villa Oplontis near Naples, and the recent extensive underground finds in Naples. Remains distant from Rome capture the imprint of the culture and the strength of its model.

SLAVERY

Alongside benign accounts of the Roman Empire, it is important to note its total reliance on slavery, although a reliance on slavery was also true of other empires, while the Romans, at least, established firm laws about slavery, including the possibility of personal eman-cipation. Given the arduous physical nature of much work in Roman society, the widespread nature of slavery allowed a politics in which there were slaves at the bottom of the ladder, while non-slaves could enjoy citizenship and status, and, under the republic, a measure of democracy. Roman generals boasted of making slaves. Julius Caesar wrote of selling tens of thousands of Transalpine Celts into slavery, while Lucius Aemilius Paullus, the conqueror of Macedon in 168 BCE, reportedly sold into slavery 150,000 of the population of Epirus, which he had plundered in 167 BCE. These sales brought them great wealth. The key requirements for slaves were for constitution, rowing galleys, household service, agricultural tasks, for example as shepherds in Apulia, mining (a particularly grim fate) and as craftsmen. Some slaves were born to existing slaves, and others obtained from war, conquest, trade or as punishment. There were both private slaves and slaves of the state.

There were frequent slave revolts, the most famous being that of the Thracian-born Spartacus, who was enslaved for desertion from the army and became a gladiator before leading a major uprising in 73 BCE. He built up a large army, possibly 90,000 strong, and, advancing along the length of the Italian peninsula and devastating the great estates, vanquished a number of Roman forces before being defeated and killed in 71 BCE at a battle in Lucania by the Praetor, Crassus. As an instance of the exemplary punishment the Romans sought and demonstrated, large numbers of Spartacus's followers were crucified and their bodies left hanging along the Appian Way. Such punishment was to be more famously inflicted on Jesus. Another type of punishment, usually the fate of defeated leaders, was to be paraded through Rome as one of the spoils in a 'triumph', as a victorious general was honoured. The defeated leaders were then generally killed, as happened to Vercingetorix, who was strangled. Violence was very much part of the Roman way.

The Spartacus rebellion remains very important to modern views on ancient Rome, notably as a result of Stanley Kubrick's film *Spartacus* (1960) and Rome was made dramatically accessible by this means. From this perspective, slavery was a crucial depiction of the wrongness of a political system that also crucified Jesus, a point repeatedly made by Christians when they referred to Rome before its conversion to Christianity. Similar assumptions and values were advanced in other films, such as *Ben-Hur* (1925 and 1959), *Demetrius and the Gladiators* (1954), *Gladiator* (2000), and the American television series *Spartacus: Blood and Sand* (2010).

There were other slave revolts in Italy, notably in Sicily in 139–132 BCE and 104–100 BCE, but they were all crushed. The former led to a fall in the grain shipments from Sicily that kept the Roman population quiescent, and the anger of the Romans was shown in the slaughter of the last 20,000 of the rebel slaves when they surrendered in 132 BCE. Sicily was also a key wine-producing region. More generally, the murder of masters by slaves helped lead to a fear of slaves, resulting in the law that in such cases all the household slaves should be executed. Despite laws that sought to restrict brutality, for example the *Lex Petronia*, which denied masters the right to sell their slaves to fight wild beasts in the arena, there could also be a casual brutality to slaves with the latter generally treated as if they were animals. The spectator sport of gladiators fighting each other to the death was part of this brutal world. There was also the brutality to animals seen in games in which they were killed for entertainment.

THE ROMAN SYSTEM

Slavery was the most dramatic instance of the inherent inequalities of Roman life, inequalities repeated daily and very apparent in all the details and ideas of life. To be a citizen might be to have a basis of equality, but, as with Britain in the nineteenth century, the situation was very different for rich and poor, men and women, parents and children, eldest sons and others. Thus, although not slaves, free tenant farmers were in a bad position economically as well as having to pay rents and taxes. They were to become serfs. In contrast, major landowners and tenants-in-chief were in a far more attractive situation.

This helped make the equality propounded by Christianity particularly subversive. Long persecuted, with Christians publicly martyred, monotheistic (one God) Christianity also challenged the system of the Olympian gods, a polytheistic system that allowed the incorporation of the emperors into the religious pantheon. Christian churches from the period, such as the fourth-century basilica in Aquileia, have impressive mosaics depicting biblical scenes. There would have been more remains bar for later rebuilding. Although certain rural areas continued to follow pagan Roman cults until the end of the sixth century, most of Italy was Christianised by the end of the fourth.

Emperor-worship did not prevent the removal of individual emperors by murder, conspiracy or rebellion. This was already true with early emperors, with Caligula, Claudius and Nero. Emperors who were most effective, for example Vespasian (r. 69–79), Titus (r. 79–81), Trajan (r. 98–117), Hadrian (r. 117–38) and Septimius Severus (r. 193–211), won victory in battle, and the resulting prestige proved the lubricant of obedience. As a consequence, defeats challenged stability, and most clearly so when emperors were killed on campaign, as with Julian the Apostate (r. 361–3), who was killed in battle against the Sassanid Persians.

ROMAN MAPPING

The Romans inherited Greek knowledge about the world. Their realisation that their known world was only a small portion of the globe meant that the Greeks appreciated that the world needed exploring and mapping. Writing in about 15 CE, Strabo described the Greeks' interpretation of geographical thought as developed by, and under, the Romans. He wrote about Crates of Mallos, a Greek philosopher who, in about 150 BCE, had made a large globe in Rome at least three metres (nine feet) in diameter that depicted four balancing continents, one in each quarter of the world, but all separated by water. The idea that the world had to balance encouraged the long-standing belief in a great Southern Continent.

Ptolemy (c. 90–c. 168 CE), a Greek geographer who worked in Alexandria under Roman rule, drew up a world gazetteer that included an estimate of geographical coordinates. Ptolemy's depiction of Britain benefited from Roman conquest from 43 CE.

Prolific surveyors, the Romans were capable of drawing to scale and they used maps for a number of purposes. There was a close connection in the Roman world between mapmaking and imperial conquest and rule, and between what purported to be world maps and pretensions to world power. The value of display was captured by the large-scale plan of the city of Rome, the *Forma Urbis Romae*, which was incised on a wall for public view.

The Romans' accumulation of information reflected the range of their military and governmental systems. It was necessary to understand the empire if it were to be administered effectively. Flavius Vegetius, the author of the fourth-century CE *Epitoma Rei Militaris*, stated that a general must have 'tables drawn up exactly which show not only the distances in numbers of steps, but also the quality of the paths, shorter routes, what lodging is to be found there and the mountains and rivers'.

The *Tabula Peutingeriana*, a twelfth-century copy of a fourth-century CE Roman road map, was a route planner, not a topographical map, and therefore adopts a strip form. The map depicts the mountains and shows roads centring on particular cities, such as Taranto.

A less well-known source is the *Ravenna Cosmography*, a list of more than 5,000 place names covering the empire, drawn up in about 700 CE by an anonymous cleric at Ravenna. It has been suggested that the compiler had access to a range of official maps.

DECLINE

The Romans had never been invariably victorious. Indeed, there had been a series of spectacular defeats, notably of Crassus by the Parthians at Carrhae in 53 BCE, and of Varus by the Germans in the Teutoburger Wald in 9 CE, a defeat in which three legions had been lost. These defeats had put paid to particular attempts at expansion or had done so at least for a while. In contrast, attacks from 'barbarians' outside the empire became pressing from the late second century CE, with the Marcomanni and Quadi invading northern Italy in 167–70. The Roman world was an attractive target. It suffered a particularly harsh invasion crisis in the 250s that led to a territorial division of the empire as local solutions were sought for its defence.

Nevertheless, the invasions were a protracted process, and, for a long time, the Romans were successful in recovering from attack. The Emperor Aurelian (r. 270–5) brought a measure of recovery, and, thanks to him, Rome itself in the 270s received a new multi-towered wall. Diocletian (r. 284–305) sought to provide delegated leadership by co-opting colleagues, creating a system of two senior and two junior emperors. However, this system eventually led to a permanent division between the eastern and western parts of the empire. The centre of power moved to the new capital of Byzantium (later Constantinople), founded by Constantine I in 330. He had converted to Christianity in 312, a conversion followed by the downgrading of paganism. This conversion greatly disrupted notions of continuity, and the divisiveness that resulted weakened the empire when it should have been concentrating on external threats. Byzantium became the city of the new, and Rome that of the old.

THE GREAT QUESTION

'It was at Rome, on the fifteenth of October 1764, as I sat musing amidst the ruins of the Capitol, while the bare-footed friars were singing Vespers in the Temple of Jupiter, that the idea of writing the decline and fall of the City first started to my mind.'

Edward Gibbon explained, in his *Memoirs*, the genesis of *The Decline and Fall of the Roman Empire*, a multi-volume study which first appeared between 1776 and 1788 and became the greatest work of post-Classical history. It was understandable that Gibbon should focus on Rome because its decline was the great question for European historians. The reasons still divide historians, and notably the degree to which internal factors contributed and also the extent to which the 'barbarians' brought cataclysmic change as opposed to greater continuity.

The less wealthy and populous Western Roman Empire proved less able to cope with 'barbarian' attack, especially because mistrust helped prevent the East from supporting the West. The failure to hold the Rhine and Danube frontiers led to pressure on Italy, pressure that was difficult to meet as so much of the army was committed to the frontiers or to other provinces. Under pressure from the Huns further east, the Visigoths under Alaric invaded Italy in 401, sacking Rome in 410 after the city, whose wall had held off Alaric, was starved into submission. Italy was then extensively ravaged by invaders: Goths, Huns and Vandals, a Germanic tribe who plundered Rome in 455 and seized Sicily in 468. Under Attila, the Huns, in 452, destroyed the major city of Aquileia, from which people fled to the shelter of nearby coastal marshy areas and eventually to Venice.

There was also political instability, with nineteen emperors in the West between 394 and 476. Power was generally held by military leaders, several of whom, including Odoacer, were 'barbarians'. Moreover, military, political and administrative links with former provinces ended. Odoacer deposed Romulus Augustulus, the last Roman emperor in the West, in 476. The emperors had taken refuge at Ravenna, which was less exposed to attack than Rome, but that could not be held. 'Barbarian' pressure on Rome was not due to problems unique to the latter. There was a more general process of attack on settled societies, one also seen with Han China. At the same time, some of the issues debated, such as the impact of Christianity, were specific to Rome.

Imperial Rome was gone but, from the sixth century, Byzantium was able to regain and maintain control over much of southern Italy until the end of the eleventh century. This helped provide an afterlife for both the Roman Empire and for the links with Greece that had contributed to Rome's cultural dynamism. The power or influence of Byzantium was also seen further north, notably in Ravenna and Venice. Ravenna is well worth visiting for the Byzantine mosaics, the Klimts of the Ancient World, preserved in its World Heritage Sites. Particularly impressive ones from the fifth century can be visited in the *Mausoleo di Galla Placidia*, the *Battistero degli Ariani*, the *Battistero Neoniano*, the *Museo Arcivescovile* and, from the sixth century, in the *Basilica di San Vitale* and the *Basilica di Sant' Apollinare Nuovo*. Byzantine-Greek abbeys were found across much of Italy, for example the *Monastero Esarchico di Santa Maria* at Grottaferrata, south-east of Rome, which was founded in 1004.

REMEMBERING ROME

Moreover, the memory and image of Imperial Rome were to play a key role in later presentations of Italy. This was especially the case with the Holy Roman Empire, a central political presence and symbol in Europe from its inception at Rome by Charlemagne in 800 to its end in 1806. Rome's influence was more wide-ranging. Imperial figures, such as Napoleon I, drew on the legacy of Imperial Rome, or their view of it; whereas republics and limited monarchies proved readier to look to Republican Rome. Thus, the new American republic had a senate. Furthermore, the painters of revolutionary France, such as Jacques Louis David (1748–1825), who had studied in Rome, drew on the iconography and images of the Roman republic, as in his *The Oath of the Horatii* (1784) and *The Intervention of the Sabine Women* (1799). Napoleon I, for whom David was court painter, enjoyed Roman echoes.

In the nineteenth century, Europeans appropriated Imperial Rome as a model as they spread their empires. Officials, both colonial governors and diplomats, were apt to adopt a proconsular role, regarding themselves as bringers of civilisation, assumptions also seen with American expansionism. In particular, the British Empire sought to echo that of Classical Rome.

The *Risorgimento* ('Rising Again') was strongly grounded in the idea of a Roman revival, and Roman glory and heritage were always mentioned in its speeches, letters and works. Thus, it is no surprise that for the Fascists, who came to power under Benito Mussolini (1883–1945) in 1922, the concept of national rebirth through the sacrifice of blood could be given a greater historical resonance, sense of purpose and validation, by looking back to Imperial Rome. This was a major theme in the language, mindset and iconography of Italian Fascism. The *fasces* or axes used as a symbol of Fascism were a direct reference to ancient Rome. Marshal Rodolfo Graziani (1882–1955), who was appointed Vice-Governor in Cyrenaica (eastern Libya) in 1930, presented his very harsh 'pacification' of the colony, the last stage of its conquest, in terms of 'Romans' subduing 'barbarians', and in 1932 referred to the enforced peace as a *Pax Romana*.

The 2,000th anniversary of the birth of Augustus Caesar, the first Roman 'emperor' (b. 63 BCE, r. 27 BCE–14 CE), was celebrated with great pomp in 1937–8. Mussolini began the celebrations by opening a large archaeological exhibition, and closed it by inaugurating the restored *Ara Pacis Augustae*, a large altar, built in 13 BCE, devoted to the goddess of Augustan Peace, to commemorate the peace that followed Augustus's victories in France and Spain. Scholarly works were also sponsored. In 1935, the *Consiglio Nazionale delle Ricercha* embarked upon a major project to map the Roman Empire. There was archaeological research, notably in Libya, where such research had started in 1911 as soon as the Italian conquerors landed in Tripoli. Libya was depicted as a former part of the Roman Empire, and thus as Italian by inheritance.

The celebrations in 1937–8 also commemorated the brutal conquest of Abyssinia (Ethiopia) in 1935–6, a conquest that had led the victorious Mussolini to proclaim the establishment of the Second Roman Empire. By exalting the first (Classical) empire, the regime praised itself, a device Mussolini was especially apt to adopt. The imperial style of rule was one he sought to annex and redefine, a style that contrasted with both the more limited scale of the Italian monarchy and the constrained powers of his predecessors as Prime Minister. To Mussolini, his Rome, the 'Third Rome', was to be the centre of Fascist faith and activity.

The archaeological exhibition opened by Mussolini in 1937, the *Mostra Augustea della Romanità*, was organised by the Ministry of Popular Culture and was subsidised by Mussolini from his special funds. On a vast scale, the exhibition included casts of statues, models of architecture, engineering and military machines and large maps of the empire, all with particular emphasis on Augustus and the legions. The exhibition served as a demonstration of the Fascist regime's alleged role in restoring Italian greatness, and became an approved site for tourists. Hitler visited it twice. So also with films. In *Scipione l'Africano* (1937), a film in which many troops took part as extras, Scipio Africanus's defeat of Hannibal at Zama in 202 BCE was presented as the precursor of Mussolini's conquest of Abyssinia.

Mussolini declared, 'Rome is our starting point, it is our character, it is our myth', and personally took part in the clearing of the city centre in order to showcase Roman remains such as the Theatre of Marcellus, which had earlier been crowded with subsequent buildings. It was excavated in 1926–32. There was a similar process elsewhere. In Rimini, buildings later constructed around the *Arco di Augusto* built by Augustus were demolished in 1935.

Today, the range of Roman remains across Italy is extraordinary. It also includes much that cannot be readily seen and that has been more influential, such as field systems, the routes of roads, and the location of cities, dams and bridges. The imprint of Rome is also present in the impact of Christianity, which was established under the empire. That the Catholic Church is based in Rome is entirely due to this legacy. So also is Rome's role as a major pilgrimage centre. Tourists are in a sense heirs to those pilgrims.

CHAPTER TWO

A Multiplicity of States: 476–1402

Attempts to maintain the grandeur of Rome continued as Italy attracted attention, both from Byzantium (the Eastern Roman Empire) and from the 'barbarians'. Of the latter, Theodoric, King of the Ostrogoths, conquered mainland Italy from Odoacer, another 'barbarian', in 488–92, following with Sicily in 493. Theodoric respected the Roman legacy and restored ancient movements including in Ravenna. However, although his kingdom was powerful, it did not last.

The Byzantines, under the Emperor Justinian I (r. 527–65) and his highly talented general Belisarius, seized much of mainland Italy, Sicily and Sardinia (as well as south-east Spain and Tunisia) in 535–55, in a series of brilliant campaigns in which the Vandals were among those crushed, and also defeated a Frankish invasion of Italy in 554. The Byzantines, however, failed to conquer the rest of Italy. This began a pattern of a failure of any power to extend and consolidate control over the whole of Italy, a pattern that lasted until 1870 when the kingdom of Italy gained control of Rome. In the 660s, Constans II briefly moved the Byzantine capital to Syracuse in Sicily, but his assassination led to its return to Byzantium.

In turn, a new 'barbarian' people, the Lombards, invaded from across the Alps in 568. They had overrun most of Italy by 751, when they captured Ravenna, a centre of Byzantine power. Again, however, there was no control across the entire peninsula, a formidable task. The Lombard king was based at Pavia in northern Italy and had only limited authority over the Lombard duchy of Spoleto in central Italy and that of Benevento in southern Italy, while, after the Lombard advances, Sicily and the extreme south of the peninsula (Calabria and southern Apulia) remained under Byzantium. The Lombards converted to Christianity in 654. Such conversion was a means by which the influence of aspects of the Roman world was maintained and strengthened.

The Lombards were defeated by the Franks under Pépin in 753–6 and again, and lastingly, by Charlemagne in 773–4. In an important symbolic claim of descent, Charlemagne had Pope Leo III crown him Holy Roman Emperor in Rome in 800, thus resuming a heritage cut short in 476. An image of Italy was being recreated, but at the behest of an outside power and on its terms. Rome and as much of Italy as possible was to be linked to the Frankish Empire. In practice, Charlemagne's capital at Aix-la-Chapelle (Aachen), and not Rome, was the true centre of this empire.

This coronation was important to the Franks, but also to the papacy. Its ecclesiological authority as head of the Church was asserted, demonstrated and advanced by such an action. This was an authority consistently defended both against Byzantium and also against other prelates in the Western Church. Papal policies, which were intended to provide unity in the Church, however, were, in the long term, greatly to contribute to the fragmentation of political authority and power in Italy.

The situation might have brought a measure of stability, but the Frankish Empire was divided from 817 among Charlemagne's descendants. Much of Italy went to his son Lothar, as part of a middle kingdom that, in turn, was divided, creating a kingdom of Italy. In 951, the kingdoms of Germany and Italy, two of the three parts of Charlemagne's inheritance, were reunited by Otto I of Germany. In practice, however, Italy was now divided, with independent states in the south, particularly Benevento, Capua and Salerno, as well as the Papal States. Much of the south – Apulia, Calabria and Naples – was under the control of Byzantium, while Sicily had been conquered from them by the Moors in 827–965.

THE ARAB CONQUEST OF SICILY

A struggle within Sicily in 826–7 led to Arab intervention. Euphemius, a Byzantine naval commander, rebelled against rule from Constantinople and proclaimed himself emperor. Resistance by some of the district governors led him to call on Arab help. The Arabs then took over. Palermo, which they captured in 831, was made their capital, in place of Syracuse, the Byzantine capital, which did not fall until 878. Taormina fell in 902 and the last Byzantine position, near Messina, in 965. The Arabs brought citrus fruit, rice and mulberries to Sicily and used slaves to cultivate sugar cane there. Large-scale Arab immigration from North Africa and Spain created a new social and political élite, but the immigrants soon saw themselves as Sicilian, and ready to resist direction from North Africa. Many of the indigenous inhabitants converted to Islam, and while elements of Byzantine culture survived, this was as part of a society that was Islamic and used Arabic. The late tenth century was a period of prosperity and autonomy. However, ethnic difficulties, notably between Arabs and Berbers, and between new immigrants and others, as well as political fragmentation in the eleventh century, prepared the way for successful Norman intervention.

Whether a more united Italy could have held off the Moors is unclear, but presupposes that power could have been readily deployed, which is improbable. There were also Moorish gains elsewhere, principally the port of Bari in Apulia from 841 to 871, as well as raids along much of the Italian coastline, including of Rome in 846. However, in 849, a big Islamic fleet was completely destroyed by a fleet from the cities of Naples, Salerno, Amalfi, Sorrento and Gaeta, and, after that victory, no Islamic settlement was established in the part of Italy that was not under Byzantium. The latter part was that closest to Moorish power in North Africa, while Byzantium itself had to focus on challenges in the core parts of its empire. As a result, its Italian possessions were vulnerable.

Slave-raiding played a major role, as Moorish society relied on slavery. This threat encouraged the location of settlements in Italy not on the coastal plain but rather, as on Sicily, on upland sites that could more readily be defended and from which the sea could be scrutinised. As a reminder, however, of the need to note the range of possible explanations, the avoidance of diseases, such as malaria, that were common on coastal lowlands was also a factor. Water on the coast could also be brackish. The Moors were the major threat, but in 860 Viking raiders sacked Pisa.

The instability of the fifth century had led in Italy to the collapse of city life in many places. However, some cities survived, notably Rome, Naples and Ravenna, and there was significant development in particular locations, especially Amalfi, which had a site relatively protected from attack by land and which became an important maritime republic that operated widely in the Mediterranean. Venice followed. Within all settlements, the requirements of the Church affected the built environment.

More generally, after the marked decline of the fifth century and subsequent problems, there was population growth in both town and country, and a significant degree of recovery from earlier decline and disruption, notably recovery in the tenth to thirteenth centuries. Monasteries were founded. There were, however, unfortunate aspects. In particular, the revival of agriculture led to more deforestation and thus accentuated soil erosion.

Any summary of the major developments during the 'Dark Ages' (early Middle Ages), as well as subsequently, captures the interplay between the drive for greatness, including unity within a greater whole, and the strength of regional and local particularism. The greater whole was presented in part by the papacy and Christendom, but, at the political level, suffered much from Italy being on the fault line between rival political systems. That was an aspect of Italy's geography and, more positively, also offered the economic and cultural benefits of links with other civilisations. Northern Italy very much looked across the Alps or, rather, was looked to from across the Alps. This was particularly true of the links between the Holy Roman emperors and northern Italy, notably the March (region) of Verona. The key route, the Via Imperii, ran through the Brenner Pass. In contrast, Sicily and Apulia were strongly drawn in different directions, Sicily both to nearby North Africa and eastward to Greece, and Apulia to nearby Greece. Venice looked down the Adriatic to Byzantium, but also northwards and westwards.

Southern Italy

In the eleventh century, a new element arrived in Italy in the shape of the Normans, in some respects the last stage of the 'barbarian' invaders because the Normans were descendants of the Vikings who had settled, from 911, in Normandy in northern France. Small groups of adventurers at first became important in Italy as professional soldiers, serving in the incessant conflicts in the south. They then seized power. Richard of Aversa succeeded in becoming Prince of Capua in 1058. The most dynamic was Robert Guiscard (c. 1015–85), the sixth of the twelve sons of Tancred d'Hauteville, a poor Norman noble, eight of whom sought their fortune in southern Italy. Rather as Piedmont was to do in the 1850s, and Mussolini was unsuccessfully to seek to do, the Normans exploited the rivalries of the other powers, notably the Holy Roman Emperor, the Pope and Byzantium, each of which also manoeuvred against the others. In 1059, Pope Nicholas II recognised Guiscard as Duke of Apulia, in return for the promise of Norman support against the Roman nobility, from whose control the popes, notably those of a reforming tendency, were trying to extricate themselves. In 1060, Guiscard drove the Byzantines from Calabria and in 1071, despite Venetian backing for the Byzantines, he captured the cities of Bari and Brindisi, the main remaining centres of Byzantine power in Italy. The Lombard principality of Salerno followed in 1077.

In 1081, Guiscard crossed the Adriatic, and he died while preparing to attack Constantinople.

The Byzantines used the Normans as mercenaries in an unsuccessful attempt to recapture Sicily from the Moors in 1038. Muslim Sicily was eventually reconquered by Robert Guiscard's youngest brother, Roger. Palermo was captured in 1072, and Roger completed the conquest of the island by 1091. His son, Roger II of Sicily (r. 1105–54), gained control of the duchy of Apulia on the death of his cousin William in 1127, and proceeded to unite the whole of southern Italy under his rule. In 1130, he took advantage of a schism in the papacy to secure the agreement of one of the two contending pontiffs to the creation of a new kingdom. He was then crowned as King of Sicily on Christmas Day 1130. This was a Norman Conquest that, while it had taken far longer, easily matched that of England in 1066 by William the Conqueror.

As an indication of long-standing issues with political consolidation, Roger, however, faced serious opposition to establishing his position, both within his new kingdom and more widely. The Emperor (the Holy Roman Emperor), who had claims over Italy, refused to accept the new kingdom and invaded in 1137. The papacy also opposed the step, because the Pope who had acknowledged Roger as king in 1130, Anacletus II, subsequently lost the schism and his actions were thus viewed as illegitimate by his victorious opponent. Fighting in the south continued until 1139, with key occasions including Roger's capture of Capua (1134), Naples (1138) and Bari (1139).

Sicily and southern Italy was an area of notable cultural interchange, especially with Moorish, Byzantine and northern European strands. This fruitful interchange was seen in the architecture and court of Palermo, and in intellectual activities such as mapmaking. With his capital at Palermo, from which Naples was more accessible by sea than from Syracuse, Roger also made Sicily particularly well administered.

THE *BOOK OF ROGER*

The cosmopolitan nature of Sicily was shown in the great triumph of Islamic mapmaking, the world map of al-Idrisi, finished in 1154 for Roger II and engraved on a silver tablet, which was destroyed in 1160. Al-Idrisi also produced a geographical compendium ('*The book of pleasant journeys into faraway lands*'), also termed the *Book of Roger*, which included a world map, as well as seventy sectional maps. He explained that Roger wished that he 'should accurately know the details of his land and master them with a definite knowledge'. Al-Idrisi drew on Ptolemy's information.

POLITICAL STRUGGLES

Further north, Italy suffered from a bitter and long-standing power-struggle between the German-based Holy Roman Empire and the papacy. In theory, the two were aligned, each as the helper of the other. In practice, there were serious differences in Italian power politics, as well as important ideological tensions, which focused on, and were expressed as a struggle for, primacy. The papacy saw itself as an organising principal, and would-be coordinator for Western Christendom, and as superior to the Byzantine Church.

In the Investiture Crisis, the ambitious and determined Pope Gregory VII (r. 1073–85) united the opponents of the Emperor Henry IV (r. 1084–1106), and thus weakened imperial authority. Henry was obliged to show contrition and seek pardon in a famous scene at Canossa in 1077, although this led only to a brief pause in the disputes. The papacy was backed by most of the communes (towns), whereas the emperors tended to be supported by the aristocracy and to support his own anti-pope. Milanese writers sometimes appealed directly to the Roman republican past against the imperial pretensions of the Germans.

However, in turn, the popes had rivals in both the Church and locally. As a reminder of the simultaneity of Italian history, this struggle occurred at the same time as those in southern Italy discussed above. The Pope called on Robert Guiscard for support, but when the latter came to rescue him from an imperial siege in 1084, his army proceeded to sack Rome. Gregory was driven from the city, and died in exile in Salerno in May 1085.

Rivalries continued, dividing cities and interacting with existing factional struggles. As a result of these interactions, feuds were focused, complicated, sustained and strengthened. From the early thirteenth century, such factions, both then and subsequently, were often described as either Guelfs (the party of the papacy) or Ghibellines (the imperial party). However, this association with the emperors and their opponents could frequently be tenuous and based on an attempt to win outside support rather than being the cause of local divisions

On several occasions, emperors sponsored anti-popes who contested the authority of the pope. However, the idea of a universal pope and an undivided Catholicism was not challenged, and, on each occasion, schism was eventually resolved. In turn, the struggle between the emperors and their opponents allowed the papacy to expand its territory in Italy, although it also obliged them to defend their territorial position. Partly as a consequence of such disputes, Italy has far more castles within the modern country than on or near its frontiers, and notably so as compared to England.

In northern Italy, another emperor, Frederick Barbarossa (r. 1152–90), who was committed to maintaining and expanding imperial power in Italy, was defeated by the Lombard League of Cities at Legnano in 1176. Formed in 1167, the League included Como, Bergamo, Novara, Vercelli, Milan, Brescia, Alessandria, Piacenza, Mantua, Parma, Reggio, Modena, Ferrara, Bologna, Imola and Rimini. Barbarossa (the nickname means Redbeard) was forced at the Peace of Constance of 1183 to recognise the autonomy of these cities as an aspect of imperial sovereignty. Another papal schism was involved in this struggle.

Barbarossa's son, the Emperor Henry VI (r. 1191–7), married in

1186 the heiress to the kingdom of Sicily, which ruled southern Italy and Sicily, and subsequently established his authority there, only to die young. This death was another of the very many might-have-beens of Italian history, a process that continues to the present.

Son of Henry VI and Constance of Sicily, the ostentatiously ambitious Frederick II, known to contemporaries as *Stupor Mundi* ('the Amazement of the World'), was highly talented. Brought up in southern Italy, and King of Sicily from 1198, he became Emperor in 1220. Frederick sought to consolidate imperial power in Italy, but was excommunicated and declared deposed by Pope Innocent IV in 1245 and opposed by the Lombard cities. In Sicily, where he spent much of his time, Frederick bloodily suppressed a Muslim rebellion that had begun in 1189. This rebellion had left the mountainous interior of the island in practice an independent state that resisted the Christians and sought help from Muslim powers elsewhere. In 1220–4 and again in 1244–6, Frederick launched a series of campaigns that destroyed the Muslim community of Sicily. His opponents elsewhere in Italy, including the Lombard League, which was revived in 1226, were more successful, though he defeated them at Cortenuova (1237). In Dante's view, Frederick, who ruled until 1250, was the last true emperor because his successors never came to Italy to be crowned in Rome. On the Sixth Crusade, Frederick took possession of Jerusalem and crowned himself king there in 1229.

Keen on the arts and on intellectual life, Frederick founded the university of Naples, which still goes by his name, in 1224. He had been taught by, among others, an imam, spoke six languages, including Arabic, and had Arab, Greek and Jewish scholars in his court. Frederick was also a very significant figure in terms of architecture. He helped introduce Arab and Greek science into Italy, and Europe more generally, and developed early Italian vernacular language and literature.

Frederick's eldest son, Conrad (r. 1250–4), continued the struggle with the papacy, but the position of his son, Conradin (r. 1254–8), was usurped as King of Sicily by Frederick's illegitimate second son,

Manfred (r. 1258–66). This allowed Pope Alexander IV (r. 1254–61), taking forward long-standing papal opposition to imperial power, opposition developed under Innocent III (r. 1198–1216), to declare the throne forfeit. The throne was offered by the French-born Urban IV (r. 1261–4) to Louis IX of France, who passed it on to his brother, Charles of Anjou, who was made King of Sicily by the French-born Pope Clement IV (r. 1265–8) in 1266. As part of a crusade, Charles defeated Manfred at Benevento in 1266 (Manfred was killed) and Conradin at Tagliacozzo (1268), executing the latter in Naples. He was beheaded in the *Piazza Mercato* and buried in *Santa Maria del Carmine* in Naples. This execution ended the Hohenstaufen state in southern Italy and transferred the kingdom of Sicily to the Angevins, the rulers of Anjou, who were a junior branch of the French royal family.

As a reminder of the rapid changes of fortune that so often characterised Italian history after the fall of Rome and that made political consolidation very difficult, the full effect of that transfer lasted only until 1282. Then, in what is called the Sicilian Vespers because it began at the start of vespers, the sunset prayer, Sicily, now heavily taxed by Charles of Anjou, revolted and turned to the House of Aragon, the rulers of eastern Spain. Pedro III of Aragon became Peter I of Sicily. Sicily and Naples remained separate until the death of Joanna II, the last Angevin ruler of Naples, in 1435, when it was united with Sicily under Aragonese rule. During the fourteenth century, and especially after the death of King Robert of Naples in 1343, political division and a breakdown in law and order seriously damaged the economy of the mainland south. Meanwhile, subjugating Sardinia after bitter conflict in the fourteenth century, the Aragonese enslaved large numbers of Sards despite their being Christian.

Under the Angevins, Neapolitan church architecture developed in a distinctive direction, notably with the construction of wide-bodied churches, several of which can be seen in the old city, especially that of the Franciscan convent of *Santa Chiara* founded by King Robert. These churches were an instance of the cultural interchange seen in Italy, and this interchange contributed to its variety. In the south, interchange was particularly apparent with other Mediterranean societies, including, increasingly, Spain and southern France as well as the more traditional links with Greece.

The Frankish rulers had granted the papacy much of central Italy in the eighth century, but, lacking the military power to intimidate and provide protection, it had proved very difficult for the popes to wield effective control outside the immediate area near Rome. The lands to the east of the Apennines were in effect independent. Similar problems arose with the lands bequeathed to the papacy by the pious Countess Mathilda of Tuscany, who died in 1115, not least because the emperors refused to recognise the validity of her donation. In the 1140s and early 1150s, Arnold of Brescia, a cleric critical of papal wealth and power, made an unsuccessful attempt to establish a new Roman republic, only to be executed in 1155 at the orders of the Emperor Frederick Barbarossa during a brief period of rapprochement between pope and emperor.

The Papal States had experienced a very chequered existence in the early Middle Ages. Under the dynamic and ambitious Innocent III (r. 1198–1216), there was a major attempt not only to improve papal government but also to give meaning to papal territorial claims (as well as ideological demands), and this attempt continued under his successors, sharpening political rivalries within Italy. Thanks to obtaining imperial renunciations of territory and granting papal 'bulls' of protection, papal authority spread to the Adriatic and then north to the River Po. While much of this area remained under vassals, the popes began to organise their territory more effectively, creating provinces governed by rectors. The calibre of papal administration was higher than that of most territorial princes, but it faced serious limitations. For example, given to Pope Stephen II in 756 by the Frankish ruler, Pépin the Short, the duchy of Spoleto had been in effect divided among autonomous towns. The papacy also faced opposition from populism, including in Rome itself. In 1347, Cola di Rienzi successfully persuaded the citizens of Rome to rebel against aristocratic rule.

After being driven out, he tried again in 1354, only to be killed as a result of a hostile rising.

Notwithstanding rumours about Boniface VIII (r. 1294–1303), most medieval popes after Gregory VII (r. 1073–85) were personally pretty virtuous, especially about sex, but there was no need to be decadent like the second Borgia pope, Alexander VI (r. 1492–1503), in order to try to benefit nephews, some illegitimate sons, and other family members, granting them Church positions and lands, and backing them in Italian power politics. Popes such as Innocent IV (r. 1243–54), who wrote dense treatises on canon law as well as proclaiming the Seventh Crusade in 1244, also engaged in such dynastic politics.

Boniface VIII sought to reassert papal superiority over temporal powers, which angered Philip IV of France who attempted to have him kidnapped in 1303, a policy also to be followed by Napoleon. Boniface's French successor, Clement V (r. 1305–14), under pressure from Philip IV, removed the seat of the papacy to Avignon in 1309. The papacy did not return to Rome until 1377, and, a few months later, the disputed election of a new pontiff led to a new and particularly serious schism that lasted until 1415. In his *The Divine Comedy*, begun in about 1307, Dante referred to the rulers of France as the Giant standing alongside the Whore that represented the corrupt papacy. The Great Schism built on the legacy of Charles of Anjou's conquest of southern Italy and Sicily in encouraging anti-French feeling. This was analogous to the anti-Spanish feeling seen in the seventeenth century.

In another direction, the energy of the Church was shown by its ability to tap the dynamism represented by the foundation of the new orders of friars, notably the Franciscans established by Francis of Assisi and gaining papal recognition in 1210. They followed an active form of ministry, as opposed to the withdrawal from the world seen with monasticism. The latter was a key field of Christian activity in which Italy had earlier been very important, as seen with prominent Benedictine monasteries such as Montecassino, which St Benedict founded in 529, and the ninth-century *Monastero Maggiore* in Milan. Montecassino enjoyed its 'golden age' under the rule of Desiderius of Benevento, abbot from 1058 and pope (as Victor III) in 1086–7. Monasteries, cathedrals and other churches have left Italy with an impressive amount of Romanesque architecture, for example the eleventh-century *Duomo Vecchii* (old cathedrals) in Brescia and Vercelli.

As a result of the friars, new churches and other ecclesiastical buildings appeared in towns, such as the *Basilica di San Francesco* in Assisi dedicated to St Francis and built in 1227–1367, and the *Santa Corona* church in Vicenza finished in 1261 to house a relic from Christ's Crown of Thorns. These and other such buildings provided much space and patronage for artistic activity, notably for painted frescoes and altarpieces. Key painters of the period included Cimabue (*c.* 1240–*c.* 1302) and his pupil Giotto (*c.* 1266–1337), each of whom took forward the representation of the human shape, especially by introducing characterisation and individuality, as with the 1303–5 frescoes at the Scrovegni chapel in Padua. Giotto was an important contributor to the frescoes of the church at Assisi. Italy also saw the foundation of numerous universities, particularly Bologna (1088), Vicenza (1204), Arezzo (1215), Padua (1222), Naples (1224), Rome (1245), Siena (1240), Piacenza (1248) and Perugia (1308), although some did not last long: Vicenza closed in 1209 and Piacenza was also short-lived.

Alongside a stress on the friars should come one on lay piety, as also for the later Counter-Reformation of the sixteenth century. Confraternities of the devout laity played a key role in social welfare. At the same time, this lay piety could have a heretical fringe as with Catharism (the Albigensian heresy), which spread from France into northern Italy by means of missionaries. Cathar churches and schools were established.

Northern Italy continued to owe nominal allegiance to the empire. However, the cities of the region, notably Milan, had long had considerable rights of self-government and, in some, this had led to the development of republican communes. These looked back, in a search for legitimacy, to ancient claims of independence, claims that led to the manufacture of an appropriate history.

THE ORIGINS OF MANTUA

In his *The Divine Comedy*, begun in about 1307, Dante Alighieri (1265–1321) provided an account of the origins of Virgil's home town, an account that emphasised the vitality of individual origin-myths and the role of the occult. Manto, the sorceress, is described as travelling and finding, in a marshy part of the Mincio valley, unoccupied land where she settled: 'In time the scattered people round about collected at that town, secure and strong by virtue of the marshland on all sides, where, over those dead bones, they built a town.' In fact, less dramatically, the city was settled by the Etruscans in the tenth century BCE.

The interaction of domestic urban politics with international power politics was amply shown in the case of Florence, from which the Ghibellines, the imperial party, had been expelled in 1267 and defeated in 1289 when they tried to overturn this result. Dante fought in the battle of Campaldino. Guelf success was followed by a democratic constitution in 1284 that disfranchised Florentines who claimed any degree of nobility, although, from 1296, they were allowed to regain the franchise by joining a guild, which was the way in which Dante entered the government in 1300. The Guelfs of Florence divided into two factions that year (Black and White), one of which sought the support of Boniface VIII who persuaded Philip IV of France's brother, Charles of Valois, to take control. This intervention on behalf of one of the factions in 1301 led to Dante's flight into exile in 1302. Dante eventually came to put his hopes in Henry, Count of Luxembourg, the Emperor Henry VII (r. 1308–13), who intervened in Italy, being crowned in Rome by two papal legates. He besieged, but failed to capture, Florence, before dying of fever in Pisa.

Dante's *De Monarchia* argued that the emperor and the pope both depended directly on God and had separate functions, so that the pope should have no temporal authority. This was a view that was to have some influence among critics of the papacy, and was to be advanced by Niccolò Machiavelli (1469–1527) and, especially, his friend Francesco Guicciardini (1483–1540), who declared, in his *Ricordi*, the need for total separation between state and church. However, it was not a view that gained much political traction until the late eighteenth and, even more, nineteenth centuries. In canto six of *The Divine Comedy*, Dante bewailed the state of Italy:

Ah, Italy enslaved, a house of grief,
A ship without a pilot in a storm,
No queen of provinces – a bawdy-house!
. . . Now your folk are never free from war,
And men devour each other, though they live
Within one wall . . .
Ah clergy, you who ought to be devout
And leave the saddle to the Emperor,
If you attended to the word of God!
See how this beast has turned to vice, because
It has not been corrected by the spurs,
Not since you took the bridle in your hands.

While Florence remained a republic, many other cities had, by the late thirteenth century, fallen under the control of seigniorial families. This was largely due to internal factions and a consequent need for stronger government, which led to a leading figure being given greater powers, or to an individual seizing them and seeking to make them hereditary. For example, the della Scala, who had ruled the city of Verona since 1263, were at the height of their power in the mid-fourteenth century. Cangrande I della Scala (r. 1308–29) extended the family's sway until, with the Visconti, they dominated Lombardy. He was a patron of Dante, Giotto and Petrarch. Mastino II della Scala (r. 1329–51) added control over Lucca, and later Parma, but fatally over-extended his resources, leading to the family's ultimate downfall in 1387.

For the Visconti, Ottone Visconti, Archbishop of Milan (d. 1295), established the foundations of family power and, from 1395, the Visconti were hereditary dukes of Milan. Azzo d'Este (1205–64) established Este authority in Ferrara, and the office of Signore of Ferrara was made hereditary in the family. Modena and Reggio (1406) were annexed by the Este. The Gonzaga seized power in Mantua in 1328, and the *Palazzo Ducale* there is a testimony to their strength and wealth, as is the *Basilica di Sant' Andrea*, commissioned in 1472 from Leon Battista Alberti by Ludovico II Gonzaga in order to contain the golden vessels allegedly holding earth soaked by the blood of Christ.

Alongside rule by princes, control by other cities was an issue. Thus, Massa Marittima, a mining centre in southern Tuscany, was taken over by Siena in the early fourteenth century. As yet, Venice had not begun to expand on the Italian mainland or *terraferma*. Instead, her efforts were concentrated on the Dalmatian coast of modern Croatia, where her presence is still visible, and in the Aegean. There, Venice benefited greatly from the crisis of Byzantine power that she herself played a large part in causing with the storming of Constantinople in the Fourth Crusade in 1204. As the Crusaders lacked sufficient money to pay Venice to take them to the Holy Land in 1203, the Venetians were able to get them first to capture the Dalmatian port of Zara and then to attack Constantinople. The Venetians gained control of important positions in the Byzantine Empire, occupying Crete in 1212. These campaigns demonstrated the expertise and capability of Venice in the execution of complex combined operations.

Only in 1339 did Venice change policy with the annexation of the town of Treviso on the *terraferma*. Separately, the struggle between the Genoese and Venetians for maritime supremacy resulted in four wars, beginning in 1253, which culminated in the War of Chioggia from 1378 to 1381. Galleys, which carried crossbowmen, had replaced lateen-rigged ships in the Italian war fleets in the early thirteenth century. Raiding, the capture of ports and islands, and the effective use of galleys over extended distances, made these wars essentially a series of combined operations. In order to blockade and starve Venice into submission, the Genoese, showing great boldness, seized the island of Chioggia, on the doorstep of the core of Venice, the *isole realtine*. This enabled them to support their galleys in a close blockade of the lagoon. They also worked in close cooperation with land forces from Padua, which attacked Venice from the west.

The Venetian response was carefully planned and well executed. The three channels linking Chioggia with the Adriatic were all blocked by stone-filled cogs under cover of darkness, while Venetian galleys and troops from the mainland launched a diversionary attack on Brendola, which protected Chioggia from the south, leaving the garrison isolated and eventually forced to surrender. Venice thus drove Genoa from the northern Adriatic, which was the basis for Venetian expansion on the mainland. The conflict showed the importance of logistics, with the Genoese trying to cut off grain supplies to Venice from Sicily, and of money: Genoa had the financial muscle to continue building and paying for replacement galleys and crucial mercenaries.

The fragmented power structure of northern Italy contrasted (in theory) with the more consolidated position in the south. In the north, the 'state' was essentially a city or group of cities that controlled the surrounding *contado*, usually with the cooperation of the locally prominent. In contrast, in the south in the twelfth and thirteenth century, the kingdom ruling Sicily and Naples matched the governmental range, power and structure of developed states elsewhere in Europe, for example France and England. However, whereas the fourteenth-century rulers of England exercised authority and power across all of the country, the power of those of France was contested, notably, but not only, by the dukes of Burgundy and by the claims of the rulers of England. Similarly, after the split of the kingdom of Sicily in 1282, government in the mainland kingdom of Naples became increasingly problematic.

Papal authority and power in the Papal States was greatly compromised during the papal 'Babylonian Captivity' in Avignon. Nevertheless, Innocent VI (r. 1352–62) made the energetic Gil Álvarez Carillo de Albornoz, Archbishop of Toledo, a cardinal, papal legate and vicar general of Italy. In the 1350s and 1360s, Albornoz greatly restored papal authority, bringing Giovanni de Vico, Lord of Viterbo, Galeotto Malatesta, the ruler of Rimini, the Montefeltro of Urbino, the da Polenta of Ravenna, Giovanni Manfredi of Faenza and the city of Ancona to submission in 1354–7 and regulating the administration of the Papal States. In the 1360s, Albornoz was able to gain control of Bologna, but he found the suppression of mercenary bands very difficult, and in 1366–7 was faced by a general rebellion in Campagna.

Papal authority in the Papal States was not really restored until the time of Pope Martin V (r. 1417–31), a member of the Colonna family, whose election effectively ended the Great Schism. When he became pope, papal authority was largely restricted to Rome and its environs, while 'vicars', in practice hereditary lords, controlled most of the Papal States. Drawing on the support of Naples, Martin was able to defeat the *condottiere* (mercenary leader) Braccio da Montone, who controlled Umbria, in 1424, the same year in which Martin gained control of Bologna.

The most powerful state in northern Italy was Milan under the Visconti, of whom the most dynamic was Gian Galeazzo Visconti (1351–1402). In 1378, he succeeded his father, Galeazzo II, as joint ruler with his uncle Bernabò, but, in 1385, he had Bernabò seized and became sole ruler: Bernabò was killed the following year. Such actions gave a lurid character, both within and outside Italy, to Italian politics.

The determined and murderous Gian Galeazzo then rapidly expanded his inheritance, in particular by seizing Verona and Padua, which made him also the most powerful ruler in north-east Italy. Visconti power was then extended into Tuscany with the acquisition of Siena. Bologna was temporarily captured, taking advantage of the weakness of papal power east of the Apennines. In 1387, Gian Galeazzo began Milan cathedral, a vast work on Gothic lines, including much marble, that was only finished in 1892, subsequently being restored and strengthened in the 1960s to 1980s. In 1396, Gian Galeazzo began the *Certosa* (Charterhouse) *di Pavia* as a mausoleum and private chapel, although it was not finished until the sixteenth century, and thus shows the transition to Renaissance style. Gian Galeazzo played a key role in the development of permanent diplomats, a system backed up by an effective chancery, which served as an embryonic ministry of foreign affairs. Italy was to play the crucial role in the development of modern diplomacy. The title Duke of Milan, purchased from the Emperor in 1395, confirmed Visconti power, but it was really based on the large army he built up. Gian Galeazzo compared himself to Julius Caesar, but his opponents saw him as a tyrant like Nero. As so often, the Roman world provided the crucial frame of reference.

CONTINUITIES

Alongside the rise and fall of rulers and cities came the continuities of society in a world operating within consistent technological constraints. Economic processes changed only slowly during the many centuries covered in this chapter. Buildings moreover were used throughout, and often reused. In Syracuse, the cathedral was built by the seventh century over the Temple of Athena, which had been built in the fifth century BCE. In Orvieto, the church of Sant' Andrea, where Martin IV was crowned pope in 1281, was built in the seventh century upon the site of a Roman temple built on walls that were Etruscan. Rebuilt from the twelfth century, the church benefited from additions in the late fifteenth century and in the 1920s.

Moreover, the strength and continuation of the dominant ideology ensured that the same topics were covered by artists. The *Triumph of Death* and *Last Judgement and Hell* frescoes of 1336–41, attributed to Buonamico Buffalmacco, in the *Camposanto* in Pisa, a burial site, were stories frequently reproduced elsewhere.

At the same time, alongside continuities, there was change. Trade expanding across and beyond the Mediterranean, and the subsequent development of local industries, notably textiles and metallurgy, made northern Italy the most advanced economic region of later medieval Europe. The south, by contrast, stagnated, and became more and more a source of foodstuffs and raw materials for the cities of the north, which, notably Genoa and Venice, controlled its external trade. Furthermore, the economic structure within particular cities altered, as did their relative position.

There was a search for advantage in which geopolitics, environment, conflict and personalities interacted. For example, Florence, which had not been at the cutting edge in the twelfth century, developed important advantages in the thirteenth: population growth interacted with major developments in trade, manufacturing and banking. By 1300, the population may have been 120,000, making Florence one of the four most populous cities of Italy alongside Genoa, Milan and Venice. However, the Black Death (bubonic plague), which arrived in 1347–8 and reoccurred periodically thereafter, hit Italy hard. Almost 60 per cent of the Florentine population fell victim to the plague in 1348. In turn, the plague hit hard at the population and economy of the nearby town of San Gimignano, leading to its takeover by Florence in 1353.

CHAPTER THREE

The Age of the Renaissance: The Fifteenth Century

Art in the service of a moral world was the theme of the *Ospedale degli Innocenti*, the foundling (abandoned children) hospital opened in Florence in 1445. Initially funded by a bequest by Francesco di Marco Datini, a wealthy merchant, and supported by Florence's Silk Guild, the building was constructed from 1419, the architect being Filippo Brunelleschi, who also created the imposing dome for the city's cathedral. The portico was intended by the architect to represent a welcoming into both a new life and the city. It offered a vision of hope, as did the artistic works commissioned for the building. And yet each individual child left there for care was also an admission of failure, of misery, and of personal, family and community shame.

COMPETING STATES

Neighbouring city-states, particularly Florence and Venice, feared Visconti expansion, and, when Gian Galeazzo died unexpectedly in 1402, they used the opportunity to increase their territories at the expense of Milan. However, smaller city-states, such as Pisa and Siena, which had survived as independent republics into the fourteenth century, increasingly became unable to preserve their status without powerful protectors.

Venice was the principal beneficiary of the collapse of Visconti power. It expanded on the mainland, overthrowing the da Carrara family of Padua, and seizing the cities of Belluno (1404), Vicenza (1404), Padua (1405) and Verona (1405). Friuli and Udine followed in 1420. In another forward advance, Venice took Brescia, including thirty-four communes of the *Magnifica Patria* on Lake Garda in 1426, and Bergamo in 1428. Venice's governing élite was divided about the value of engaging in war for these gains, but, in the event, the expansionist party won. This expansion was initially welcomed in Florence and Rome as a way to restrict Milan's power. Ravenna was added by Venice in 1441, but lost in 1509 after a very troubled rule. These gains brought Venice economic advantages, including iron and wool production, and prosperity, as well as providing new administrative responsibilities. Venice's provinces were governed by members of its patriciate.

Milanese power was revived by Gian Galeazzo's son, Filippo Maria Visconti (r. 1412–47), and the latter's son-in-law, Francesco Sforza (r. 1450–66), a *condottiere* (mercenary leader), who used his military strength to establish himself in Lombardy and to found the Sforza dynasty. In gaining power, Sforza, who was allied with Venice, suppressed the short-lived Ambrosian Republic. An effective ruler of Milan, Sforza also gained control of Genoa, although this was not a permanent acquisition.

Further south, Florence expanded its power in Tuscany, acquiring Arezzo (1384) and, in the aftermath of Gian Galeazzo's death, the formerly powerful independent republic of Pisa (1406). By then, Pisa was no longer a major maritime power able to challenge Genoa, not least because of the silting up of the River Arno. Lucca, however, fought off a Florentine attack in 1429 and remained a medieval city-state after a brief princely interlude under Paolo Guinigi.

Within cities, there was much conflict as factional and political interests were pursued. At the same time, the situation varied by city, in part due to its political situation. In Verona, control by Venice limited violent conflict, but it was frequent in Bologna, while Florence adopted an intermediate position.

RENAISSANCE

Meanwhile, this was the period of the Renaissance, a movement of great importance to European, indeed world, culture. The Renaissance saw a strengthening of interest in, and knowledge about, the achievements of pre-Christian Classical thinkers, artists and authors. For centuries, learning in Western Christendom had been largely confined to the monasteries and was mostly concerned with theological issues. Much intellectual effort centred on matters of religious doctrine, while painting, architecture and music were also largely in the service of the Church. This situation continued during the Renaissance, but there was also a greater engagement with lay issues and concern with lay patrons.

The improving financial conditions of the middling orders, notably in the cities, from the thirteenth century, allowed wealthy citizens to seek a better education for their children, particularly their sons. Education was highly significant. A key figure was Vittorino da Feltre (1378–1446). Born in Belluno, he came from a poor family and became one of the great humanists and possibly the greatest schoolmaster of the Renaissance. He studied in Padua and taught there. Later, Vittorino moved to Mantua, where he set up a school that, from its happy atmosphere, became known as *La Casa Gioiosa* (The Joyous House). At the school, he taught not only the Gonzaga children and the sons and daughters of other prominent families, but also many poor children, free of charge and treating them all as equally important. The school taught Greek, Latin, mathematics, music, art, religion, poetry and philosophy, abolished physical punishment, and placed special emphasis on physical activities. The school acted as a significant model for many others across Europe.

Education and money encouraged the new growing middle class to commission artists to decorate their homes, while many also liked to spend time reading and talking about cultural topics. Mathematics was important because it helped improve auditing. Double-entry bookkeeping developed in Italy.

Literature, including philosophy, was important in Renaissance 'quality time'. This kind of activity and education did not neglect Latin, but relied much more than in the past on the Italian language.

At the same time, artistic patronage allowed scholars to widen their researches into monastic libraries where they focused on Latin and Greek texts that had hitherto been overlooked.

From the fourteenth century, a group of Italian scholars, inspired by the poet Petrarch, proposed a new educational syllabus, based on Classical literature, which they called *studia humanitatis*. This syllabus was to comprise five key subjects: rhetoric, poetry, grammar, history and moral philosophy. Theology played no part, although the humanists (as these scholars became known in the nineteenth century) did not go so far as to reject Christian doctrine. Instead, they shifted the emphasis from debating how a person should serve God to asking how the virtuous man should act. Humanism became a more broadly diffused cultural practice and commitment.

The Renaissance saw an efflorescence of artistic activity. Raphael, Michelangelo and Leonardo da Vinci were all key figures and their fame has lasted to the present. They built on the achievements of a much broader group that had taken forward an important skillset. This was seen, for example, in the understanding and presentation of perspective, particularly in Masaccio's frescoes in *S. Maria del Carmine* in Florence (*c.* 1425–8) and in the depiction of the human body, as with the sculptures of Donatello, notably his *St George* (*c.* 1416–17) and his *David* (*c.* 1440–50), both held in Florence's Bargello museum. Architecture was also influenced by antiquity, as with Filippo Brunelleschi's cathedral dome at Florence, a work, the largest dome in the world, erected in 1420–36, that provided a distinctive skyline for the city.

Cultural creativity was to the fore in a number of different contexts, Venice, Rome and Florence being especially significant. Florence was particularly to the fore in the fifteenth century (*Quattrocento*), as with Lorenzo Ghiberti's bronze doors for the Baptistery. In contrast, Rome and Venice became more important in the sixteenth century (*Cinquecento*), notably with the work of Raphael and Michelangelo in the former, and of Giorgione, Titian and Tintoretto in the latter, and with those only the most prominent of many painters.

The significance of particular contexts helped produce the diversity and energy of the Renaissance. The Florentine historian Francesco Guicciardini (1483–1540) discussed the idea that Italy's territorial divisions resulted in a diversity and competition that led to virtuosity. There was certainly a benefit from these divisions for independence, for at least some cities, and this provided opportunities for a distinctively Italian urban culture. At the same time, the city was a contested, indeed intensely political, environment, and some outcomes proved more favourable than others for artistic achievement and intellectual activity. In particular, the attempt of élites to present themselves as aristocratic proved important in many cities.

Cities, whether republican or courtly, were not the sole context of artistic activity. There was also the significance of monarchical Italy, in the shape of Naples, of the south and, likewise, of rural and seigneurial patrons. More work needs to be devoted to these subjects. A very different artistic legacy from the period is the sanctuary of St Francis of Paola in the unappealing Calabrian town of that name: the fifteenth-century saint gave rise to a sanctuary with wall paintings illustrating his miracles.

Renaissance thought represented both an attempt to understand new (and revived) information and a drive to systematise it in order to provide a natural philosophy that could be used to comprehend and expound knowledge. The Renaissance advanced an ideal of good government, although a more ruthless pragmatism could also be shown, most readily by the Florentine Niccolò Machiavelli in his *Il Principe* (*The Prince*, 1532), a guide to winning power that was in parts bitter, ironic and perceptive. Old and new ideas coexisted and interacted, as in understandings of science and astrology, notably of the alleged impact of the cycles of the Heavens on human life, a subject to which much attention was devoted.

The attempt to rationalise the world, indeed to use the study of the natural world and Christian devotion to understand each other, was a goal that was intended to ensure a harmony that would bring peace and fulfil divine goals. This purpose linked intellectual speculation with religion, and also with alchemy and magic. Harmony, the counterpoint of order, was believed to be inherently a good, as well as being a means of good. In the *Septe Giornate della Geografia* (*The Seven Days of Geography*, 1482), the Florentine humanist Francesco Berlinghieri produced a poem describing the world, illustrated by twenty-six engraved maps, that followed the order of Ptolemy's second-century *Geographia*, but also offered a morality he deemed appropriate, providing Christian moral perceptions that looked to Dante's *The Divine Comedy*.

Art was very much part of the process. The use of mathematics to order spatial relationships was seen in the development of perspective. Greater precision in representation was part of the process of showing God's work and the human sphere. Artists could also be mathematicians, notably with Leon Battista Alberti (1404–72), while Brunelleschi provided perspective views of features within Florence. City views reflected the application of humanist learning, the glorification of the city as harbinger of the new culture, and the revival of ancient city republics, especially in the new form of Venice. The city as a whole, a unit that could be grasped visually through pictures and could, and should, be adapted by new architectural projects, was a concern of Renaissance rulers, architects and artists. The knowledge of perspective renewed interest in vistas and related harmonies. In Urbino, a major centre of Renaissance painting, the contemporary interest in the creation of perfect, proportionate and whole entities was manifested in a fascination with idealised cities, perhaps best known in the form of a perspective view of an imaginary townscape, usually attributed to Piero della Francesca (*c.* 1400–92).

There were also attempts to build such townscapes. The *Addizione Erculea* in Ferrara, designed by Biagio Rossetti at the end of the fifteenth century, is one of the first urban plans clearly based on perspective. Rossetti sought to balance the humanist principles relating to form and volume in architecture, with open space, local traditions and the needs of an organised city. In 1459–62, the Tuscan village of Pienza was rebuilt at the orders of Enea Piccolomini (later Pope

Pius II) to the design of Bernardo Rossellino, who applied Alberti's ideas. Closely associated with the Gonzaga, Sabbioneta was a sixteenth-century example of the ideal city based on humanist principles. It was built from nothing by Vespasiano Gonzaga, whose intention was to create a new Classical city of art and culture.

The Renaissance understandably dominates our interest in the Italy of this period. It was indeed impressive, a powerful affirmation of the human ability to envisage a new-moulded world and to try to advance this vision. The improvability, even, to some, the perfectability, of mankind appeared a prospect.

Yet, as with 'Golden Age Holland' in the seventeenth century, this was only the culture of a portion of society. Most particularly, art patronage was, in large part, an aspect of a luxury economy that served princely courts, the Church and urban élites. Cultural display was a way to show political and social status, and this function became increasingly important from the mid-fifteenth century as civic and public art declined. This process was very much demonstrated by the Medici in Florence, although civic and public art remained important in Venice, while another aspect of public art was provided by the Church.

Many other cities also deserve mention. They include Mantua under the Gonzaga and particularly at the time of Isabella d'Este, Francesco Gonzaga's wife, a major cultural and political figure in the Renaissance and one of the greatest patrons of artists. Under the Este, Ferrara was a significant centre of Renaissance Italy. So also with Urbino under the Montefeltro, for which the *Palazzo Ducale* is the key site. Federico da Montefeltro was educated in Mantua by Vittorino da Feltre and was particularly interested in mathematics and architecture.

The first printing press was introduced to Italy in 1464–5 by two German émigrés. Pope Paul II (r. 1464–71) proved an enthusiastic patron. Printers at first used a Roman font that was similar to the appearance of manuscripts. Initially, in Venice, a major centre of publishing, books were sold to a humanist élite who also read manuscripts, and print runs were only about 300 a book. However, from the mid-1470s, there was a change in marketing, appearance, print runs and pricing in Venice, and this change was well established by the 1480s. Books on religious and legal topics were printed in a Gothic font and for a wider market, with an emphasis on utilitarian purposes.

POWER POLITICS

As the work of the painter Andrea Mantegna (1431–1506) for the Gonzaga showed, art was not incompatible with warfare. Indeed, Leonardo da Vinci was supported by warrior-rulers including Francis I of France and Cesare Borgia. The latter used Leonardo as a military engineer. The competing ambitions of Italian states led to much warfare, ensuring that there are impressive fortifications from the period such as the *Castel Sismondo* in Rimini, which was designed by Sigismondo Malatesta, and the *Castello Estense* in Ferrara.

The costs of war encouraged peace negotiations, as did the Turkish challenge to Italy after the fall of Constantinople in 1453. This threat led Pope Nicholas V (r. 1447–55) to try to bring peace in Italy and then form an anti-Turkish league. By the Peace of Lodi (1454), Italy's leading powers – Milan, Venice, Florence, Naples and the Pope – recognised each other's boundaries and laid the basis for over two decades of peace. The War of the Milanese Succession was ended, the recent major expansion by Florence and Venice consolidated, and the attempt by René of Anjou, with the support of France and Francesco Sforza, to revive the Angevin claim to Naples was thwarted.

Italy experienced a quarter-century of relative calm until Venice went to war with Ercole I, Duke of Ferrara, from 1480. Although it faced a coalition of almost all the other Italian states, the settlement that ended the war in 1484 left Venice with some minor gains. More ominously, the Venetians had tried to induce Charles VIII of France to invade Italy with the promise of their help to conquer Naples.

This attempt foreshadowed the French invasion of 1494, an

invasion that launched what were to be called the Italian Wars. These wars reflected not only the divisions of Italy, but also a new, or rather renewed, willingness of outside rulers to intervene. Initially the most important was Charles VIII, who benefited from France's earlier success against England in 1449–53 and the overthrow of Charles the Bold of Burgundy in 1477. Thus, as so often, Italian history was in part a product of the fate of great-power rivalries, both elsewhere and in Italy, a situation that means that Italian history can only accurately be told in this broader context.

The balance of forces within Italy was disturbed, and external powers returned to the peninsula, when Ludovico Sforza, Duke of Milan, asked Charles VIII for help because he feared that Alfonso II of Naples (r. 1494–5), brother of Ferdinand of Aragon, was fomenting an Italian alliance against him. Charles responded promptly, arriving in Italy in the early days of September 1494 with an army composed of 30,000 troops supported by 150 cannon. Charles captured Naples in 1495 at the close of a campaign that had led to the expulsion of Piero II Medici from Florence in 1494. Charles asserted the Angevin claim to Naples and also claimed that he was providing a base for a crusade to the Holy Land. Some Italians with French and Guelf sympathies welcomed his arrival.

However, his success aroused opposition both within Italy, where there was growing suspicion that he aimed to seize the entire peninsula, and from two powerful rulers who had their own ambitions to pursue: Maximilian I, the Holy Roman Emperor, who ruled Austria and the other Habsburg territories, and Ferdinand II of Aragon, ruler of Aragon, Sicily and Sardinia, half-brother of Ferrante (also called Ferdinand I) of Naples (r. 1458–94), and husband of Isabella of Castile. Ferdinand, who combined Italian interests with Spanish resources, joined Venice, Ludovico Sforza, Duke of Milan from 1494, and Pope Alexander VI (r. 1492–1503) in the League of St Mark. Spanish troops moved from Sicily into mainland southern Italy in 1495, and the French were driven from Italy in 1495–6. This success further encouraged Ferdinand's interest in southern Italy.

FORTIFICATIONS *ALLA MODERNA*

The increased effectiveness of cannon against the stationary target of high stone walls led to the redesign of fortifications to provide lower, denser and more complex targets. Some of these defences can still be seen today. Bastions, generally quadrilateral or pentagonal, angled and at regular intervals along all walls, were introduced to keep the besieger from the inner walls and to provide gun platforms able to launch effective flanking fire against attackers. The defences, strengthened with earth to minimise the impact of cannon fire, were slanted to help deflect and defeat cannon balls. To a degree drawing inspiration from the idealised radial city plans offered in Renaissance art and utopian political tracts, many new-style fortifications were built, including in Civitavecchia (1515), Florence (1534), Ancona (1536), Genoa (1536–8) and Turin (from 1564).

THE FACTS OF LIFE

Much of life remained grim, as far from the values of the Renaissance as that of the Middle Ages had been from the ideas of chivalry. Sanitation and diet were major problems for the bulk of the population. Their housing conditions, in particular the habit of sharing beds, were conducive to a high incidence of respiratory infections. This was a consequence of the lack of privacy that was produced by the limited nature of the housing stock.

In Renaissance Italy, louse infestation was related to crowding, inadequate bathing facilities and the continual wearing of the same clothes. Cleanliness was associated with wearing clean shirts and linen, rather than washing, but both were only possible for a minority. Whatever their wealth, humans had few defences against a whole range of the natural world, from lice, bedbugs and fleas to tapeworms.

The habit of washing in clean water was perforce limited, while the proximity of animals and dunghills was unhelpful. Like the rest of Europe, Italy was a society that conserved, rather than disposed of, its excrement. Animal and human waste were gathered for the purpose of manure, a crucial replenishment of soil fertility; but this manure was a health-hazard, notably through contaminating the water supply. Effluent from undrained privies and animal pens flowed across streets, and on and beneath the surface, into houses through generally porous walls. Typhus was one result.

Alongside the availability, in towns from Roman times, of public fountains and public taps in streets, clean drinking water was an issue across much of Italy, especially in coastal regions and lowland areas without deep wells. River water was often muddy, while pump water could be affected by sewage. As elsewhere in Europe, this accounted for the importance of fermented drinks.

As elsewhere, and reminding us anew that a history of Italy is in part a history of Europe, poor nutrition also contributed to the spread of infectious diseases by lowering resistance. Furthermore, malnutrition limited sexual desire and activity, hindered successful pregnancy, and, if chronic, delayed sexual maturity and produced sterility in women. Problems of food shortage and cost ensured that the bulk of the population lacked a balanced diet, even when they had enough food. Diet was a particular problem for the urban poor, who found fruit and vegetables, let alone meat and fish, expensive, and who were also frequently ill-clad. The peasantry consumed little meat or fish.

Disease was not only affected by nutrition. Harsh weather, notably, but not only, in the winter, could weaken resistance. It was exacerbated by shortages of firewood and by the damp, cold, cramped and insanitary nature of much accommodation.

The persistence of disease ensured that weak sections of the community remained especially vulnerable. The real killer of babies was puerperal fever, the cause of which was not understood until the nineteenth century. However, politico-social factors were also significant in famine and disease. Subsistence crises were not simply the result of exceeding the amount of food available, but also had their roots in the unequal distribution of resources and in the limitations of governmental action. Animal health, moreover, was a serious problem. The primitive nature of veterinary science was an issue, and the usual response was the slaughter of animals and the prohibition of their movement.

The situation at the level of the individual was of a hostile and unpredictable environment, of forces that could be neither prevented nor propitiated, and of the efforts of years swept away in an instant. The line between independence and calamity, between being poor and falling into pauperdom, could be crossed easily, fast and frequently. Most individuals had few assets.

Renaissance art did not capture the grim working conditions of the age. For example, fishing was dangerous, while many places of craft work and industrial employment, including those involved in the production of works of art, craft and architecture, were damp, poorly ventilated, badly lit or dangerous. Exposure to hazardous substances, such as lead and mercury, was a serious problem, while construction work was very dangerous. Millers worked in dusty and noisy circumstances, frequently suffered from lice and often developed asthma, hernias and chronic back problems. The notions of health and safety at work were barely understood and the issues involved were generally not grasped.

Agriculture was highly vulnerable to the weather and to disease. There were few improved crop strains, and rainy winters produced diseased and swollen crops, while late frosts attacked wheat and other crops. The absence of pesticides, and the difficulties in protecting crops and stored foods, were serious issues. Mice and rats posed major problems. The facts of life were frequently deadly.

At the same time, a definite effort was made to ameliorate, even improve, circumstances and consequences. This was an aspect not only of traditional care, both religious and civic, for the unfortunate and others, but also of the Renaissance as an aspiration for, and form of, the application of knowledge. Thus, in Venice, much money was spent on curing the sick, and for the defence of the city and the

Adriatic coastal ports as a whole from disease. Measures were taken not only to prevent infections arriving by ship but also for general hygiene.

Because of the plague, Venice pioneered and developed systematic projects for prevention. Already, in the thirteenth century, the Venetian *Capitolari* had defined the general rules for health workers and their role in the care of the patients. It became very active in the fourteenth century, giving advice on cures and on how to wash garments, and also seeking to control the many charlatans and fake doctors in the city. Venice had also, in the *Scuola di Rialto*, a preparatory school of natural philosophy leading to medical study, and in 1485 the *provisores super salute* (doctors, apothecaries and barbers) became an established centre of hygiene for the general health of everybody. Several hospitals followed: the *Ospedale dei derelitti* (for the poor), *incurabili* (the terminally ill), *della Pietà* (for children) and *San Giovanni e Paolo*.

Hospitals had long existed. For example, the still-working *Ospedale di Santo Spirito* began its medical activity in Rome in 1198 as a development of what had previously been the hostel for British pilgrims. However, more hospitals followed in the Renaissance, including those established in Bergamo (1449), Verona (1515) and Brescia (1521), while Francesco Sforza founded the *Ospedale Maggiore* in Milan in 1456.

Knowledge was pursued, disseminated and applied. In the early fifteenth century, partly in order to solve the problem of several infectious diseases, the University of Padua promoted the study of medicine and anatomy, and became an innovative centre for these disciplines. In 1545, a botanical garden for medicinal plants was included. The spread of printing made it easier to communicate information. Several texts on medicine were published, especially in Venice, for example the *Consiglio per la peste* by Pietro da Tossignano, which was included in *Fasciculo de Medicina* published in Venice in 1494, and Pietro Tommasi's work on preventive medicine.

Yet, traditional remedies also remained significant, notably folk remedies and spiritual intervention. In the *Chiesa di Sant' Agostino*

(Church of St Augustine) in San Gimignano, Benozzo Gozzoli painted a fresco showing Saint Sebastian intervening to protect the city against the 1464 plague epidemic. Such beliefs remained important, and part of the ritual of particular communities and their sense of identity.

CHAPTER FOUR

The Italian Wars: The Sixteenth Century

WAR TO THE FORE

The French were not prepared to see defeat in 1495–6 as final. To do so would be to surrender royal *gloire* and to compromise regal status. Charles's successor, Louis XII (r. 1498–1515), invaded the duchy of Milan in 1499, claiming the duchy on the grounds that his grandmother had been a Visconti. The Venetians also invaded the duchy. The major positions fell to the French in August–September, while Genoa accepted a French governor. French troops were also sent to help Alexander VI's illegitimate son, Cesare Borgia (c. 1476–1507), in Romagna where he sought both to consolidate the papal position and, in the end unsuccessfully, to create a new principality for himself.

However, disaffection with French rule led to a rallying of support to Ludovico Sforza who regained Milan in February 1500. In turn, the strength of the French response and the evaporation of Swiss support led to the collapse of Sforza's army. Swiss mercenaries, trained and effective pikemen, the heavy infantry of the age, were key military players, but they had to be paid. Ludovico was sent a prisoner to France, where he died in 1508, and Louis's power was reimposed in Milan. Louis and Ferdinand II of Aragon partitioned Naples by the Treaty of Granada (1500), and the French captured the city of Naples in 1501.

However, the new territorial order proved precarious. Disputes with Ferdinand in 1502 led the French to try to take the entire kingdom, only to be heavily defeated by the Spaniards in 1503. As a result, in 1504, Naples entered a personal union with the kingdom of Aragon under Ferdinand, while Louis renounced his claims to Naples by the Second Treaty of Blois of 1505.

The battlefield of Europe, Italy was increasingly dominated by France and/or Spain. These were the only powers with the resources to support and sustain a major military effort. Pope Julius II, a *perpetuum mobile* of papal plotting, formed the League of Cambrai in 1508, with Milan, Austria, Mantua, Savoy-Piedmont, the Swiss and France, in order to attack and despoil Venice. It was France's role that was decisive, notably in defeating a much smaller Venetian army at Agnadello (1509). Indicating the consequences of defeat in battle, much of the Venetian *terraferma* then rebelled, only for Venice, in this crisis, to display resilience and regain control.

Italian rulers adapted, if possible, to foreign invaders and sought to employ them to serve their own ends. For example, the Este of Ferrara aligned with the French against papal expansion. Thus, there was no inherent conflict between these rulers and foreign powers. The latter were able to find local allies, but these, in turn, could affect the relationship between France and Spain. Thus, in 1511, there was one of the dizzying changes of alignment typical of the period, and notably so in Italy, changes that Italian rulers helped to cause but from which they suffered: Julius II formed the Holy League, with Spain, Venice and Henry VIII of England, in order to drive the French from Italy. The French beat the Spaniards at Ravenna (1512), but Swiss intervention against France, and opposition to the French in Genoa and Milan, helped the Spaniards to regain the initiative. The French retreated across the Alps, while the Spaniards overran Tuscany, and Massimiliano Sforza was installed in Milan. Local politics was set by big-power confrontations.

In 1513, the French invaded across the Alps anew, supported by the Venetians who were afraid of Milanese expansion. The Swiss came in to help Sforza against the French, but were defeated at Novara, and the *terraferma* was ravaged by the French to the shores of the Venetian lagoon. Such activity drove home the cost of war.

Soon after coming to the French throne, the dynamic Francis I (r. 1515–47) invaded the Milanese anew, defeating the Swiss at Marignano (1515). The French then occupied Milan until 1521. However, the election in 1519 of Charles I of Spain – heir of Ferdinand and Isabella, and heir of Maximilian and of the Aragonese, Castilian, Habsburg and Burgundian inheritance – as the Holy Roman Emperor Charles V seemed to confirm the worst French fears of Habsburg hegemony: Spain, Naples, Sicily, Sardinia, the Low Countries and Austria were now under one ruler. Francis declared war on Charles in 1521, only to lose Milan (1521) and be defeated at Bicocca (1522). This led Venice to turn to Charles (1523), and in early 1524 it helped his forces drive out a fresh French invasion of Milan.

A renewed French invasion later in the year led to the French capture of Milan and to alliance with Venice and Pope Clement VII (r. 1523–34). The Spaniards, however, crushed the French at Pavia (1525), capturing Francis who agreed peace on Charles's terms, enabling Charles to invest his ally Francesco Sforza with the duchy of Milan. Once released, Francis repudiated the terms, claimed, with reason, that his agreement had been extorted, and agreed with Clement VII, Francesco Sforza, Venice and Florence to establish the League of Cognac (1526), which led to the resumption of war. Again, rapid changes in alignment were the order of the day.

In 1527, a truce between Pope Clement and Charles V left the latter's army unoccupied. Charles was short of money to pay his troops who marched on Rome and sacked the city in the 'Sack of Rome', inflicting very heavy damage. Contemporaries compared it to the fall of Rome to the Goths in 410. The French invaded Italy anew, but repeated French failures, including in a siege of Naples, led Francis to accept the Treaty of Cambrai (1529), also called the Peace of the Two Ladies because of the role of Luisa of Savoy-Piedmont and Margaret of Habsburg. Francis abandoned his Italian pretensions, while, although Francesco Sforza was restored to Milan, the right to garrison the citadel was reserved to Charles. Venice, which had gained control of a number of ports in Apulia in 1495–1509 and 1528–9, finally restored them to Naples, while Ravenna and Rimini were restored to Clement VII.

Charles V's victory at Pavia, followed by the Treaty of Cambrai, ensured a major change in the Italian perception of his role. In place of the view of Charles as a powerful Italian ruler among other powerful such rulers, and as an alternative leader to the French king, came the perception of Charles as a dominant force, one able to draw on international strength and local support. In the person of Charles, Spanish control of Naples seemed fixed.

Charles's power was clearly demonstrated in the successful siege of Florence in 1529–30, after which he restored the Medici to power in the person of Alessandro de'Medici. They were to turn this into a key episode in the transition of Florence, from a republic with strong republican institutions, into a duchy, later a grand duchy, so that the city became the capital of a territorial state. This transition entailed a measure of continuity as the same families continued to enjoy influence. Nevertheless, there was also the standard absolutist repertoire from coercion, for example new fortresses, to consensus, the latter being affirmed by the idea of authority as endorsed by religion, a view very much taken by Cosimo I as ruler (1537–74). An attempt to restore the republic in 1537, when Duke Alessandro de'Medici was assassinated, failed. In turn, his cousin, Lorenzino de'Medici, who was responsible for the murder, was killed at the behest of Charles V in 1548: the republican exiles were linked to France and Turkey. As so often, domestic politics were linked to international power politics, with subversion being a standard means to pursue interests.

War resumed after the death of Francesco Sforza in 1535 led to a disputed succession in Milan. Francis invaded Italy in 1536, but the inability of either side to secure a particular advantage led to a truce. In 1540, Charles invested his son Philip (later Philip II of Spain) with the duchy of Milan, which represented the transfer of part of the imperial (then Austrian) legacy in Italy to Spain. In 1544, the French invaded northern Italy again, but the decisive fighting that decade took place north of the Alps. So also in the 1550s.

The wars not only saw a clash between the major powers, but also related struggles involving others. Thus, in the 1550s, Spain fought Pope Paul IV (r. 1555–9), and also supported Florence in attacking and annexing Siena. This was an instance of the extent to which divisions within Italy interacted with those between the major powers. In 1552, Siena had rebelled against Spanish control and, in cooperation with France, seized the citadel from the Spaniards. Florence under the Medici was, from the late 1520s, an ally of the Habsburgs. In turn, cooperation with the Turkish fleet enabled France to occupy Corsica in 1553–4: Genoa, the ruler of Corsica, was an ally of Spain.

Charles V divided his empire between his brother, Ferdinand I, the new Holy Roman Emperor, who received the Austrian part of the inheritance, and his son, Philip, who got the rest: Spain, the Italian territories including, crucially, Milan, the Low Countries and the Spanish territories in the New World. Milan was thereby permanently detached from the Holy Roman Empire. In turn, in 1559, by the Treaty of Cateau-Cambrésis, Henry II of France (the son of Francis I) accepted a peace by which Philip was left in control of Milan, Naples, Sicily and Sardinia. Savoy and Piedmont, which France had seized in 1536, were returned to Duke Emmanuel Philibert of Savoy (r. 1553–80), a nephew of Charles V and a loyal and successful general to him. The return of Emmanuel Philibert's possessions was a restoration of his rights to a relative of Charles, the reward of a local general and the creation of a client state. Siena had to accept the control of Florence. Cosimo I acquired the title Grand Duke of Tuscany from Pius V in 1569, a title subsequently ratified by the Emperor. The Habsburgs had won the Italian Wars, and, despite conflict earlier, in the 1610s, 1620s and 1630s, this triumph was not to be seriously challenged until the 1640s.

International rivalry continued to play a role in Italy in the late sixteenth century, but Spain was dominant. France and the Turks provided help to the Corsican rebellion against Genoese rule in 1564, while the Genoese were backed by Spanish troops. The rebels, under Sampiero Corso, used the difficult terrain to their advantage with guerrilla tactics, but, aside from the professionalism of the Spanish troops, the Corsicans were divided, a product of the long hold of factional feuds, and by 1569 Genoese control had been re-established.

These feuds were also significant elsewhere, notably in Sardinia. In the 1560s, a local rebellion in Finale on the Ligurian coast drove out the harsh ruler, Alfonso Del Carretto, but when, in 1571, Philip II intervened, he took over the principality for himself. In Casale Monferrato, Spanish troops helped the ruler, Duke Guglielmo of Mantua (r. 1560–87), suppress resistance to his attempts to limit tax and judicial exemptions. Corsica, Finale and Casale were all important for the articulation of Spanish power. Genoa acted as the bank for the Spanish Empire, Corsica in French hands could be a threat to the movement of Spanish troops to Italy, Finale was their landing port, and Casale a fortress that protected their march north.

Not all revolts provided opportunities for the display of Spanish power. In 1573, Guidobaldo II, Duke of Urbino, harshly repressed a revolt against new taxes without Spanish assistance. The contested succession to Alfonso II, the last Duke of Ferrara (r. 1559–97), led Cesare d'Este and the Pope to raise armies, only for the former to back down when he did not receive French support. Pope Clement VIII (r. 1592–1605) occupied Ferrara, and the Este continued as dukes of Modena until the male line died out in 1803. Meanwhile, the new political order was imposed with citadels, such as those built by the Medici. Urban republicanism continued in Venice, Genoa and Lucca, but it was not the prime model in northern Italy, let alone elsewhere.

THE COUNTER-REFORMATION

Meanwhile, alongside Spain, Italy was the centre of the Counter-Reformation, the energising of Catholicism by a reform movement directed both against Protestantism and for a revival of Catholicism. Protestantism itself had scant support in Italy where Catholic orthodoxy was very much maintained by the Church authorities including the Inquisition. Thus, Domenico Scandella or Menocchio (1532–99), a literate miller from Montereale in Friuli who rejected the Christian creation account and, instead, asserted pantheistic beliefs, was burnt at the stake for his heresies on the orders of Pope Clement VIII. A new body that served to strengthen papal power, the Inquisition found its authority contested in some territories, notably Venice, and accepted elsewhere, as in Naples.

Launched in Trent, the capital of a prince-bishopric, where a Church council opened in 1545 lasted until 1563, the Counter-Reformation had particular cultural energy, with an active programme of church building and decoration. The new commitment, as well as the reconstruction and strengthening of the Papal States after the Italian Wars, were symbolised in Rome by the Baroque reshaping of the city. This was notably, but not only, the case under Sixtus V (r. 1585–90). There were also changes in devotional patterns, particularly with an increase in emphasis on the Eucharist. As a consequence, the significance of internal church features changed. Thus, in St John in Lateran in Rome, there was a greater stress from 1599 on the new altar of the Blessed Sacrament. More generally, architecture was a product of changing functions and of altered responses. This was also seen in this period in the development of fortifications built *alla moderna*, a term, referring to ravelins and other geometric anti-cannon features, later described as *trace italienne*.

The political significance of artistic motifs was clearly shown across Italy, and notably in Venice where there was a rejection of the style of church architecture that was seen to betoken papal authority. Instead, the emphasis there was on religious and cultural reform, notably in the reconstruction of the church of San Salvador, which was more austere than St Peter's in Rome. So also with cathedrals in the *terraferma* such as the *Duomo Nuovo* (1604) in Brescia. Its height, hence power, had to be greater than that of the early medieval civil *Palazzo Broletto* and *Torre del Pegol* (people tower) next door.

Medieval buildings were given frescoed interiors, and new altars and paintings, during the Counter-Reformation, as with the cathedral in Verona. More generally, the art of the Counter-Reformation expressed the range of the latter and drew on a number of traditions, including reforming zeal, humanist erudition and sensual refinement. The light and dark of the at-once naturalistic and theatrical paintings of Michelangelo Merisi da Caravaggio (1573–1610) reflected these tensions. This was notably so of his *Conversion of St Paul* and the *Crucifixion of St Peter*, both in Rome's *Chiesa di Santa Maria del Popolo*, and of his *Le sette opera di Misericordia* (*The Seven Acts of Mercy*) in Naples in the *Pio Monte della Misericordia*, a charity established in 1601 to provide loans to the poor.

Religious practice was not restricted to religious institutions. In Milan, a centre of the Counter-Reformation under the talented archbishops of the Borromeo family, there was an emphasis on educating children. Charles Borromeo (1538–84), appointed to Milan by his uncle, Pius IV, at the age of twenty-two, made a major effort to support poor relief during the famine of 1570 and the plague of 1576. He was canonised in 1610, and much celebrated in paintings.

More generally, charitable activity was regarded as important alongside the maintenance of orthodoxy, while preaching was seen as important in order to combine moral living with spiritual renewal. The Counter-Reformation can be treated in a positive light, in terms of instigating Church reform through existing institutions. The Church played a crucial role in social care, and in combining lay spirituality with ecclesiastical bureaucracy.

However, far less positively, attempts to restore Church unity, by means of doctrinal compromise with Protestantism alongside Church reform, were pushed aside in favour of the definition of existing Catholic teaching. This was a rigid and intolerant approach that prefigured that which was to be taken by the papacy in the nineteenth century and for most of the twentieth. Pius IV (r. 1559–65) issued the Tridentine Creed in 1564 and instituted the Index of Forbidden Books, while Borromeo drew up the *Catechismus Romanus* (1566). In 1570, Pius V excommunicated Elizabeth I of England, beginning another religious war. Pius also implemented the Tridentine decrees. He was made a saint in 1712.

The Church, however, was never a monolith, and this contributed to the fluid nature of the Counter-Reformation, notably the role of local initiatives. Local sacral traditions were strongly supported, as in Florence. As an instance of diversity, the Counter-Reformation strengthened the patriarchal character of Italian life in some respects, while also providing more space for female spirituality and religious projects. Women were not invisible in the Church. Religious foundations for single women who did not wish to become nuns were intended to protect women whose virtue was endangered by the absence of adequate family protection.

Rulers subscribed to the new norms of the Counter-Reformation. Moving his capital from Chambéry to Turin, in the 1560s, Emmanuel Philibert also moved the Holy Shroud, a relic of Christ's death that gave the dynasty particular prestige and that still can be seen in Turin cathedral. Moreover, the dukes of Savoy-Piedmont sought to patronise shrines whose saints could be seen as working for the state as a whole, and not for only part of it.

DECLINE?

The Italian Wars remain important to the standard account of Italian history, one that presents a series of 'lost centuries' of foreign rule and relative decline, a period only ended with the *Risorgimento* (national independence and unification) of the nineteenth century. These centuries certainly saw a series of wars, with Italy being particularly affected in 1494–1559, 1611–59, 1673–8, 1689–97, 1701–13, 1717–20, 1733–5, 1741–8 and 1792–1815, while Venice was involved in major wars with the Turks, culminating with those of 1645–69, 1684–99 and 1715–18. Italian states lost their surviving foreign territories, the Turks conquering Naxos in 1537, Cyprus in 1570–1 and Crete in 1645–69 from Venice. Genoa lost Chios to the Turks in 1566, and sold Corsica to France in 1768, while, from 1798, first France and then Britain ruled Malta which, before being ruled by the Knights of St John, had been a dependency of Sicily. The Ionian Islands went from Venice in 1797 and were gained by Britain in the Congress of Vienna (1814–15), being eventually transferred by Britain to Greece in 1863.

Linked to this is the idea of cultural decline and social stultification after the Renaissance, and as part of a more general relative decline of the Mediterranean, as the key routes of trade and cultural interchange no longer ran across and around the blue sea. As with most commonly accepted historical interpretations, there was, and is, a measure of truth in this. In particular, it would be foolish to pretend that Mediterranean societies played as central a role in the age of developing Atlantic oceans as they had done in the past. In practice, however, Italy shared in the more general trends of European society, notably population growth in the sixteenth century, relative stagnation in the seventeenth and renewed growth in the eighteenth.

ECONOMY AND SOCIETY

Yet, these trends played out in particular ways as a result of the situation of individual states and economies. The kingdom of Naples benefited greatly in the sixteenth century, thanks to the ability to export, particularly silk, metal goods, ships, shoes, wine and olive oil, but was badly hit in the sixteenth and seventeenth centuries by the need to finance Spain's lengthy wars through taxation, loans and the farming of taxes, with a resultant impact on liquidity. If Spain paid for protection, it normally asked for 'a present' to be given. The kingdom was squeezed by Spain for money, goods and men, as much as possible and without mercy. The *donativo*, the 'present', began in 1504 with 311,000 ducats, and it later became normal. Between 1532 and 1553, Naples sent Spain a total of 6.5 million ducats and, subsequently, the tax went up, becoming, in the 1560s, 1.2 million to be paid every two years. By 1607, the debt was 8 million ducats. Moreover, in Naples, the population increase of the sixteenth century meant that land was taken out of production for wine or mulberries (for silk), both export goods, and was transferred to grain production.

Across Italy, agriculture was the principal source of employment and wealth, the most significant sector of the economy, the basis of the taxation – government, ecclesiastical (tithes), seigneurial and proprietorial (rents) – that funded most other activities. Land and its products provided both the structure of the social system and the bulk of the wealth that kept it in being. The impact of agriculture extended to the towns. In much of Mediterranean Europe, and notably in Sicily, agricultural workers lived in towns, rather than in dispersed settlements, in part because the peasants feared brigands who normally attacked at night-time.

Moreover, the links between agriculture, industry and trade were close. The limited advances in the state of technological and scientific knowledge ensured that manufacturing was based on natural products. The age of synthesised products, notably in fabrics, had not yet arrived. The staple industrial activities were concerned with the manufacture of consumer goods – food, drink, clothes, shoes and furniture – that relied on raw materials produced in the countryside, such as wool, animal hides and timber.

As the bulk of the population lived in rural areas and engaged in agricultural activities, it is not surprising that the prosperity of these activities played a significant role in determining the nature of the purchasing power in the communities of Europe. Rural wealth created a market both for industrial goods and for expensive agricultural products, such as meat. Conversely, poverty, the commonest state for the bulk of the rural (and urban) population, acted as a permanent limitation on the markets for goods, products and services. Any rise in the cost of agricultural products, especially grain, affected the urban population, reducing purchasing power, both in the towns and among much of the rural population, and restricting the market for manufactured goods. Alterations in the prices of agricultural products were a constant feature, essentially for seasonal reasons, the price of foodstuffs generally rising to a peak in the early summer as last year's harvest was used up. Harvest variations dictated additional price changes that were often very sharp. The consequences contributed to a sense of uncertainty. The prevailing systems of farming did not produce enough to create a reliable margin of safety in the event of harvest difficulties, and few regions of Italy produced a sufficiently large marketable surplus to help areas where grain production failed. Slow and expensive transport limited the effect of those which did.

The extension of the cultivated area, whether achieved by the clearing of trees, the removal of stones or the digging of irrigation ditches, was essentially the product of labour-intensive methods. Deforestation, however, helped make the climate drier, which affected the soil. Malaria was a serious problem. The entire coast was affected from Tuscany to Sicily, as well as many rural areas, for example the plain around Rome. The resulting high mortality rate hit the rural economy and helped explain why so much of the countryside was poorly populated apart from upland settlements.

POWER AND AUTHORITY

Alongside states, there were the strategies of landowners and urban oligarchs, strategies that played the key role in shaping the system and character of power in Italy's localities. In 1526, for example, the aristocratic Colonna family intimidated Pope Clement VII (r. 1523–34) before occupying Rome. In the city of Brescia in the Venetian-ruled *terraferma*, on a pattern that was more generally typical, the close-knit families that sustained the city's most important governmental responsibilities owed their political pre-eminence to family continuity, antiquity, both in terms of time served on council and in terms of social status, wealth, professional standing and beneficial marriage connections. All five factors were tied to the behaviour of households and to lineage. The stability of these families was important to the maintenance of political order. Family ties were crucial in both alliances and disputes among the Brescian élite. They also proved a formidable challenge to the effective administration of justice, and thus to Venetian control. Powerful families at the fore in town government sought to run aspects of it, such as the judicial apparatus and the grain-provisioning system, in their own interests. Grain provisioning was always a key aspect of government and power, indeed one that looked back to ancient Rome.

There were social and political tensions behind the facades of power. These facades, which drew on the theatres of power that helped focus artistic patronage, provided myths of control, but the reality, as on the Venetian *terraferma*, was of the strength of local factions interacting with loose and flexible governance. For example, in 1640–5, a dispute between the Brescian oligarchy and the Venetian state over the fiscal demands of the latter provided the occasion for a campaign from within Brescia by well-off, but disenfranchised, groups challenging the élite and proposing a more broadly based government. The Venetian state eventually chose to compromise with the local oligarchy, and the Brescian protesters, who anyway lacked self-confidence, cohesion and popular support, were rendered powerless by this decision. Near Brescia, the communes of the *Magnifica Patria* on Lake Garda had a great deal of independence.

Thus, the political system of the *terraferma* – local particularism and, especially, the power of urban-based aristocracies – continued to prevail, as it did across most of Italy. This resilience of the old aristocratic order was indeed a major strand in Italian society, urban and rural, although its attitude towards entrepreneurialism depended on the particular culture of the territory in question. In Naples, Sicily, the Papal States, Parma, Modena and Savoy-Piedmont, the emphasis was on landowning as a mark of nobility, but in Lombardy, Liguria, Venetia and Tuscany, the nobles were traditionally involved in trade and industry. The old aristocratic order remained very important into the nineteenth century and, in part, to the present day. Indeed, despite the end of the monarchy, a degree of secularisation, and the decline of the aristocracy discussed in Giuseppe di Lampedusa's famous and atmospheric novel *Il Gattopardo* (*The Leopard*, 1962), aspects of the old order and the related influence have in part survived far more than many Italians find it comfortable to note.

The interactions between these local worlds and central government were far from fixed in their character and provided much of the context of politics. Rulers sought to establish their officials as the intermediaries between themselves and the localities, but, to be effective, these officials had to accommodate themselves to the locally powerful.

The Florentine Health Board was established on a permanent basis in 1527. It can appear as a major new adjunct to government, not least because, although initially created to respond to the plague, it had become, by the early seventeenth century, a more wide-ranging body for the maintenance of public health. The Board dispatched physicians to examine particular epidemics and also sought to use systematically collected information, demanding, in 1622, that local authorities report on the state of sanitation. This reflected the view that open privies, stagnant water, and the failure to remove human and animal waste were responsible for 'miasmas' in the air, 'miasmas' that were thought to cause epidemics because epidemics were not understood. However, neither the local authorities nor the people were ready to respond to the advice of the Board. In practice, policy-making in public health was not greatly carried forward in Tuscany during the sixteenth and seventeenth centuries. Nor was there much that could be done about the traumatic plagues that hit Italy in 1575 and 1630. Troop movements from Germany were decisive to the spread of the 1630 plague.

Tuscany was a relatively small state, where, as also with Parma in the late eighteenth century, the possibilities for effective government were greater than in larger states, but compromise with the élite was nevertheless the key element. This is clear from the administration of criminal justice under the first three Medici grand dukes, who ruled from 1537 to 1609. Unwilling to meet the high costs of rigid enforcement, and unable to control the poor, the grand dukes found that compromise secured acknowledgement of their power to administer justice. Local officials played a crucial role in the capture of fugitives and the reporting of crime, but local police forces were small, poorly paid and generally enmeshed in local networks of family alliances. The Medici sought to create loyalty among local élites by upholding their interests against those of their competitors. The scale and organisation of violence, although possibly not its incidence, seem to have been much greater outside than within Florence. Authority was more effective in the city, and violence there was committed mainly by individuals and small groups of close kin, rather than by the locally potent families and factions that, on a long-standing pattern, feuded in the smaller cities and the countryside. The resulting system was neither modern nor 'absolutist', as the term is currently generally understood in works that stress the rise of the modern state and the emergence of bureaucratic organisations. Both are misleading concepts for this period.

Alongside institutional developments, there was a high level of violence across Italy. Frequently associated with the social élite, brigandage remained a marked feature of Sicilian society. In the Veneto and Lombardy, there was a rise in violence and a revival of feuds at the close of the sixteenth century. Feuding and banditry helped determine the standard pattern of rural homesteads: the ground floor had no windows and served as a barn, the door of which was made of very heavy timbers and iron strapping. The stairway from the ground floor to the upper floor, where the family lived, was very steep, narrow and eminently defensible. The *cascina* in the north or the *masseria* in the south were a form of small fortified village, as the houses of this type were surrounded and protected by a defensive wall, and the settlement had only one entrance.

Another form of bleakness was provided by the economic changes that hit many farmers. In particular, as land was acquired by estate-holders and townsmen, many farmers became day labourers. This was a process that helped define much of Italian society to the present and that was particularly important until the large-scale movement from the land after the Second World War.

Authority and power were also seen in more intimate settings. The responsibility of the heads of households for their members extended into moral and social spheres. The head of a household had an official description, *capofamiglia*, and he set the rules for everybody in the family. Most of these were over thirty-eight and all who were not heads were legally dependent. Designated as *figlio di famiglia* (child of the family), they could not contract for land or enter into any other form of contractual relationship. The phrase had several meanings according to different contexts and different periods. In medieval times, *figli di famiglia* referred to *non liberi* (not free), people who lived on lands they did not own and had to obey a common master. From here, the phrase came to mean all the servants working for a household or just for a person, as opposed to the contemporary meaning of the children of important families.

People working as artisans and merchants lived in different conditions to those on the land. Houses were different for particular levels of society. In the countryside, there was more of a practice of sharing a room, whereas tradesmen and merchants tend to use the ground floor for tools, workshops and goods, and to live above. Geographical differences were also always a factor.

Nuclear families appear to have been preferred, but family combinations were encouraged by a lack of land, the effects of death and family-based economic systems. Many agricultural and industrial tasks could be accomplished by children. At Altopascio in Tuscany, four- and five-year-olds tended livestock. Their likely futures were poor, and certainly not better than those of their parents.

CHAPTER FIVE

Baroque Italy: The Seventeenth Century

THE PLAYTHING OF THE GREAT POWERS

Italy continued to be affected by what must have seemed incessant conflict. In 1610, Charles Emmanuel I of Savoy (r. 1580–1630) assembled an army to support French schemes in Italy against Spain, but the assassination of Henry IV of France in Paris that year as he was preparing for war lessened the crisis. However, Charles Emmanuel was then financed by Venice in order to distract Spanish forces in Lombardy from attacking the republic: the Venetian government correctly alleged that Spain was plotting to overthrow the republic.

In 1613 war broke out between Venice and Austria. Venice had difficulties with Dalmatian privateers, the Uskoks of Senj, who were protected by the Austrian Habsburgs. A Venetian fleet attacked the privateers in their ports. This maritime war expanded to the Italian mainland where Venetian forces attacked Austrian troops at Gradisca, a city in neighbouring Friuli. Spain prepared its forces in Milan in order to assist the Austrians, while Charles Emmanuel I demanded the marquisate of Monferrato in pursuit of a succession claim. Spanish opposition to his expansion ensured that war broke out in 1613. Although the weight of forces favoured Spain, the Spanish army from Milan was defeated. Surviving for the moment, Charles Emmanuel actively pursued a Venetian alliance. The Senate in Venice decided that this Savoyard distraction served it better than an active war between Venice and Spain. Rather than declaring war on Spain, Venice covertly subsidised the Savoyard army, and Charles Emmanuel's war occupied Spanish resources in Italy.

The Spanish (in other words Neapolitan) fleet appeared in the southern Adriatic, but the Venetian fleet was more than adequate to meet the challenge. The war stalemated, but the threat of French intervention compelled Philip III of Spain (r. 1598–1621) to end the conflict before his Italian territories were threatened by an alliance of France, Savoy-Piedmont and Venice. In 1617, the powers came to terms. Charles Emmanuel, who had invaded the Monferrato in 1613, 1615 and 1617, did not gain it in the peace.

France and Charles Emmanuel tried to seize Spain's ally Genoa in 1625, only to be driven back by the Spaniards who were concerned about its significance for Spanish strategic links. In 1627, the end of the direct male line of the Gonzaga family produced a contested succession for the duchies of Mantua and Monferrato. Spain, again concerned about the wider strategic situation of particular Italian territories, intervened in force in 1628 in what became the War of the Mantuan Succession, and France, in turn, sent in an army. So, also in 1629, in support of Spain, did Austria, the army of which spread plague.

As a reminder that Italian politics were an aspect of wider strategies, these interventions were determined by other events, for example French success against the Huguenots and that of Austria against the Danes. The Swedish invasion of northern Germany in 1630 led to the negotiation of peace in northern Italy in 1631, only for war to resume in 1635 as part of a large-scale conflict between France and Spain. French invasions of Lombardy in the late 1630s failed.

The Habsburg cause in Germany during the Thirty Years War (1618–48) was actively supported from Italian resources. Pope Paul V (r. 1605–21) pledged 20,000 florins per month for the duration of the conflict, Tuscany maintained a cavalry regiment in Germany throughout the war, and thousands of Italians fought in the Habsburg armies in Germany. The greater part of Habsburg forces and finances were drawn from Italy.

Under the new French first minister from 1642 to 1661, Cardinal Richelieu's protégé and successor, the Italian-born Cardinal Mazarin (born Giulio Raimondo Mazzarino), operations in Italy played an important role for France. Amphibious expeditions were significant, giving France a range and flexibility otherwise limited by the need to cross the Alps. In 1646, the French captured Piombino and Porto Longone on the island of Elba, important bases that controlled naval movements, but attempts to take Genoa, Finale and Orbetello, and thus cut links between Spain and Italy, failed. So did attempts to exploit anti-Spanish rebellions in Naples and Sicily in 1647–8.

Italy played a major role as part of wider strategic calculations. The 'Spanish Road', the system by which Spanish forces were moved from the Mediterranean, via Lombardy, north through the Alps, most of them ultimately to the Low Countries, had two sea routes to Finale in Liguria. The longest, and less safe, was from Barcelona, and the safer one from Naples, a major stronghold of the Spanish crown. Troops embarked in Naples – which, rather than any dream of reviving Angevin power in Naples, explains French support for rebellion there – and sailed, or were rowed, north. They stopped in Gaeta, Orbetello, Elba or Piombino, and then Finale. To cut the maritime route was strategically highly significant.

The Neapolitan rising of 1647, led by Tommaso Aniello or Masaniello, was in large part a response to the fiscal demands of a Spanish government desperately short of funds for the war, notably a tax on fresh fruit. Divisions within Naples, which led to the killing of Masaniello, helped the Spaniards recapture the city in 1648. The episode became the setting for Daniel Auber's dramatic opera *La Muette de Portici* (1828), which also shows an explosion of Vesuvius.

In the 1650s, Spain regained Porto Longone and Piombino, defeated the French at Pavia in 1655, and overran the pro-French duchy of Modena, whose duke had abandoned Spain. Peace came in 1659, the Peace of the Pyrenees, with Spain still dominant in Italy. It is overly easy to forget this, as also to ignore Austria's success and position in Italy in the 1810s–40s. Spanish resilience is an important part of Italy's history in the sixteenth, seventeenth and eighteenth centuries. Religion was significant. It is no accident that Spain was able to recreate its power and authority in Italy, where Protestantism scarcely existed, but earlier had no comparable success in the Low Countries, where Protestantism was far stronger.

Smaller-scale conflict also continued in Italy. In 1642–4, Tuscany, Modena, Venice and Parma joined against Pope Urban VIII (r. 1623–44) in the Castro War over the fate of Italian fiefs and the extent of papal pretensions. The war was over possession of the duchy of Castro, a Farnese territory but claimed by the Barberini papacy in lieu of unpaid Farnese debts. The duchy was envisaged as a potential Barberini duchy, giving the family the same dynastic status as had been obtained by the Farnese in the 1540s thanks to the acquisition of Parma-Piacenza. Urban VIII thus continued the practice of pursuing family benefit from holding the papacy. In the event, the papal forces were heavily defeated. Such divisions helped explain the difficulty of ensuring any practice of a united Italian policy. Earlier, in 1608, Tuscany had taken over the fortress-town of Pitigliano, which had been a fief of the Orsini family.

Italy was drawn into the major war France launched against Spain in 1673, although the key area of hostilities was the Low Countries. A fleet and army were sent to help the revolt against Spanish rule in Sicily launched by the city of Messina in 1674. In 1675, the siege was raised by the French. However, thanks in large part to Dutch naval help for Spain, the revolt was finally quashed.

Louis XIV of France (r. 1643–1715) was more successful when he relied on cash, purchasing the powerful fortress of Casale from the Duke of Mantua in 1681. This extended Louis' power far beyond what was subsequently seen as the natural frontier of the Alps and provided a base for acting against the Spaniards in Milan. In 1689, war resumed with Spain and, in 1690, Victor Amadeus II of Savoy-Piedmont (r. 1675–1730), fed up with French tutelage, and eager to dislodge the French from Pinerolo and Casale, joined the league against Louis. The French defeated Victor Amadeus at Marsaglia in 1693, but he was still able to seize Pinerolo after a long siege and to invade the Dauphiné region of France. Keenly and necessarily looking to his own advantage, and hearing rumours that at least some of his allies – Austria, Spain, England and the Dutch – might be negotiating a secret peace with France, Victor Amadeus was determined not to be the victim of a deal. In 1695, by means of a secret agreement with Louis, Victor Amadeus ensured that he, and not allied forces, captured besieged Casale, while, in 1696, he abandoned his allies by the Treaty of Turin, enabling Louis to transfer forces to other fronts. Deprived of Casale and Pinerolo, the French could not overwinter their forces in Italy, which was a major strategic gain for Savoy-Piedmont.

The imminent death of the childless Charles II of Spain encouraged international negotiations in 1698, with Italian territories treated as bargaining chips and Italian rulers playing no role in the negotiations. Under the 1698 partition treaty, the Treaty of The Hague, Spain, Sardinia, Spanish America and the Spanish Netherlands were to go to Joseph Ferdinand of Bavaria, who had Habsburg ancestors, while Naples, Sicily, and the *presidios* (Tuscan fortified towns) were to go to Louis' heir, the Dauphin Louis, and the Milanese to Archduke Charles, the second son of the Emperor Leopold I, the ruler of Austria. However, in 1699, Joseph Ferdinand died after a short illness, which gave rise to rumours of Austrian poisoning. This death led to a new partition treaty in 1700, the Treaty of London, with the Dauphin getting the same as in the first treaty, plus Lorraine, then an independent state whose duke was allocated the Milanese, while Archduke Charles received the rest. Neither the Emperor nor the Spaniards accepted this, and Charles II left the entire inheritance to Louis' second grandson, Philip, Duke of Anjou, who became Philip V of Spain on Charles II's death later that year.

Meanwhile, Venice remained in the front line of the struggle with the Turks. A major conflict was launched in 1645 when the Turks invaded Venetian-ruled Crete. The operation resolved itself into a long and seemingly intractable siege of the Venetian fortress of Candia, one greatly complicated by attacks on Turkish supply routes across the Aegean Sea by Venice and its allies: the papacy, Malta and Tuscany. There was also persistent fighting in Dalmatia between Venice and the Turks. Candia finally fell in 1669. In the subsequent War of the Holy League (1684–99), the Venetians again fought the Turks in the Aegean and Dalmatia. From the war, Venice acquired the entire

Peloponnese in the 1699 peace treaty, only to lose it to the Turks in a new conflict in 1715.

Priding itself on being different to the rest of Italy, Venice emphasised its independence and its republican constitution. Its intervention in the Peloponnese and its campaigning in the Aegean served to underline Venice's continued interest in the Greek world. This was a geopolitics very different to those of Savoy-Piedmont and Milan.

INTELLECTUAL CRISIS

The Counter-Reformation led to a clear reaction against free speculation in intellectual matters. In many respects, it was a Counter-Renaissance, although such a description unduly simplifies the Renaissance. Prominent Italians could suffer. Astronomical research had encouraged an interest in mathematical understandings of the cosmos and its workings. This was particularly seen with the work of Shakespeare's contemporary Galileo Galilei (1564–1642), Professor of Mathematics at Padua, and then Mathematician to Grand Duke Cosimo of Tuscany. His earliest publication, *Le operazioni del compasso geometrico e militare* (1606), focused on military engineering, not navigation, but there was an emphasis on using an instrument (a compass) and on the importance of applying mathematical rules. Subsequently, Galileo's empirical research focused on the newly invented telescope. First appearing at The Hague in 1608, this was an instrument greatly improved by Galileo. His research helped make Copernicus's ideas about the solar system relevant and convincing. Moreover, in revealing what he had discovered with his telescope, which, by the close of 1609, magnified twenty times, Galileo's *Sidereus Nuncius* (*The Sidereal Messenger*, 1610) transformed the understanding of the moon by showing it to be like the Earth: uneven and with mountains and valleys.

Such a similarity challenged the view of an essential contrast between the nature and substance of the Earth and the Heavens, an argument made by Aristotle. Drawing on his authority, the thinkers of medieval Christendom saw the moon as being like the planets, perfect in shape and orbit, and unchanging, whereas the Earth was prone to change and decay. As a result, the Earth was the appropriate setting for redemption and the Christian message. By revealing that Jupiter had four satellites, Galileo also showed that the Earth's moon was not unique.

In 1613, Galileo's astronomical ideas were attacked on scriptural grounds. A self-conscious rationalist as well as an empiricist, he subsequently fell foul of Church authority, in part because of his *Dialogue on the Two Principal World Systems* (1625–9), which compared the Copernican and Ptolemaic systems, and supported the former. In 1633, the Inquisition (founded in 1542) condemned Galileo for holding that the Earth moves and that the Bible is not a scientific authority. In addition, his views on atomism were a challenge to the Catholic doctrine of transubstantiation, and thus practice of the Mass, the nature of matter being significant in both cases. Galileo was confined to house imprisonment. The Inquisition had been introduced into Tuscany as part of the process in which Cosimo became duke, identifying himself with the authority of the Church, more particularly the papacy, which had long sought to extend its authority northwards. Condemnation by the Inquisition, a papal institution, saved Galileo from being tried by the Tuscan government on issues related also to religion, a trial that might have led to a death sentence. Thus, rival jurisdictions played a major role in the crisis of Galileo's life.

Galileo had able followers, notably Alfonso Borelli and Evangelista Torricelli, but they had to avoid the Copernican issue. Moreover, the *Accademia del Cimento* founded in Florence in 1657 largely focused on 'safe' experiments, a process encouraged by Church oppression, which became more notable towards the end of the century.

In addition to the coexistence of a more sophisticated understanding of nature and natural forces with a continued belief in occult forces, the obscurantism associated with Counter-Reformation Catholicism took many forms. Richard Creed, a Catholic visitor, noted of the Church of St Nicolas of Tolentino in Rome in 1700:

> The fathers [priests] make little cakes as big as a farthing, and stick seven of them together; and so call them the seven loaves; they bless the flour and make them with holy water and so give them to the people to eat when they are sick; and if they recover they say the cakes cured them; if they die they say the cakes saved their souls.

Such remarks may appear humorous, but the net effect was to produce an Italy in which free enquiry was constrained. Moreover, this was particularly so in contrast to England and the Netherlands. The threat of being punished as heretical was a major issue. It led authorities, both secular and ecclesiastical, to be uneasy about being seen in any way to encourage heresy. Thus, Venice, a long-standing opponent of papal pretensions and of Habsburg views and ambitions, did not wish to be discredited.

THE STATE

The combination of war with foreign rule over much of Italy ensured that options for the Italian nobility were increasingly in the service of foreign rulers. The exception was Savoy-Piedmont, in which the state was more closely focused on international competition while militarism there was more central to the prevailing political ethos. In

Savoy-Piedmont, the standing army professionalised the nobility and more closely integrated it with the state than was the case elsewhere in Italy. Joseph Spence, a British visitor, commented in 1740 that the aims of this state was 'to keep always prepared for war; to weigh the strength of the greater powers that may fall out; and to join with that power, by whom they may get most in Italy, and whose increase of power can prejudice them least'.

In a period stretching from the sixteenth century to the end of Medici rule in Tuscany in 1737, the number of independent territories in Italy declined. Thus, in 1540, Perugia came under papal rule, while, in 1624, the Della Rovere family ceded the duchy of Urbino to the pope. Whatever the Italian state and the ruler, the nobility was increasingly integrated into developing state forms and patterns of discipline.

SOCIETY

In his *De Morbis Artificum Diatriba* (*Diseases of Workers*, Modena, 1700), the first study on workers' health problems and social medicine, Bernardino Ramazzini, Professor of Medicine at Padua, revealed the serious consequences of employment for health. He pointed out that disorders could result from the strain of unusual physical demands or postures, such as those required of tailors and weavers. He discussed the phthisis acquired by stonemasons and miners, the eye troubles of gilders and printers, the sciatica of tailors, lethargy of potters, and particular problems of bath attendants, chemists, fishermen, tobacconists, vintners and washerwomen. This was very much a different view of the Baroque.

More generally, aside from such usual problems, the seventeenth century was a particularly grim period in Europe as a whole. In part, this was linked to the 'Little Ice Age' and a global cooling, possibly related to sunspots, that cut growing seasons and brought a crisis for agricultural production. It is, however, very difficult to assess standards of living in a quantifiable fashion.

Italy was hit particularly hard, notably by disease, for example the plague epidemic in Naples in 1656, and war. As a result, there were frequent acts of public contrition designed to propriate God. More mundanely, Richard Creed noted in Milan in 1699 the efforts made to avoid the plague: 'they take so much garlic to prevent it for the future that they are fit to poison one'.

Less attractively, Jews were treated as a problem. Thus, in Modena, where they had lived since at least 1025, they were enclosed in a ghetto in 1638. Lent sermons blamed them for the death of Christ. Protestants were also treated unfavourably. Although Tuscany's commercial policies allowed Protestants and Jews in Livorno, they were unpopular, while they were expelled from Genoa in 1747.

The wars and epidemics of the period hit economic demand, encouraged currency debasement and hyperinflation, and helped drive up debts. These debts caused serious crises for many, including aristocratic families forced to sell estates.

Culture

At the same time, Italy was the centre of the Baroque, a bold cultural drive, as much as a style, that began in Rome. The key figures, both working in Rome, were Gianlorenzo Bernini (1598–1680) and Francesco Borromini (1599–1667). Masters of a flowing sculptural style of architecture, at once dramatic and charming, they provided the architectural settings for the typically highly decorated Baroque interiors, notably altars of marble, gold and precious stones, and *trompe l'oeil* ceiling paintings. Less famous locations and works also received the Baroque treatment. Thus, *San Domenico*, a fourteenth-century church in Perugia, was rebuilt in the Baroque style, as was the twelfth-century cathedral of Spoleto.

THE BIRTH OF OPERA

Born in Cremona, Claudio Monteverdi (1567–1643) was in the employ of the Duke of Mantua from 1602 to 1612 and, during that time, developed a new type of entertainment, opera, with

Orfeo (1607) and *Arianna* (1608). In *Orfeo*, Orpheus moved Pluto to pity with song. There had been significant precursors, notably interludes between the acts of plays, and verse dramas accompanied by music, with Italy important in both from the fifteenth century. Mantua, Ferrara, Florence and Venice were all significant centres of musical innovation. Monteverdi produced a musical unity, drafting his music on a large scale. From 1613, he lived in Venice, writing for the public theatres. *The Coronation of Poppea* (1642) is frequently seen as his masterpiece.

Venice saw the construction of many opera houses from 1637. Indeed, at least sixteen were built by 1700. As a result, many operas had to be written to match demand. A pupil of Monteverdi, Pier Francesco Cavalli, who wrote about forty operas including *Calisto* (1651), and Marc Antonio Cesti were key figures in mid-century. Major opera houses were also built for princely courts, including in Parma (1618). The operas of the period were often spectaculars, with 'architectural' sets providing the background for such episodes as supposed fires and floods.

The cultural role of the Church could be ambivalent. Mary Magdalene was sung by the soprano Margherita Durastanti at the first performance of Handel's oratorio *La Resurrezione* in 1708. A complaint by Pope Clement XI (r. 1700–21) that a female singer had been allowed to take part in a sacred work led to her replacement by a castrato for the second performance.

Rulers sought to identify themselves with the Church. Cosimo III of Tuscany (r. 1670–1723), who sent artists to Rome for their training, commissioned a reliquary to hold the skull of Saint Cresci. Victor Amadeus II began work in 1717 on a huge church at Superga to commemorate his victory at nearby Turin in 1706. The site, outside the walls, was chosen because it was from there that he had ascertained the weakest point in the French position. Behind the church, consecrated in 1727, which still dominates the Turin skyline, a monastery was built that was designed to serve as the mausoleum for the dynasty, the monks offering perpetual prayers for the salvation of its dead members. This arrangement was similar to the Escorial in Spain, Mafra in Portugal and Klosterneuburg in Austria.

Although the building of great churches, which served as the setting for major royal events such as weddings, was the most obvious example of the royal patronage of ecclesiastical art, many monarchs were also generous patrons of existing foundations and, for example, commissioned much church music. The sensibility of the seventeenth century entailed an exuberant ostentatious religiosity. There was a parallel with *opera seria*, the world of Classical mythology, serious heroism and solemn music brought to life by Italian composers and singers.

The cultural influence of ancient or modern, secular or religious Italy on foreigners could be profound. Gilles-Marie Oppenordt (1672–1742) developed his style in Rome in 1692–9 while supported by the French Academy. His first decorative works, altar designs for *Notre Dame* and *Saint-Germain des Prés* in Paris, were completely governed by Roman models, while his architectural work on the *Palais Royal* in Paris was heavily influenced by the architecture of Borromini and northern Italy. Italian works served as models for artists and collectors elsewhere. In 1701, the Austrian Prince Johann von Liechtenstein asked the Florentine bronze-caster Massimiliano Soldani for reduced copies of the statues in the grand-ducal collection.

Religion

In 1714, Cardinal de La Trémoille, the perceptive French envoy in Rome, suggested to Louis XIV that the dispute between Pope Clement XI and Victor Amadeus II of Savoy-Piedmont, who had recently been granted Sicily in the Utrecht peace settlement of 1713, was having a detrimental effect on Catholicism in the island. La Trémoille claimed that the use of papal interdicts, which had been placed on Sicilian bishoprics, would cause the people, 'otherwise ignorant of the principles of religion', to forget them entirely, and alleged that he had witnessed the same process in the diocese of Sorrento, south of Naples: the people no longer troubling themselves, not attending Mass nor taking the sacraments. In this view, the Church was a barrier against a loss of faith among a populace whose religious faith was superficial.

However, in practice, Catholic belief was buoyant in Italy, with the people adhering tenaciously to a demonstrative Baroque piety. It was centred on local saints and their shrines, and most clearly so in the south. From 1743, the Dominican preacher and theologian Daniello Concina (1687–1756) was to argue that Venetian society was de-Christianised. In practice, across Italy attendance at Mass was high, as was the taking of the sacraments, and there was enormous support for processions, cults of the saints and the Virgin, confraternities, pilgrimages and relics.

ITALIAN IDENTITY AS HOSTILITY TO SPAIN

The seventeenth century contributed *antispagnolismo* to Italian historical consciousness. Hostility to Spain had a number of bases, historical, thematic and regional, but the shared argument was that Spanish rule was an occupation, that this occupation was harmful, and that, in particular, it both represented and further caused a failure to accept modernity. Already present in the seventeenth century, notably among Neapolitan critics of Spanish rule, these arguments were to be crucial to Enlightenment thinkers opposed to the Counter-Reformation in the eighteenth century; and also, in the nineteenth century, to the *Risorgimento* and to Liberal Italy, not least by placing, for castigation, the allies of Spain, notably the papacy and the nobility of the south. Moreover, in the twentieth century, Fascist commentators opposed the Spanish link as a demonstration and exploitation of Italian weakness, and a cause of weakness.

These accounts were all useful for views of the Italian nation, but they underplayed the complexity of the links between Spain and Italy, as well as the range and extent of local participation in this Italo-Spanish world. Moreover, these accounts assumed that there was a clear Italian alternative, which was not a view offered at the time. Instead, the alternative to Spain in the seventeenth century was, frequently, that of an alignment with France. There was no Italian nation state in prototype or prospect. However, a perception of Italy existed abroad, as was, moreover, the case with Germany, which also was divided into many territories. In the 1700s, British troops referred to Prince Eugène of Savoy as 'ye old Italian prince'. Within Italy, there was a shared identity that was commonly accepted, or at least by those who were a bit literate. There was, however, no equivalent to the federal practices offered by the German constitution, notably the imperial Diet, imperial courts and the regional system of imperial circles that raised troops for the imperial army.

CHAPTER SIX

The Old Order: The Eighteenth Century

Never was government more hated and more feared than is the Austrian in the Milanese on account of the oppressions the people live under, which are more than they are able to bear, and more burthensome than under any of their former masters [Spain the last]. They would be glad of an opportunity of getting rid of it had they anybody to help them, but the Emperor [Charles VI] has 30,000 men to keep them in awe.

John Mills, British visitor, 1726, on governing Italy

POWER POLITICS

The first half of the century was an age of war in Italy. The wars led to major changes in the control of Italian territories, and thus of dominance within Italy as a whole. All destructive, these wars resulted in much disruption as well as attempts to increase governmental powers and effectiveness, both on the part of independent states, notably Sardinia (Savoy-Piedmont), and in the Italian dominions of foreign powers, for example the Milanese (Lombardy).

The following section is detailed, but it is significant for what it tells us about the nature of Italian politics before unification and the causes of the geopolitics of the period. Fighting in Italy in the eighteenth century began in 1701 as France sought to block an Austrian invasion of Milan. For the Emperor Leopold I (r. 1658–1705), who was prepared to accept a partition of the Spanish Habsburg inheritance, Spanish Italy was the key objective for the Austrian Habsburgs, and notably Milan. In 1701, the Grand Alliance of The Hague brought

Austria, France, England and the Dutch together to support a partition awarding Spanish Italy to Leopold. In opposition, Louis XIV, who supported the inheritance of the entire Spanish monarchy by his second grandson, Philip, Duke of Anjou (Philip V of Spain), won the alliance of Victor Amadeus II of Savoy-Piedmont, who was surrounded by France in the west, Spanish Lombardy in the east, and pro-Spanish Genoa to the south. Victor Amadeus signed an alliance treaty, which was to expire on the last day of 1703, explaining to Leopold I that he had no choice in order to avoid occupation. Victor Amadeus always intended to change sides as soon as the treaty expired, and did so in return for Anglo-Dutch subsidies and the promise of part of the Milanese.

Italian territories were up for grabs. To win over Max Emmanuel of Bavaria (r. 1679–1726), the Austrians in 1702 offered the possibility of an exchange of Bavaria for Naples and Sicily, only for Max to press for the Milanese, which he also demanded from Louis in 1704 with the addition of a broad corridor to it through the Tyrol.

The war settled the matter. The French army besieging Turin was defeated by an Austrian-Piedmontese army under Prince Eugène and Victor Amadeus in 1706. This was a major achievement that the House of Piedmont was to play up repeatedly, one that underlined the linkage of ruler and war. As a result of the defeat, the French evacuated Italy. In turn, Naples was seized by the Austrians in 1707 and Sardinia, with the help of British naval power, in 1708.

The future of the Milanese played a key role in secret negotiations during the war, while Italy as a whole provided a rich field for diplomacy. In 1711, the French proposed that Victor Amadeus be given the Milanese and made King of Lombardy in order to win him over, following, in 1712, with the idea that their ally Max Emmanuel receive, in addition to the return of Bavaria, Sicily or, failing that, Sardinia. Victor Amadeus's demands for an extended Alpine barrier were rejected by the French as leaving the French province of Dauphiné vulnerable.

In the event, by the Treaty of Utrecht of 1713, the Emperor

Charles VI (r. 1711–40), ruler of Austria, gained Spanish Italy bar Sicily, which was to go to Victor Amadeus, giving the House of Savoy the title of kings, which was of major importance for the unification of Italy. Victor Amadeus was the 'cousin' of Queen Anne (r. 1707–14) because his wife, Anne-Marie d'Orléans, was the daughter of her aunt Henrietta. She was pleased he became a king while the British government wanted a weak ally to hold Sicily. The treaty also brought Victor Amadeus a settlement of his Alpine frontier that was less generous than he had sought, but more geographically consistent than the old frontier. The Habsburg gain of the duchy of Mantua was acknowledged: the Duke had allied with the Bourbons, been judged a traitor, and deprived of his state and title, finding a refuge in Venice, where he died.

Charles VI did not want to yield Sicily, but accepted the terms in 1714. Philip V of Spain (r. 1700–24), however, did not sign any treaty with Charles, and his (second) marriage in 1714 to Elizabeth Farnese, niece of the childless Duke of Parma, a duchy Vienna claimed as an imperial fief, indicated that he was still interested in Italy.

Hostilities broke out anew in Italy in 1717, with the successful Spanish invasion of Sardinia, only four years after the Peace of Utrecht, followed in 1718 by a Spanish invasion of Sicily. There was war in Italy in 1717–20, 1733–5 and 1741–8, and tension for the remainder of the period through to 1748. This was essentially because, in the case of Italy, both Austria and Spain were dissatisfied, while the satisfied powers were the weak, small Italian states, such as Venice, that had nothing to gain from change. The prizes offered by the anticipated extinction of local dynasties, the Farnese dukes of Parma and the Medici grand dukes of Tuscany, which ended in the male line in 1731 and 1737 respectively, exacerbated the dispute between the major powers, because Philip V sponsored the claims to both of Don Carlos, born in 1716, his eldest son by his marriage to Elizabeth Farnese, while Charles VI sought to exercise jurisdiction over these territories as imperial fiefs.

THE FIGHT AGAINST SMALLPOX

There were more deadly enemies than other humans. Smallpox was a serious killer, especially of children, and was responsible for mortality crises, including in Milan in 1707 and 1719 and in Verona in 1726. It was endemic in Italy in the 1750s and in Venetia in the early 1760s. Smallpox was also no respecter of rank. In 1777, it claimed the brother of Ferdinand I of Naples, leading the King to have his children inoculated.

The disease was difficult to conquer. Resistance to inoculation against smallpox, frequently on the grounds of tempting divine providence, was not always uninformed. A British traveller, the Reverend Norton Nicholls, wrote from Rome in 1772, 'The smallpox has raged like the plague here and made dreadful havoc. They are much prejudiced against inoculation, and have a ridiculous notion that the disorder may return again so, but not after having had it in the natural way.' In fact, the spread of inoculation in Italy after 1714 might be related to the higher frequency of smallpox, as inoculated persons, when not isolated, were a source of infection. Vaccination, rather than inoculation, played a major role in defeating smallpox, but was not introduced until the nineteenth century.

The conflicts and diplomacy of the period were to result in the transfer of control over more than half of Italy, mostly with no attention to the wishes of local rulers or inhabitants. Italian rulers did seek through diplomatic means to advance and defend their interests, but they were generally unsuccessful. Cosimo III of Tuscany sought support in 1710 for the eventual re-establishment of republican government, before deciding to back the succession of his daughter after that of his childless sons. In 1713, the latter course was decreed and recognised by the Senate of Florence and the Council of Two Hundred,

but Cosimo was to have less success in achieving international guarantees for his daughter. Charles VI rejected Cosimo's claim in 1714. In
1716, Cosimo chose the Este family of Modena as the successors to his
daughter, hoping for a union of the territories, which might, indeed,
have created a significant Italian state able to act as an alternative to
Savoy-Piedmont. Charles VI was also unwilling to accept this.

The wishes of other Italian rulers were also ignored. Charles VI
refused to recognise Victor Amadeus II as King of Sicily, refused to
guarantee the integrity of his possessions and, in 1716, sent troops
into Novi in the republic of Genoa in furtherance of a border dispute.
Charles's control of Milan, Mantua and Naples provided the base for
such action.

The limited room for manoeuvre enjoyed by Italian rulers was
indicated by the enforced exchange of Sicily for poorer Sardinia that
Victor Amadeus was obliged to accept in 1720 as a consequence of the
settlement ending his 1717–20 war with Spain that had begun with the
Spanish invasion of Sardinia. The exchange was of great long-term
significance for the future of Italy as it ensured that Savoy-Piedmont
was linked to a territory that had scant influence on it. In contrast,
as Sicily had shown with the Hohenstaufens in the late twelfth and
thirteenth centuries, it was wealthier, more populous and more his-
torically resonant. That situation would probably have had a major
impact on the Savoyard-Piedmontese state, and therefore on the
course of the *Risorgimento* and of subsequent Italian history, not least
by ensuring a stronger link between the *Risorgimento* and an important part of the south. In contrast, the *Risorgimento* was to be perceived
in the south as a takeover.

The exchange of Sicily for Sardinia satisfied Charles VI's wish to
reunite Sicily to the kingdom of Naples. Meaningful resistance came
not from Victor Amadeus, but from more powerful rulers concerned to
keep Charles out of Sicily. Victor Amadeus had owed the island to the
support of France and, in particular, Britain. A British naval squadron
took him there in 1713. However, George I (r. 1714–27) did not continue
the anti-Austrian policies of Queen Anne's Tory ministers while, after

the death of Louis XIV in 1715, Victor Amadeus complained bitterly about the French failure to restrain Austria in Italy.

Victor Amadeus's diplomacy was rendered redundant by the unexpected Spanish invasion of Sicily in 1718, the failure of most Sicilians to support the King and the rapid Spanish conquest of most of the island. The Spaniards landed 20,000 troops in Palermo, whereas Victor Amadeus had 10,000 scattered over the island and only 1,400 of them in Palermo. Spanish fortunes were affected not by Victor Amadeus, but by the actions of other powers determined to ensure that changes to the Utrecht settlement took place only with their consent. The British fleet, whose preparation had failed to dissuade the Spaniards from invading, destroyed most of the Spanish fleet off Capo Passero in Sicily in 1718. Meanwhile, Charles VI had signed a treaty with Britain and France that provided for the exchange of Sicily and Sardinia, and for Don Carlos's reversion to Parma and Tuscany once their native dynasties had died out.

Some of the local population sometimes took a role. In the case of Naples, most opinion was loyal to Spain until the death of Charles II of Spain in 1700 and accepted the succession of Philip V, though there was an abortive coup in favour of the Austrians in 1701. Yet, there was no opposition to the Austrian conquest of 1707. Pragmatism was matched by a consistent wish to secure as much autonomy as possible for the kingdom of Naples and its élite under whoever came to be king. Full independence was not anticipated, and its advent in 1734 was unexpected; the point was to avoid complete, direct subordination to an oppressive monarch.

Charles VI did not really want the establishment of Don Carlos in Italy. The Austrian rejection of Spanish pressure led Spain in 1729 to settle with Britain and France by the Treaty of Seville on condition that they supported Spanish garrisons in Parma and Tuscany. It might seem surprising that this apparently relatively minor issue was so important in the diplomacy of Italy and Europe in this period but for Spain, which had little confidence in international guarantees, they were the only secure basis for Carlos's succession, while, for the rest of Europe, they were seen as a possible means by which Spain, newly reascendant under Philip V, might destroy the existing Italian system and launch herself on a career of Italian conquest. As part of an Anglo-Austrian peace settlement, Austria agreed in March 1731 to accept the Spanish garrisons. An Anglo-Spanish fleet convoyed the Spanish troops to Livorno (Leghorn) and Carlos, similarly escorted, followed. As Duke Antonio of Parma had died in January and the pregnancy of his widow, on which Europe's diplomats waited, had been shown to be false, Carlos became the new duke.

France was opposed to the new Austrian-dominated European order and in 1733 joined with Spain to attack Austria. This Bourbon effort was to be aided by the alliance of Victor Amadeus's heir, Charles Emmanuel III, who had gained the throne when his father abdicated having married his mistress Anna. In 1731, under the influence of Anna, Victor Amadeus sought to regain the throne only to be arrested and imprisoned while Anna was taken to a house for reformed prostitutes and later to a convent. Austrian difficulties stemmed in large part from Italy where British diplomacy had failed to solve Austrian differences with Charles Emmanuel over the overlordship of the frontier region of the Langhes and differences with Spain over Carlos's vassalage and the size of the Spanish forces in Italy. These issues were serious irritants in a society where rank and recognition were crucial indicators of status and power, but it is also clear that Philip and his wife were looking for an opportunity to return Italy to the Spanish sphere of influence.

The Treaty of Turin, signed with Charles Emmanuel in 1733, provided that Carlos should have Naples and Sicily, and Charles Emmanuel the Milanese. French and Sardinian forces easily overran the Milanese that winter. The following summer, Carlos conquered Naples, and the Austrian forces in southern Italy were defeated at Bitonto. This was one of the most decisive campaigns of the century, and led to a short-lived loose Italian unification under Bourbon hegemony, albeit with Savoy-Piedmont taking a role. Philip V ceded his rights in Naples and Sicily to Carlos, who, in consequence, proclaimed himself King of Naples. Though Charles Emmanuel was already governing the Milanese under the Treaty of Turin, and sought to conquer Mantua, still held for Charles VI, Philip wanted both, and his wife thought that Parma, Tuscany, Naples and Sicily should be the inheritance of her sons. To a certain extent such demands were negotiating counters, but they also indicated the bold wish to reallocate territories that characterised much of the diplomacy of Italy's history for centuries.

The Austrian attempt to reconquer northern Italy was defeated at Parma and Guastalla in 1734, and in 1735 they were reduced to the defence of the water-girt fortress of Mantua (the city sits alongside three lakes), in which they were aided by serious Sardinian–Spanish differences. Austrian pressure on Britain to send naval assistance was evaded. However, French determination to beat her allies to a separate peace with Austria was aided by a willingness to compromise over Italy. Compromise and equivalents were an integral feature of the treaties of the period, but that of 1738 depended on Sardinian weakness and Spanish inability to continue fighting on her own. The peace left Carlos, now Charles VII of Naples, with Naples, Sicily and the *presidio* towns, but, in exchange, Parma went to Charles VI and the Tuscan reversion to Duke Francis of Lorraine in return for the acquisition of Lorraine by Stanislaus, the father-in-law of Louis XV of France, who thereby gained Lorraine for France in 1766. As in the Partition Treaties of 1698–1700, Italy was required by the major powers to provide the equivalents and the equalling-out that compensated for gains elsewhere. With the death of Gian Gastone in 1737, Francis, who had married Maria Theresa, heir to Charles VI, in 1736, succeeded to Tuscany. Charles Emmanuel had to return the Milanese to Austria, but his gains included some of it, not least the area around Novara, increasing the vulnerability of what remained with Charles VI.

War over the Austrian Succession broke out after the death of Charles VI in 1740. Lacking sons, Charles sought to leave his entire inheritance to Maria Theresa, his eldest daughter, but other rulers saw this as an opportunity for gains. However, hostile Bourbon action in Italy was affected by British naval action, the threat of the bombardment of Naples forcing Charles VII of Naples in 1742 to declare his neutrality in one of the most striking displays of naval effectiveness that century. Initially, Charles Emmanuel was neutral, only to turn against Spain in 1742 when its army advanced into the Po valley. British pressure on Maria Theresa obtained the promise of Piacenza and part of the Milanese for him by the Treaty of Worms of 1743, while Britain provided generous financial support to both her allies and naval backing for Charles Emmanuel. Charles Emmanuel had decided to gain concessions in the Milanese by alliance with Austria and Britain, rather than opposition to them. A month later, the Second Family Compact committed France to help conquer Milan, Parma and Piacenza for the benefit of Philip V's second son by Elizabeth Farnese, Don Philip. Spanish forces occupied Charles Emmanuel's duchy of Savoy in 1743, holding it for the rest of the war, but Bourbon attempts to storm his Alpine defences failed. The Italian war was far from static. Winning the alliance of Genoa in 1745, the Bourbons defeated Charles Emmanuel at Bassignana, captured Asti, Casale and Milan before the end of the year, and then signed an armistice with him before Christmas.

Keen to expel the Austrians from Italy, the French foreign minister, René Louis, the Marquis d'Argenson, proposed that Charles Emmanuel become King of Lombardy and leader of an Italian federation. D'Argenson's argument that the Italian rulers sought liberty against the excessive and tyrannical power of Austria, and that the Bourbons should exploit this, was countered by Philip V with the claim that the league was impossible or would take many years to negotiate, that it would depend on Bourbon armed support, that any league required a number of near equal powers which Sardinian (Savoy-Piedmont) power prevented, that Charles Emmanuel would not maintain the projected 'Republic of Sovereigns', but would seek to despoil it, and that he would despoil, not help, Don Philip. These arguments are interesting given the eventual role of France and Savoy-Piedmont in furthering and obtaining Italian unification respectively, and the extent to which other Italian dynasties, notably the Neapolitan Bourbons, were indeed despoiled. Emmanuel Philbert had moved his capital from Chambéry to Turin because the presence of a strong kingdom of France prevented any attempt to increase the power of the House of Savoy whose dream was to re-establish the duchy of Burgundy. The policy of expansion in Italy did not succeed until Victor Amadeus, whose direction to his son and heir, Charles Emmanuel III, was 'Italy is like an artichoke, to be eaten leaf by leaf'. This attitude was understood by Philip V, whose first wife had been a daughter of Victor Amadeus, and who also distrusted the House of Savoy's close link to Britain.

D'Argenson's project was rendered academic anyway by Charles Emmanuel's decision not to pursue the French option, which led, in 1746, to the Austrian recapture of Asti, Casale and Milan and to the Austro-Sardinian victory at Piacenza, another of the century's decisive battles that is largely forgotten. However, the Austrians did not drive Charles VII from Naples, as they had hoped. Moreover, after they had been expelled from captured Genoa by a popular revolt in December 1746, they failed to regain the city. This revolt led to partisan warfare by local peasants and the use of workers' brigades. Priests were trained to fight, and women worked on the fortifications. The fervour showed in this rising tends not to receive the attention it deserves in Italian public history, in part because of the focus on the later and national narrative of the *Risorgimento*. More generally, Genoa's history is widely neglected outside both Liguria and Italy.

The British played a role in Italy throughout the war thanks to the navy. In 1742, they succeeded, and in 1743 failed, to protect Nice, then part of Charles Emmanuel's dominions, in 1744 provided supplies to the Austrian army operating south of Rome, while also preventing France and Spain from sending troops by sea to Italy, and in 1746 helped the Austrians and Sardinians to conquer Genoa and regain Nice. British warships also transported Sardinian troops to back a

Corsican rebellion against Genoese rule and, when Genoa rebelled, assisted in the blockade. Despite Austrian reluctance, Charles Emmanuel, in the eventual Peace of Aix-la-Chapelle (1748), received the lands he had been ceded at Worms, bar Piacenza, while Don Philip gained Parma, Piacenza and Guastalla, creating a new Bourbon territory and dynasty in Italy, albeit not one on the scale of Naples and Sicily.

As Genoa in 1746–8 showed, Italians were affected by the issues, as well as the processes, of power politics. The response was often one of localism. In Sicily and Naples, there was scant support for Austrian rule or that of Savoy-Piedmont. Instead, there was considerable affinity with Spain, notably with its culture. Thus, the world of potent patron saints and of a committed popular piety continued to span Spain and southern Italy, looking towards the situation in the following century.

ECONOMY AND SOCIETY

British travellers were unimpressed by the nature of rule, and notably of the rulers. Richard Creed presented Francesco, Duke of Parma from 1694 until 1727, as a harsh figure: 'the Duke is the great landlord and all his subjects are his slaves and pay him what he demands'. Of the Duke of Mantua, Creed wrote:

Ferdinando Carlo Gonzaga the second [r. 1665–1707]; he is a very plain man to look at, just like an English famer, and every day drives himself all the town over in a little calash with one footman; he has four pistols in it; he is about 50 years old, but he is a man of pleasure. He has at least eighty misses in his keeping, and he keeps them handsomely; and they perform his operas; for they are all handsome and all sing or dance; he has about 70 children in town; but none by his Duchess; he is very absolute, imprisons who he pleases; he hangs and raises money at his pleasure; he spends all, for he has no heirs.

William Mildmay presented Giovanni Gastone (r. 1723–37), the last of the Medici grand dukes of Tuscany, as enjoying seeing carried out the sexual acts, particularly sodomy, which his drunkenness had rendered him unfit to perform.

The economy was of greater consequence to the population, but it is not easy to determine general trends. The population certainly grew, and markedly so compared to the seventeenth century, with the opportunities that it offered and the problems it posed. Whereas Venice's population remained constant at about 137,000 during the century, that of Turin rose from 44,000 to 92,000, that of Sicily from 1 to 1.5 million, that of the mainland kingdom of Naples doubled to over 5 million, and that of Italy as a whole from 13 to 17 million.

Relative economic decline was most notably seen in the penetration of the Mediterranean by foreign goods and merchants, such as the English and Dutch traders who benefited from the designation of Livorno in Tuscany as a free port in 1675. The English, already active for a long time as brokers in Venice, hit its entrepôt trade with the Turkish Empire.

At the same time, research on a number of areas, such as Lombardy and the Veneto in the seventeenth century, or Venetian trade and the Veneto's industry and agriculture in the eighteenth, has indicated a considerable degree of economic resilience, adaptability and growth. As so often, it was the variety of Italian circumstances that were most obvious. In Lombardy, a naturally fertile agrarian region, rice cultivation increased from the 1730s, partly as a result of the activity of the leasehold farmers and partly because there was sufficient local capital to support the necessary irrigation. In the second half of the eighteenth century, there were clear signs of Lombard agricultural expansion, especially in the rise of rice, silk, cheese and butter exports, although rice required a level of irrigation that put pressure on water supplies. There were also significant improvements in the Veneto where the growing of maize spread widely. The production of olive oil in Apulia and Calabria was highly commercialised and export-oriented. The vine was an important cash crop, and, in the eighteenth century, it spread in Friuli.

However, in general, the Italian position was bleak, substantially a matter of traditional methods and extensive cultivation, rather than agricultural changes and intensive methods. The mixed farming of the Lombard plain, with animals providing manure (and therefore enhancing soil fertility) and milk, made little progress elsewhere, and efforts to encourage the cultivation of the potato had little impact. The principal problems – harsh terrain, denuded soil, poor water supplies, inadequate communications and a lack of investment – continued to dominate the peninsula, and very much contrasted with the situation in England and the Netherlands. In Tuscany, the plough produced only a shallow upheaval of soil, and the real soil preparation was achieved by the use of shovels. In Altopascio in Tuscany, the average age on marriage rose from 21.5 prior to 1700 to 24.17 between 1700 and 1749, and was matched by a decline in the average number of children per couple. This rise probably owed much to the depressed incomes that paralleled the fall in the price of wheat at the beginning of the century.

Famines could bring massive mortality, leading for example to a sharp rise in the death rate in Bari, Florence and Palermo in 1709, and in the kingdom of Naples in 1764. The last led Ferdinando Galiani (1728–87) to write in 1769 a strong attack on the free trade in grain, which, he correctly argued, benefited cities at the expense of rural areas. The famine certainly revealed the inadequacies of public relief and food provisioning systems. The famine of 1764–8 may have been responsible for the fever epidemic that hit central Italy in 1767. Famine could also lead to riots, as in Palermo in 1773 and Florence in 1790. In addition, poor harvests seriously disrupted economies and threatened revenues. The rise in population, which was concentrated in the second half of the century, made the grain supply a particular problem.

Faced with calamities, communities and individuals turned to the Church. Pope Clement XIII (r. 1758–69) responded to famine in the 1760s with prayers and ceremonies. In 1765, all public diversions were suspended in Florence and public prayers held for the return of good weather, as they were in Milan in 1765 and 1766. In Terracina in April 1769, a miraculous image of the Virgin was carried in procession, attended by great crowds, in the hope of securing better weather. In 1755, the Venetian authorities, faced with a lack of drinking water, exposed a statue of the Virgin.

The major cause of increased production was not enhanced productivity, but the expansion, especially from the mid-eighteenth century, of the cultivated area. Although commercial farming spread in most of Italy in the second half of the century, and, as in England, common lands were enclosed, subsistence agriculture continued to be the norm. In southern Italy in particular, grain production remained very much a part of the traditional subsistence agriculture, which still prevailed in many parts of the interior. Except for the city of Naples, its markets were generally local. Benefiting from rises in grain prices, the aristocracy was essentially parasitic, diverting rural rents to urban expenditure. Marquis Domenico Caracciolo, Viceroy of Sicily in 1781–6, blamed the aristocracy for the poor state of local agriculture. There was far less commitment across Italy as a whole and in the south in particular to new agricultural methods than in the case of the English aristocracy.

The failure to match England, Catalonia and the Low Countries in developing a more productive agrarian economy was not, however, for want of some effort. Guillaume du Tillot, the talented French-born leading minister in the duchy of Parma in the 1760s, encouraged the cultivation of hemp, flax, sainfoin, potatoes, mulberries and vines, and the improvement of animal breeding, and sponsored the publication of a work on bee-keeping. In the 1780s, a Calabrian aristocrat, Domenico Grimaldi, demanded a state loan for new presses for the olive oil industry and proposed that the king should appoint instructors to tour the countryside and demonstrate their use. However, it proved difficult to translate new ideas, such as those of the numerous agricultural academies or the artificial incubator developed in Parma in the 1760s, into action. There was a lack of interest by small-scale farmers, in part because there was not the widespread continuity and control by farmers seen through the inheritance of family farms, as in Catalonia and some of the Low Countries, or through regularly renewed leases, as in England. This situation made the attitude of the aristocracy more significant. Governments got their incomes from taxing rural provinces, but did little to raise this income. More generally, there was a lack, or weakness, of social groups committed to change.

As an instance of change, there was a modest expansion of rural domestic production, with silk and wool remaining the basic industries in most of the country. As an example of a more general process, velvet manufacture in the villages around the city was organised by Genoese merchants, the rural workers putting in long hours, and being obliged to keep their looms in repair. This situation provided much work for women.

There were also proto-factories. The town of Como in Lombardy in 1769 had 25 establishments producing woollen goods with a total of 180 workers, 155 establishments for other fabrics with about 2,000 workers, 4 dye-works with 78, 3 tanneries with 80, 4 soap factories with 23, 2 hat-works with 12, 11 looms for cotton goods with 20, and 2 looms for knitted stockings with 120. In nearby Locco, 500 women were employed in silk-making in 1774, while, that year, the town of Bellagio on Lake Como contained 6 soap-works and 7 looms for knitted cloth. In the Upper Veneto, certain sectors of the domestic-based textile industry changed from 'putting-out' to more centralised, factory-based mechanised production.

However, much of Italian industry was hampered by a weak domestic market, inadequate capital, poor communications, active foreign competition and backward techniques. In Lombardy in 1767, only 1.5 per cent of the population were industrial workers, a percentage way below that in England, although quantitative data is generally problematic for this period. Alongside industrial expansion in some areas, there had been deindustrialisation in others, for example Bologna.

VERSIFYING TOURISM

Touring Italy with Stephen Fox, a young friend, in 1729, John, Lord Hervey wrote:

> Throughout all Italy beside,
> What does one find, but Want and Pride?
> Farces of superstitious folly,
> Decay, Distress, and Melancholy:
> The Havoc of Despotic Power,
> A country rich, its owners poor;
> Unpeopled towns, and lands untilled,
> Bodys uncloathed, and mouths unfilled.
> The nobles miserably great,
> In painted domes, and empty state,
> Too proud to work, too poor to eat,
> No arts the meaner sort employ,
> They nought improve, nor ought enjoy.
> Each blown from misery grows a saint,
> He prays from idleness, and fasts from want.

COMMUNICATIONS

By the 1780s, there were more signs of change in Italy. Communications improved, although they generally remained inadequate. In 1748, over 500 labourers were employed in building a new road from Bologna to Florence, which, it was hoped, would improve trade between Lombardy and Tuscany. In the 1770s, the Neapolitan government tried to build roads to open up the provinces. Further north, at the southern end of the Alps, the Col di Tenda, in the 1780s, became the first Alpine pass opened to wheeled traffic, improving routes from Piedmont to Nice. It had taken seventeen years to build.

Nevertheless, the terrain of much of Italy was seriously unhelpful to road and river links, a situation that remained the case until the 1960s when highway-building attracted bold engineering solutions. Mountainous terrain increased the need for draught animals and limited the speed of transport. Poor roads led to long and unpredictable journeys. A critical British commentator observed in 1772:

> The road from Naples as far as Barletta is very good, for which the public is obliged for the road from Naples to Rome to His Majesty's being married; kings in these regions are not Kings of the People but the People People of the Kings.

Indeed, in southern Italy, roads were so bad that it was easier to ship olive oil. A Tuscan government enquiry in 1766 found that it cost as much to move goods overland from Pescia to Altopascio as on the water route from Altopascio to Livorno, which was six times as far. However, although, in 1777, the Martesana canal from Milan to the River Adda, and then to Lecco, was opened, there was no significant expansion in northern Italy of the canal system outside the Venetian *terraferma* where, from the fifteenth century until the Austrian takeover in the 1790s, the canal network integrated the river system. Much of Italy was not suitable for canals, but that was not the only issue, especially in northern Italy.

INTELLECTUAL LIFE

There were signs of intellectual development, but much depended on particular intellectual traditions and on political and cultural circumstances. The centres of *Illuminismo* (the Italian Enlightenment) were Naples, Milan, Tuscany in the late eighteenth century, Modena and Parma. In contrast, interest in new intellectual ideas had less support in the Papal States, Genoa, Tuscany under the last of the Medici, and Savoy-Piedmont. In 1737, indeed, Pope Clement XII (r. 1730–40) tried to prevent the erection of a mausoleum to Galileo in the Florentine church of St Croce. In 1759, Clement XIII (r. 1758–69) condemned the *Encyclopédie*, the repository of progressive French opinion. In contrast,

Giambattista Vico (1668–1744), Professor of Rhetoric at Naples, emphasised the historical evolution of human societies in his *Scienza Nuova* (*New Science*, 1725) and is still considered as the founder of history as a discipline in modern terms.

Science ranged from the extraordinary to the rational. Marcello Malpighi (1628–94), Professor of Medicine in Bologna and the founder of microscopic anatomy, believed that all men were originally white, but that the sinners had become black. Bernard Albinus (1697–1770) falsely claimed in 1737 that Negro bile was black. Compared to such rubbish, it was reassuring in 1760 to note that Lazzaro Spallanzani (1729–99), an Emilian priest who became an academic, argued the fallacy of the supposed experimental proof of the theory of spontaneous generation, the idea that inanimate matter could come alive. In doing so, he took forward the research of Count Francesco Redi who demonstrated this fallacy in the case of decomposing meat and the genesis of flies. Spallanzani proved that bacteria could not spontaneously develop and thus that spontaneous birth was not possible at all. He also studied blood circulation, the activity of the heart in it, and digestion. In Naples, Raimondo di Sangro, Prince of Sansevero, experimented in embalming and studying human bodies, the results of which can be seen alongside the amazingly lifelike sculptures in the *Cappella Sansevero*. Born in Turin in 1736, Giuseppe Luigi Lagrange was an important figure in the history of mathematics.

Other theories were more valuable, but not always easy to implement. In 1776, Marsilio Landriani (1751–1815), an official in Lombardy who had proposed the practice of eudiometry (the study of the quality of the air) the previous year, was appointed to a chair of physics in Milan, and the study was proclaimed as a useful aid to the study of public health. In practice, it was impossible in this period to measure the healthiness of the air. The relationship between this healthiness and the respirability of the air, which could be tested by assessing the quantity of oxygen in samples, was unclear. As a result, eudiometry was abandoned.

In contrast, thanks to the publications of a Venetian, Count Francesco Algarotti (1712–64), Sir Isaac Newton's ideas spread in

Italy, while, later, Italians took forward the discussion of electrical phenomena. In 1791, Luigi Galvani (1737–98) published the results of experiments that began with his observation of the effects of electricity on the muscles of a frog's leg in 1780. He advanced a theory of 'animal electricity' known as galvanism, which claimed that electricity is inherent in animal tissues. This theory was rejected by Alessandro Volta (1745–1827), Professor of Physics at the University of Pavia from 1779, who invented the battery of cells and the dry pile in 1800.

There were also contrasts between states over their willingness to embrace reforming policies. The Papal States proved especially unpromising, and the population suffered high rates of illiteracy and begging, a situation that continued into the nineteenth century. However, there were important efforts in other regions, notably Lombardy, Parma and in Tuscany under the Habsburgs. At the same time, Tillot's fall from power in Parma in 1771 was in part due to opposition to reform.

In 1771, William, 2nd Earl of Shelburne noted 'at present you may be recommended from town to town from a set of literati to the other, as formerly from convent to convent'. The 'literati' or *letterati* normally gathered in *Academie*, which were cultural clubs where they discussed many issues. Archaeology began in the period, especially in Tuscany where Giovanni Lami was a key figure. In politics, the key group was that around the Milanese newspaper *Il Caffe*. It included Count Pietro Verri, his younger brother Alessandro and Marquess Cesare Beccaria, who wrote a pamphlet condemning torture and the death penalty, leading Grand Duke Leopold of Tuscany to eliminate both, and also influencing the American Founding Fathers. Literary figures included Lorenzo Da Ponte (1749–1838) and Pietro Metastasio (1698–1782) who wrote opera libretti, while the Venetian lawyer Carlo Goldoni wrote successful comedies and the Piedmontese Count Vittorio Alfieri revived the Classical tragedian style on the stage.

Much writing on Italian history treats reform as a secular process, but that underplays the significance of ecclesiastical issues and movements. The complex situation varied by state, but the main issue was generally the government's determination to avoid the Church's intrusion in its own affairs and to limit the Church's influence. Governments wanted the Church to rule the conscience, while the state, which was composed of Catholics, was otherwise in control of itself. This had led to a clash between Venice and Rome in 1611. In the eighteenth century, the first clash occurred between Turin and Rome about Sicily. The contemporary term was jurisdictionalism – a matter of defining the jurisdiction of both Church and state – and it had its first advocate in Pietro Giannone, a Neapolitan lawyer who produced, in 1727, a history of the development of the civil laws in Naples, which was put on the Index for arguing that the Church courts had gained excessive power that was not founded in law. This approach, although not officially accepted, was welcomed by practically every Italian ruler.

Ludovico Antonio Muratori (1672–1750) and his pupils were also influential. In his *Della Regolata Divozione dei Cristiani* (1747), Muratori argued in favour of simple worship and public education and against Baroque piety, and he criticised the papacy and monasticism. A bright young shepherd, Muratori was admitted to school, became a priest and the librarian of the Duke of Modena, and wrote a history of Italy from the fall of the Roman Empire to 1749. Muratori's arguments were also those of the *Zelanti*, a group of cardinals who from 1727 pressed for a more serious and really Christian Church.

Supported by rulers and ministers opposed to papal pretensions, reform ideas circulated in Naples and Parma in the 1760s. Moreover, reform bishops and priests were influential in Lombardy in the 1770s and 1780s, when the government restricted the rights of the papacy and the monasteries, enacted toleration, suppressed the confraternities and the ecclesiastical courts, and decreed that in future all parish priests should study at the seminary of Pavia, now reorganised under reform clerics. Emperor Joseph II (r. 1765–90), the ruler of the Milanese, personally gave gold medals to leading reformers there in 1784. In Tuscany, Joseph's brother, Grand Duke Leopold, ruler from 1765 to 1790, supported the reforms of Scipione de'Ricci, the Bishop of Pistoia and Prato, in part because he saw it as a way to increase state powers over the Church. Nevertheless, the attempt to simplify liturgical practice, reorganise the Church in order to increase the power of the parish priests and attack monasticism led in 1787 to opposition from most of the Tuscan bishops and to riots in Prato, and Leopold withdrew his support.

The suppression of the Jesuits, long seen as agents of the papacy, was supported by the Jesuits' many opponents in the Church, notably the Franciscans and the Dominicans. In 1764, the Jesuit order was suppressed in France, with Spain and Naples following in 1767, and Parma in 1768. Clement XIII (r. 1758–69) sought to protect the Jesuits, but his successor, Clement XIV (r. 1769–74), was bullied by the Bourbon rulers, who seized the papal enclaves of Avignon in France and Benevento in the kingdom of Naples, into abolishing the order in 1773. This abolition reflected the declining prestige of the papacy, which, separately, had in 1742 yielded on jurisdictional issues in dispute with Savoy-Piedmont. In addition, the secular authorities took over control of censorship in Tuscany in 1743 and Lombardy in 1768.

ARTS

In cultural terms, Italy lacked the central position it had enjoyed in the sixteenth century, but remained crucially important, notably in art and music. The rulers continued to be key patrons. The Sicilian architect Filippo Juvarra (1678–1736), who had been brought to Turin in 1714 by Victor Amadeus II, rebuilt the Piedmontese palaces of Venaria Reale and Rivoli, made additions to the royal palace in Turin, and, in 1729–33, built a pleasure palace and hunting seat at Stupinigi outside the capital for Victor Amadeus. Once Naples had a royal court, a new and highly impressive country palace was built at Caserta from 1752 by the architect Luigi Vanvitelli.

Aside from the construction of new palaces, monarchs also rebuilt old ones, their changes frequently reflecting stylistic shifts. For Victor Amadeus's mother, Juvarra produced a superb facade with a grand ceremonial staircase across the front of the old *Palazzo Madama* in Turin (1718). Rulers seeking to beautify their palaces patronised a range of arts, including landscape gardening, as at Caserta, painting and the production of splendid objects.

In 1737, the first royal opera house, the *San Carlo*, was opened in Naples. It could hold more than 1,300 people. In 1740, the second, the *Teatro Regio*, was opened in Turin by Charles Emmanuel III. Designed for opera, it was reserved for the court and privileged individuals. In contrast, when La Scala was completed as an opera house in Milan in 1778, it was capable of holding 3,600 people.

Wealthy nobles could also be important patrons, notably of architecture, painting and music. Patrons generally determined the subject of the work and often influenced its composition. Count Niccolò Loschi, who commissioned Giambattista Tiepolo (1696–1770) in 1734 to decorate his villa near Vicenza with frescoes, wanted a complex set of didactic allegorical illustrations. In Venice, the so-called *vedutisti Veneti* (Venetian viewers), notably Giovanni Canaletto, Bernardo Bellotto, Francesco Guardi and Giovanni Pannini, used the camera obscura and cold colours to produce wonderful paintings. They sold them to those who wanted to bring back an image of Italy.

The arts tackled religious themes, in large part due to Church patronage. For example, Pierre Subleyras (1699–1749), a French painter who lived from 1728 in Italy, principally in Rome, was patronised exclusively by the popes, the cardinals and the religious orders. His most famous work, the *Mass of St Basil*, was commissioned by the pope for St Peter's. Pompeo Batoni (1708–87), best known for his portraits of tourists, especially British tourists, visiting Rome, also painted many altarpieces, including the *Fall of Simon Magus* for St Peter's. Many clerics, such as Pope Clement XII (1730–40) and Giuseppe Martelli, Archbishop of Florence (1722–41), were great individual patrons.

Religion also provided patronage and themes for music, while the churches offered training and employment for many musicians. Alessandro Scarlatti (1660–1725), one of the founders of the Neapolitan school of opera, provided the music in 1703 for the annual celebrations of the Feast of Our Lady of Mount Carmel at the church of *Santa Maria di Monte Santo* in Rome, becoming choirmaster of *Santa*

Maria Maggiore there in 1707. His son, Domenico, a very talented and famous composer, worked in Italy and Spain, as did Luigi Boccherini.

There were also significant developments in style and technique, for example the development of string-playing by Arcangelo Corelli, Antonio Vivaldi and Giuseppe Tartini, and the invention of the piano in about 1709 by Bartolomeo Cristofori. The Italian style had a huge relevance for, and a deep influence on, contemporary European music. Handel came to Italy in his early years, knew Corelli, competed with Alessandro Scarlatti in Rome, and produced many operas and cantatas for both the Church and the nobles. Then he exported Italian opera and many Italian singers to Britain. Vivaldi's music was carefully studied by Johann Sebastian Bach who reproduced some of his concertos.

ITALY AND ARTISTIC COSMOPOLITANISM

Italy was central to artistic cosmopolitanism in the seventeenth and eighteenth centuries. Within Europe, there was, at the level of the élite, a culture that was cosmopolitan, thematically, stylistically and in terms of artists and performers. Cosmopolitanism was aided by travel, patronage, the role of cultural intermediaries and the process of emulation. Most major French artists spent some time in the French Academy in Rome, and they were not alone. The Nuremberg painter Carl Tuscher (1705–51) worked in Italy in 1728–41 before going on to London and becoming court painter in Copenhagen. Italians were well represented in a number of courts, including Dresden, Madrid and Munich. Giambattista Tiepolo painted in Madrid and Würzburg. Italian influence was strongest in the fields of art, architecture and music, but markedly weaker in that of literature. Italy was significant as a source of artists, and for the training and inspiration it provided to those from elsewhere, and to a lesser extent, as a still wealthy society able to provide considerable patronage.

STABILITY

Tensions over change did not lead to conflict, and Italy enjoyed a particularly long period of international and domestic peace and territorial stability after the Peace of Aix-la-Chapelle of 1748, rather like that after the Peace of Lodi in 1454, but more so. This stability was greatly strengthened by an alliance between Austria and Spain. As a result, Piedmontese expansionist aspirations were effectively muzzled: no power would support Savoy-Piedmont plans to acquire sections of the Ligurian coast from Genoa. Corsica was purchased by France from Genoa in 1768, a measure that Savoy-Piedmont deplored, but was able to do nothing about, in part because Britain was unwilling to back it. A large-scale popular revolt in Corsica was suppressed by the French in 1769, providing a measure of continuity with later French policy in Italy. Thanks to the purchase, Napoleon was born French in 1769 and not a Genoese subject. There was no sign that the general situation would change. Italy appeared stable as, in effect, a system of separate states that had nothing political in common although they shared their religion, language and culture.

CHAPTER SEVEN

The Revolutionary and Napoleonic Period: 1789–1815

The year 1789 was not especially good for the people of Turin. The population figures published the following January showed that deaths had exceeded births that year by 55 per cent, in part due to an epidemic of measles. Despite immigration from rural areas, the city's population had fallen. Its foundling (orphan) hospital received over 500 children, presumably because their parents had died or could not cope with them. The government was similarly confronted by traditional problems. The large number of abuses in the administration of communal properties, despite the regulations of 1775, led to the establishment of a council to deal with the problem.

Fearful, from 1789 to 1792, of a revival of French expansionism, notably into Savoy, Victor Amadeus III (r. 1773–96) was greatly concerned about military matters. This, in turn, led in early 1790 to Genoese fears of an attack, but there was no attack.

There were few signs that the established order was soon to be disrupted, although, in the summer of 1790, the peasants on the lands of Prince Carignan near Turin rose against tax demands, while the government backed up with arrests its prohibition of public discussion of politics and its limitations of the newspapers permitted to circulate. However, these restrictions were hardly novel: Turin had long been known as a rigorously policed city where the free expression of opinion was restricted. None of this prepared the city or state for the impact of the French Revolution.

AN IMAGE OF ITALY

One of the most potent images of Italy came from the pen of Ann Radcliffe (1764–1823), a successful British novelist who never went there. In her highly successful *The Mysteries of Udolpho* (1794), her heroine went to Italy. Her sequel, *The Italian, or the Confessional of the Black Penitents* (1797), was received with enthusiasm in Britain and immediately translated into French. In it, the captured Ellena confronts a sublime account of a brooding, forceful Italian landscape.

It was when the heat and the light were declining that the carriage entered a rocky defile, which shewed, as through a telescope reversed, distant plains, and mountains opening beyond, lighted up with all the purple splendor of the setting sun. Along this deep and shadowy perspective a river, which was seen descending among the cliffs of a mountain, rolled with impetuous force, fretting and foaming amidst the dark rocks in its descent, and then flowing in a limpid lapse to the brink of other precipices, whence again it fell with thundering strength to the abyss, throwing its misty clouds of spray high in the air, and seeming to claim the sole empire of this solitary wild. Its bed took up the whole breadth of the chasm, which some strong convulsion of the earth seemed to have formed, not leaving space even for a road along its margin. The road, therefore, was carried high among the cliffs, that impended over the river, and seemed as if suspended in air; while the gloom and vastness of the precipices, which towered above and sunk below it, together with the amazing force and uproar of the falling waters, combined to render the pass more terrific than the pencil could describe, or language can express. Ellena ascended it, not with indifference but with calmness; she experienced somewhat of a dreadful pleasure in looking down upon the irresistible flood; but this emotion was heightened into awe, when she perceived that the road led to a slight bridge, which, thrown across the chasm at an immense height, united two opposite cliffs, between which the whole cataract of the river descended. The bridge, which was defended only by a slender railing, appeared as if hung amidst the clouds. Ellena, while she was crossing it, almost forgot her misfortunes.

Breaking out in 1792, the French Revolutionary War brought a period largely of peace and stability to an end, with French forces invading northern Italy late that year. There was political and social tension in Italy prior to the French Revolution, but not on the scale of France. Much discontent was traditional. For example, Cardinal Boncompagni, the Governor of the papal city of Bologna in the 1780s, was unpopular with the local nobles because he had introduced papal troops into the town and made changes in its government. In Capodistria, a town in Venetian Istria, an attempt in 1769–71 by the 'people', supported by some dissident nobles, to gain representation in the council, which was controlled by a small oligarchy, was resisted and failed due to the unrelenting attitude of the Venetian government. In Piedmont, the entrenched oligarchy similarly continued to remain relatively homogenous.

There were groups, there and elsewhere, knocking on the doors of power, some of whom were willing to appeal for French support in the 1790s, but there is little sign that they were especially numerous or that their opposition betrayed profound social tensions. In Piedmont, professional and non-noble townsmen had expanded their land-owning during the century, but without this causing marked social tension. In 1723, Victor Amadeus II had taken back feudal lands whose owners could not demonstrate their right to them, and had then sold them, and the related noble titles, to the upper middle class, creating a new aristocracy that was more commercially minded than the old one. However, John Trevor, British envoy to Savoy-Piedmont, reported from Turin in 1792:

> the misfortune is that in this country the whole society is divided into two classes, the *Court and Nobility*, and *the Bourgeoisie*, and the line drawn between them is so rude and marked that the two parties have long been jealous and might too easily become hostile; there are none of those intermediate shades which blend the whole together into one harmonious mass as in our happy country.

Alongside strains, it is important to note that loyalist movements, directed against radicalism and the French, were to attract considerable support in Italy in the 1790s, notably in Naples in 1794 and 1799.

Savoy and Nice were conquered by the French in September 1792. The poorly prepared, outnumbered and dispersed defenders retreated in confusion across the Alps into Piedmont. In response, Victor Amadeus III hired Austrian troops, while Savoy was annexed by France that November. The French threatened to invade Piedmont and the Milanese.

Neutral powers, such as Genoa, were placed under considerable strain by their fears and the contrasting demands of the combatants. Italian rulers sought the assistance of outside powers. Pope Pius VI (r. 1775–99) in 1792 approached Britain for help in deterring the threat of French attack. In addition to seeking a British declaration that the Papal States were under British protection, there was a request for a British fleet in the Mediterranean to give substance to the declaration. Tuscany seemed defenceless and rebellious to the British envoy, and its ruler, Ferdinand III (r. 1790–1801), was keen to see a British squadron anchor at Livorno. Naples was hostile to France, but, in December 1792, a far larger French fleet arrived off the city of Naples. The threat of attack led the government to agree both to acknowledge the French Republic and to be neutral. Nevertheless, the French concentrated in 1792–5 on operations in the Rhineland and the Low Countries.

From the mid-1790s, Napoleon remade Italy's politics. As commander of France's Army of Italy, he attacked and developed in 1796 the characteristics of his generalship: self-confidence, swift decision-making, rapid mobility, the concentration of strength and, where possible, the exploitation of interior lines. Victory at Mondovì (1796) knocked Savoy-Piedmont out of the war, and dramatic victories, at Lodi (1796), Bassano (1796), Arcole (1796) and Rivoli (1797), brought triumph over the Austrians. Italian rulers responded. Ferdinand III of Tuscany recognised the French Republic in 1796.

It proved difficult, however, for the French to fix their success. The brutal French exploitation of Lombardy in 1796 led to a popular rising that was harshly repressed. Napoleon's unsympathetic report made clear the scale of popular anger: 'rioting crowds in Milan had torn down and trampled the tricolor . . . five to six thousand peasants joined the rioting people of Pavia'. In response, there were mass executions and the taking of large numbers of hostages.

Napoleon advanced to within 70 miles of Vienna, forcing Austria to accept the Treaty of Leoben (1797). Austria agreed to cede the Milanese to a newly formed French satellite republic, the Cispadane Republic, and was to receive the Veneto in return, while Venice would be compensated with Bologna, Ferrara and Romagna, territories seized by France from the Pope earlier in the year. Napoleon remodelled much of northern Italy into the Cispadane and Ligurian Republics, the latter based on Genoa. Proclaimed at Reggio, the former had a green, white and red flag, later the colours of that of Italy. With the addition of Lombardy, the Cispadane became the Cisalpine Republic. This was a pretend democracy on the model later to be made familiar in Communist states. The constitution established in 1797 declared that sovereignty resided in the adult male population as a whole, but the vote was limited while the legislators of the two councils, and the directors who administered the republic, were all named by Napoleon.

Later in 1797, by the Treaty of Campo Formio, Austria accepted the French gain of the Ionian Islands and the major northern Italian military base of Mantua, while Austria received Venice, which had refused an alliance against Austria, as well as the Veneto, Dalmatia and Istria. The cession of republican Venice to Austria, brutally bringing to an end its long history of independence, was condemned by French and especially by Italian Jacobins as a betrayal of revolutionary ideals, but that was to be true of most of the Revolution. In Italy, military convenience, lust for loot, strategic opportunism, and the practice of large-scale and deadly expropriation, all encouraged aggressive action by France, as with the seizure of the Papal States in February 1798. The previous year, the residence of the French envoy in Rome had been occupied by papal police during a riot: the rioters had taken refuge there. In the ensuing disorder, General Léonard Duphot, an aide to the French envoy, was killed. Given, however, that the French had sought to provoke a revolutionary uprising, their conduct had been less than exemplary. Once in control, Napoleon proclaimed a Roman Republic. Pope Pius VI had been deported.

The year 1798 saw the move of Ferdinand IV of Naples (r. 1759–1825), whose wife was the sister of the Queen of France, into the anti-French camp. His forces briefly drove the French from Rome, only, in December, to be pushed back and to evacuate Naples in Horatio Nelson's flagship, fleeing to Palermo. Naples was left with a four-way struggle between the royalists, the advancing French, the *giacobini* (Italian Jacobins) and the *lazzaroni* (the poor who were in favour of revolutionary ideas, but not of French troops). The *giacobini* and *lazzaroni* fought each other in January in street fighting that cost over 4,000 lives, before the French and *giacobini* enforced control.

In Naples, the French established the Parthenopean Republic, another satellite regime. However, in Naples and elsewhere, these new governments were unpopular and compromised by their links with expensive and meddlesome French occupation. In Naples, the new republic introduced republican and atheistic celebrations as well as freedom of religion, refused to employ anyone who had served the king, and could not cope with shortages of bread and firewood. The republic was also weakened by the movement north of most of the French troops.

As a result, little resistance was mounted against a royalist rising under Cardinal Fabrizio Dionigi Ruffo, who formed the *Santa Fede* (Holy Faith) Army in Sicily in January 1799, landed in Calabria on 8 February, and advanced on the city of Naples. In addition, a 32,000-strong Russo-Turkish expeditionary force with forty men of war captured Corfu and then arrived on the Adriatic coast of Italy. It landed in lower Apulia and marched north, capturing the cities of Taranto and Foggia, before moving west and capturing Ariano, Avellino and Nola. At the same time, an Anglo-Sicilian force threatened Naples. On 15 April 1799, 500 (Sicilian) Neapolitan regular loyalists were landed from British ships together with British forces, seizing Castellammare di Stabia and its naval arsenal. A second Anglo-Sicilian force landed south of Naples at Salerno (where the Allies were to land in 1943) and approached Naples, seizing en route the towns of Vietri, Cava, Citara, Pagani and Nocera. Although the French troops reacted well against the attackers, subsequent Anglo-Sicilian seizures of the islands of Ischia and Procida in early May completed the blockade, and Naples was captured on 13 June. The discussion of foreign intervention in a liberation comparable to that by Anglo-American forces in 1943 does not tend to attract Italian attention.

The *giacobini* in Naples suffered from a *lazzaroni* uprising and many were murdered. The new order was imposed in Naples in June with over 100 executions. These executions tend to receive much attention from Italian commentators, not least as they provided a way to castigate the Bourbons and because those executed were reformers. Less attention is devoted to the many Italians, tens of thousands in total, killed by the French over a longer period.

The partisan approach to the past is instructive. On the left, the foreign intervention of 1943 is seen favourably because, although Anglo-American and capitalist, it supported 'positive' forces, that is to say the left. In contrast, in 1799, such intervention by the British and Russians (not the French) was/is seen as against the 'positive' forces, because a line was/is drawn from the French supporters to the *Risorgimento* and, subsequently, to left-wing groups in 1943–6 such as the Action Party. The latter claimed to be the spiritual descendants of the *giacobini*, while the spiritual 'ascendancy' of the latter was underlined by noting that they had opposed the Neapolitan Bourbons, just as Garibaldi was to do in 1860.

The monarchy was restored in Naples in 1799. Anti-French risings also occurred in other areas including Piedmont and Tuscany. Subsequently, Allied forces, including a British naval blockade of Genoa, cleared Italy of the French in 1799.

However, in 1800, Napoleon returned and defeated the Austrians at Marengo. In 1801, France and Austria negotiated the Peace of Lunéville. Piedmont and Lombardy were left in the French sphere of control and Venice and the Veneto in that of Austria. Tuscany was transferred to the Duke of Parma in compensation for Spain transferring Louisiana to France. Napoleon annexed Elba in 1801 and Piedmont in 1802.

Southern Italy again saw conflict in 1805 as the War of the Third Coalition spread. French forces occupied part of the kingdom of Naples, only to withdraw before an Anglo-Russian force that arrived in November 1805. Plans were made to defend the kingdom, but there was scant popular support, in part due to the exactions of Russian troops. Moreover, distant events in 1805 had a major impact. Trafalgar meant the defeat of a Franco-Spanish fleet ordered to intervene off Naples, but Napoleon's crushing of Austro-Russian forces at Austerlitz in the modern Czech Republic led to the collapse of the new order in southern Italy. Russia and then Britain withdrew their forces, while King Ferdinand unsuccessfully sought to assuage Napoleon's anger. At every level, Italians had to respond to more powerful outsiders.

Calabria, in turn, became a battleground with a major rising in

1806. The peasants, there and elsewhere, proved hostile to all troops and most government. Italian conservatism, however, was eventually suppressed in Calabria by French forces brutally imposing a new order, including by the deployment of 48,000 troops and the use of punitive flying columns. British observers commented on the 'marked degree of severity' shown by the French towards an 'armed populace' suffering from the 'greatest want of arms and ammunition'.

British military intervention in Calabria in 1806 proved too short-term to delay the process seriously. However, King Ferdinand had taken shelter in Sicily where he was protected by the British fleet and by British garrisons. The British commander, Lord William Bentinck, introduced British constitutionalism to Sicily. Similarly, Victor Emmanuel I of Piedmont (r. 1802–21) took refuge in Sardinia.

France no longer brought republics. Naples was entrusted in 1806 to Napoleon's brother Joseph, and in 1808, when Joseph moved to be King of Spain, to Caroline, Napoleon's youngest sister, and, as co-ruler, Joachim Murat, a Napoleonic marshal, a great cavalry commander, and Caroline's husband. The eldest surviving sister, Elisa, became Duchess of Lucca in 1805 and Grand Duchess of Tuscany in 1809, and another, Pauline, became Duchess of Guastalla. Her husband, Prince Camillo Borghese, was made governor general of the French departments in northern Italy.

Napoleon's will for dominance was much on display in Italy, where, having had himself made President of the Italian Republic (a renaming of the Cisalpine Republic) in 1802, he named himself King of Italy in 1805, with his stepson, Eugène, as viceroy. Napoleon crowned himself with the Iron Crown of Lombardy in Milan cathedral that year. Victory over Austria brought Venice and the Veneto to the kingdom in 1806, the Papal Marches following in 1808 and the Trentino in 1810. Napoleon talked of an Italian national spirit in the kingdom of Italy, but annexed much of Italy to France, including the *presidios* in 1801, Piedmont in 1802, and Genoa and Parma in 1805. The Ligurian Republic was redundant in a monarchical and French Italy. Etruria (Tuscany) was annexed in 1809. Istria, Dalmatia, Trieste and Fiume were transferred to the kingdom of Italy in 1806, and then, as the Illyrian Provinces, became part of France in 1809.

The Papal States was annexed by France in 1810. Born in 1811, Napoleon's son was made King of Rome and successor to the imperial throne. Pope Pius VII (r. 1800–23) had been arrested and taken to France, and the many clergy who refused to take an oath of loyalty were arrested. The attack on traditional Catholicism involved the closure and demolition of monasteries and convents, and the banning of many feast days and processions as part of a de facto secularism. The police were used to enforce this new order, but, thanks to such policies, cooperation was sapped and the masses feared.

Napoleon, who last visited Italy in 1807, also pressed on with the cultural pillage of Italy begun by the French Revolutionaries. Many paintings and statues were seized for France, and notably so from northern Italy, including Venice, and also from Rome. Some can still be seen in many French museums. Moreover, Italy had to produce large numbers of men for the French army, and many died when invading Russia in 1812.

As the war went badly, Napoleon, nevertheless, proved unwilling, in negotiations with Austria in 1813–14, to surrender control over the kingdom of Italy as part of the price for a peace that left him in control of France. Defeated, he was exiled in 1814 to Elba, which became a principality under his rule. In 1815, when he returned to France in an attempt to seize power, Murat sought to act in his support. Both men were totally defeated.

THE FAILURE OF ITALY'S LIBERATOR

Joachim Murat, who, as co-ruler of Naples with his wife Caroline, had sought to develop an Italian nationalism, proclaimed himself Liberator of Italy on 15 March 1815 when he declared war on Austria in an attempt to help, and benefit from, Napoleon's return to France from Elba. Murat had kept the kingdom of

Naples in 1814 by abandoning Napoleon, but, aware that the Austrians were now willing to see him deposed, the naturally ambitious Murat would not follow Napoleon's advice to wait before acting. Moving into the Papal States, on 19 March, Murat invaded central Italy in order to attack the Austrians further north, and seized Rome and Florence, while defeating, at Cesena on 30 March, the Austrians who tried to block his advance on Bologna. Murat benefited from the extent to which many Austrian units were north of the Alps and, at Rimini on 31 March, he issued a proclamation to all Italians, calling for a new order and a 'war of independence' for Italy.

However, Murat suffered from the unpopularity of Napoleon's rule and from the concentration of Austrian forces to produce an army that was able to capture Bologna on 16 April and Cesena on 21 April, and to defeat Murat at Tolentino on 2–3 May. This defeat led to the dissolution of Murat's army through desertion.

The British played a major role with their naval power, which was present off Ancona and Gaeta, as well as protecting Sicily. A small British squadron then arrived off Naples and forced the surrender of the Neapolitan navy. Murat's position collapsed and, as a result of a convention of 20 May, Murat left, to be replaced by Ferdinand IV of Sicily, while British marines and Austrian troops occupied the city on 23 May.

As a consequence of earlier betrayals, Murat was unwelcome to Napoleon. Instead, he fled, first to Toulon and then, as royal control was re-established in France, to Corsica, where he raised a few followers and took shelter in the inaccessible terrain of the interior. As the role of bandit-leader proved unattractive, Murat sought to return to his former kingdom. He duly invaded Calabria on 8 October, but was speedily defeated, captured, and, after a court-martial, executed on 15 October by a firing squad of Ferdinand's troops. His cell and tomb can be seen in Pizzo, the gloom of the former enlivened by wax models.

THE *EPOCA FRANCESE*

The Napoleonic period was subsequently to bear the weight of much responsibility for accounts of Italy's development. In particular, it was to be seen as responsible for the growth of nationalism and for the development of a bourgeoisie. Napoleon was to be praised for building roads, for introducing religious liberty and divorce, and for a range of administrative reforms. Tuscan was adopted as the standard language of the kingdom of Italy in 1809. Indeed, once the Habsburgs regained control in 1814, they showed a considerable institutional debt to the Napoleonic system. So also for the papacy as French centralisation swept away the autonomous power of local institutions in the Papal States. These had often challenged papal political authority as the ancient privileges were still respected by the popes as a part of the agreements made when these areas had accepted the popes as their rulers.

Napoleon's nephew, Louis Napoleon, later Napoleon III, argued in his *Des Idées Napoléoniennes* (1839): 'In Italy he formed a great kingdom which had its separate administration and its Italian army . . . The name Italy, so beautiful, defunct, for so many ages, was restored to provinces which until then had been severed. That name implies in itself a future of independence.'

In practice, however, the unpopularity of the Napoleonic regime, which included financial burdens and 70,000 deaths fighting for Napoleon, helped create and accentuate divisions between state and society that have been a feature to the present. Ironically, this was a period in which Italy was more united politically than at any time since the Roman Empire, and notably so in terms of an attempted political culture. This, however, was very much imposed by France, on a French model, and to the benefit of France, as with conscription, high taxation and the establishment of a gendarmerie or military police.

The French were least unsuccessful where their control was not only longer-established but also relied on cooperation with local élites, namely in Lombardy and Emilia, and less so further south, notably in rural central Italy. In Liguria, Napoleon relied on French administrators and paid scant attention to local traditions and views, but, in Piedmont, he used Piedmontese administrators (as he also did elsewhere), many in very senior positions. In Lombardy and Emilia, the former Cispadane, then Cisalpine, Republic, Napoleon gave most of his patronage to Italians and relied on considerable local autonomy. In doing so, he benefited from the degree of development and enlightenment already seen in these regions, and notably in the duchy of Parma. Far from backing the bourgeoisie, Napoleon established titles of nobility from 1808, and, in 1811, allowed *ancien régime* patricians the option of applying for new Napoleonic titles, although the latter proved less popular than the former.

The heavy burdens of enforced participation in the Napoleonic system prefigured those to be seen in Mussolini's Republic of Salò in 1943–5 with regard to the Germans. Direct comparisons can be unwelcome, but subsequently, in each case, there was to be an attempt to rewrite the past, one that deserves harsh scrutiny.

CHAPTER EIGHT

From Napoleon to Unification: 1815–60

CONSERVATISM RESURGENT

The Congress of Vienna completely redrew the borders of Italy. Piedmont was strengthened with the acquisition of Genoa, and of Liguria as a whole, as a barrier to French expansion, a barrier sought by both Austria and Britain. Opportunities for French expansion or influence in Italy were further lessened with Lombardy-Venetia becoming part of Austria, and Tuscany a Habsburg secundogeniture. Venice and Genoa were not restored to independence and Italian republicanism largely came to an end. Parma was restored to the Bourbon-Parma dynasty, but only after the death of Marie Louise, Napoleon's second wife and the Emperor Francis I of Austria's daughter. In the meanwhile, the Bourbon-Parma dynasty was 'parked' in Lucca, now a duchy. When Marie Louise died in 1847, the dynasty went back to Parma, and Lucca passed to Tuscany. The dukes of Modena were now of the House of Habsburg-Este.

There was a significant cultural restitution. In 1814–15, France had to give back many of the paintings and statues that had been seized. The Pope sent the great neo-Classical sculptor, Antonio Canova, as the chief of the papal commission and he reclaimed much. What had been stolen in Lombardy and Venice was demanded by Austria. With Allied forces occupying France until 1817, such demands were heeded.

As a result of the changes, there were fewer independent states in Italy than prior to 1792. The Papal States and Naples were restored to their former shape and rulers, although each was weakened by the extent to which the old system of government and the related legitimation were now under challenge. Ferdinand IV of Naples (and III of Sicily) returned from Palermo to Naples and suppressed the more liberal parliamentary constitution of 1812 that had been introduced in Sicily. The two kingdoms were united and Ferdinand became Ferdinand I of the Two Sicilies, the title of the new kingdom. With Britain now in control of Malta and the Ionian Islands, and very much the Mediterranean great power, the political situation in Italy ultimately rested on the Austrian army and the British navy. France had been largely removed from the equation.

Piedmont (still technically the kingdom of Sardinia) was the territory that appeared to offer the only prospect of change and, more particularly, the formation of a modern state, one able to guarantee security and provide governance. Indeed, in 1762, John Hinchliffe, a British visitor, had written to Augustus, 3rd Duke of Grafton: 'The Sardinian monarch seems to be a snowball from mountains gathering as it goes. It is the only power . . . which is at all in a rising state.' In 1831, during a period of insurrection across much of Italy, Giuseppe Mazzini (1805–72) called upon the King to lead the struggle against Austria and create a united Italy.

Napoleonic rule had proved highly unpopular in Italy, largely because of the conscription it had entailed, which had led to large-scale opposition. The army of the kingdom of Italy had grown from 23,000 in 1805 to 90,000 in 1813. The majority of those sent to fight for Napoleon in Spain, Russia and Germany died. In addition, conservatism rested on extensive popular support, and liberalism had only limited purchase, all points later commentators, both Italian and foreign, found easy to forget, both for Italy and more generally. As in Spain, Napoleon's assault on Italian religious life and institutions was highly unpopular. The reputation of the clergy was particularly strengthened by the experience of French occupation. Religious enthusiasm was seen in the post-Napoleonic world, as with the discovery of the remains of St Francis in 1818.

Although providing refuge for members of the Bonaparte family, including, from 1823, the future Napoleon III, the papacy took a markedly conservative line. Leo XII, elected in 1823, imposed strict censorship and, in the 1824 encyclical *Ubi Primum*, denounced liberalism and what he presented as the de-Christianisation of society. In 1829, his successor, Pius VIII, issued the encyclical *Traditi Humiliati*, in which he urged Church leaders to be vigilant against both false teachings and secular attempts to undermine the Church. In 1831, Gregory XVI was elected as the candidate of the *zelanti* against the liberals. An opponent of new political ideas, Gregory was willing to yield to Austrian pressure to stand firm.

Thanks to widespread conservatism, Austria, after 1815, as part of the Russian-backed policy of the anti-revolutionary Holy Alliance, was able, from 1821, to suppress liberal risings in Italy with far greater ease than the French when faced with conservative risings in Spain in 1808–13, or, indeed, in Calabria from 1806. Austrian action, which owed much to papal encouragement and to requests from other Italian rulers, including Duke Francis IV of Modena and Marie Louise of Parma in 1831, reflected a determination to control Italy, not least because of fears that radicalism in individual Italian principalities would affect the situation in Austrian-ruled Lombardy and Venetia. These fears encouraged diplomatic and military interventionism. In 1821, in response to risings by the garrisons of Alessandria and Turin, demanding liberty, Austrian and loyal Piedmontese troops defeated the rebels. Similarly that year, the Austrians crushed a rebellion in Naples by the *Carbonari* (an anti-royalist movement) and restored the previous conservative royalist regime. There had been a revolution in Palermo the previous year. Despite disturbances, Italy was then largely quiescent in 1830, a year in which there were successful revolutions in France and Belgium. The quip by Austria's Chancellor, Prince Metternich, that Italy was merely a geographical expression appeared well justified.

In 1831, there was another revolution in Italy, this time focused on the Legations (although also in Modena and Parma). These, the northern provinces of the Papal States, centred on Bologna, suffered particular neglect, being seen as a source of funds for distant Rome. Indeed, the revolts in 1831 demonstrated the point that, while liberal nationalism enjoyed relatively little support, misgovernment could lead to support for the alternative it offered. Austria suppressed the revolts in 1831 and intervened anew in 1832 to preserve papal control, maintaining forces in the Legations until 1838. Napoleon's nephew, Louis Napoleon, later Napoleon III of France (Napoleon I's son, the 'King of Rome', was, to some, Napoleon II), took part in the 1831 revolutionary movement in Italy, and it was an important influence for him.

Revolutionary plots continued, as in 1843 when Nicola Fabrizi planned an Italian-wide revolution, which was to begin in the Legations and Naples, as these were seen as the areas of greatest discontent. Confident of the situation in Lombardy-Venetia, Metternich passed on the information about the plans to Naples and Rome, only to find the governments lacklustre in their response. In the end, however, the precautions taken dissuaded the revolutionaries from rising, and only small-scale revolutionary action was taken. Tension, nevertheless, continued, and, in 1844, a revolt took place at Cosenza in the kingdom of Naples. It was suppressed. However, these allied governments were clearly too weak to confront a major rising.

Meanwhile, the failure of the radicals encouraged supporters of Italian nationalism increasingly to turn to leadership from Piedmont. Many of these supporters became more conservative as the nationalist movement responded to the Piedmontese state, a transformation very much associated with Count Camillo di Cavour (1810–61), Piedmont's Prime Minister from 1852.

In 1848, in the 'Year of Revolutions', tensions within a number of states, some of them nationalist in character, gave rise to a crisis of governance that spread across much of Europe. Rising hostility to Austrian rule was an important factor in Italy, where the *Risorgimento*, the cause of unification, became inseparable from rivalry between Austria, its opponent, and Piedmont, its supporter. In Italy, revolution broke out in Palermo in January, and there were also uprisings in Bologna, Florence, Livorno, Modena, Naples, Parma and Venice. In Sicily, the constitution of 1812 was revived and a parliament controlled most of the island. Riots in Naples led the King to grant a constitution. Piedmont, in contrast, did not have to worry about a nationalist challenge.

The most prominent Austrian commander, Field Marshal Josef Radetzky (1766–1858), a veteran of the Napoleonic Wars, restored the Austrian position. He retreated from Milan eastwards into the powerful fortresses of the 'Quadrilateral': Legnano, Mantua, Peschiera and Verona. Charles Albert of Piedmont (r. 1831–49) advanced as commander of the United Italian patriotic forces, but was outmanoeuvred and outfought by Radetzky, who employed interior lines to achieve a concentration of strength against strung-out Piedmontese forces. About a third of his army was Italian, and most of the Italians in the Austrian army served in Italy. Radetzky's crushing victory at Custoza near Verona in 1848 was followed by the recapture of Milan and most of Lombardy. In 1849, his heavy defeat of Charles Albert at Novara forced the latter to abdicate. Radetzky then blockaded Venice, and starvation and cholera led to its surrender. The role of force in securing Austrian control was made abundantly clear when Radetzky became Governor of Lombardy and Venetia in 1850–7.

Meanwhile, in May 1848, the Bourbon army overcame the insurgents in Naples with much bloodshed, and in late 1848 and early 1849, this army restored control over Sicily. In Rome, Pius IX (r. 1846–78), a reformer, had been elected. He rapidly introduced changes, notably relaxing censorship and establishing an elected local government in Rome, and granted a constitution to the Papal States in 1848. However, Pius was unwilling to join Piedmont in making war on the Catholic Habsburgs. As a result, he was overthrown in 1849 and a republic was declared. This was a dramatic rejection of the old order, and one that was significant for all Catholic Europe, much of which rallied to his help. Moved rapidly from Toulon to Civitavecchia by steam, overwhelming French forces successfully besieged Rome, which they occupied in 1849. Spanish and Neapolitan troops helped, with Pius blessing Neapolitan troops gathered on the esplanade of the Royal Palace at Naples that September. Meanwhile, Austrian forces restored papal control east of the Apennines and brought back the old order in Tuscany. Held in the *Museo Nazionale di San Martino* in Naples, Achille Vespa's painting of the papal blessing of the Neapolitan troops captured a celebration of victory that appeared to reflect a strong old order.

In 1850, Pius IX returned to Rome. He was no longer a liberal. In 1854, he defined as a dogma of faith the doctrine of the Immaculate Conception, a crucial move in the cult of the Virgin Mary, and, in 1864, issued the *Syllabus Errorum* (*Syllabus of Errors*) appended to the encyclical *Quanta Cura* denouncing freedom of conscience and parliamentary government. Pius convoked the First Vatican Council (1869–70), which issued the declaration of Papal Infallibility in 1870. With its public executions of rebels, this was a theocratic state. More positively, attempts at reform were made in the 1850s and 1860s in the Papal States, but the necessary administrative structure and resources were absent. The strength of religious fervour felt by many can be captured by listening to Rossini's *Petite Messe Solennelle* (*Little Solemn Mass*, 1863).

The Roman Republic had pushed Giuseppe Mazzini to the fore as head of the governing triumvirate. The key ideologue of the *Risorgimento*, Mazzini had a quasi-religious concept of Italian nation-hood, one that linked it to what he presented as a necessary moral regeneration. He helped make the cause internationally respectable. An inspirational figure and opinion-former, Mazzini saw liberty as a way to fulfil human capabilities and to empower Italians. His concept of liberty embraced conditions within the country that he wished to help create. In particular, drawing on the model of the 1789 French Revolution, there was to be, if not equalisation, nevertheless equal-ity before the law in order to foster social justice. Mazzini was keen on workers' cooperatives as a means to the same ends. Prefiguring Mussolini, a comparison that will not be widely welcome, Mazzini was a master of rhetoric, and also an active user of the press, in order to establish an effective appeal that brought together religious and secular language and ideas. A spiritual union between God and the people was a goal and means of his democratic nationalism. Mazzini's religion was non-dogmatic, but many of the ideas and much of the language of the *Risorgimento* showed the influence of Catholicism.

CONSIDERING ITALY

The *Risorgimento* awakened interest in Italy as a 'proper' country among British and other foreign politicians and intellectuals, with the theme presented and accepted of the nation striving for freedom and, to an extent, breaking the claims of the past. For example, the poet William Wordsworth (1770–1850), who was greatly influenced by 'the idea' of Italy, a fusion of Classical civilisation and landscape with hopes of modern regeneration, as well as praising the old republic of Venice in a sonnet, engaged with Italian poets, moralists and historians. Not only did George, Lord Byron (1788–1824) obviously enjoy living in Italy, but, with his links with the *Carbonari*, he had strong sympathies with Italian aspirations towards political freedom and might easily have died in Italy instead of as part of the modern crusade for Greek freedom. Nevertheless, Italy's reputation in Britain may have suffered in the early nineteenth century from being the place of refuge chosen by dangerous radicals with dubious lifestyles, such as Byron and the free-living poet Percy Bysshe Shelley who lived there from 1818 until his death by drowning in 1822.

Later in the nineteenth century, the cause of Italy became more popular, not least because revolution no longer seemed a serious prospect in Britain. Writers such as the Brownings, who moved to Florence in 1846 after their elopement, and, especially, historians such as George Trevelyan were very interested in Italy-present. Charles Dickens was a keen supporter of the *Risorgimento*, as were such prominent politicians as William Ewart Gladstone and Henry, Viscount Palmerston. For example, in the 1850s, Tuscan policies that were perceived as religious persecution, notably of Protestants, helped encourage support for the *Risorgimento*. More generally, anti-Catholicism played an important role, while also, however, ensuring Irish popular support for the papacy.

There were many public lectures and newspaper articles in favour of the *Risorgimento*. The local newspaper in William Bell Scott's painting *The Nineteenth Century, Iron and Coal*, finished in 1861, carries an advertisement for a 'Grand Panorama!!! Garibaldi in Italy. Struggles for Freedom . . .', a show that ran in Newcastle that March. Britain that year was the first country formally to recognise the kingdom of Italy. Giuseppe Garibaldi (1807–82) was applauded by working-class crowds when he visited England in 1864, and there was a fashion for clothes and accessories associated with him, as well as many subscriptions. A type of biscuit was named after Garibaldi.

Yet, such enthusiasm proved short-lived: once united, Italy ceased to arouse sympathetic interest and, even during the *Risorgimento*, there had been an important element of condescension, notably in Britain.

TRIUMPH FOR THE *RISORGIMENTO*

It would have surprised most commentators to know that the situation was to have changed radically by the end of 1860. In 1859, France backed Piedmont in a war in northern Italy in which the Austrians were defeated. In doing so, the French responded to skilful manipulation by Piedmont's leading minister, Count Cavour, a version of Austria's Metternich, but one standing for a cause that was different politically, although not really socially. Prime Minister in 1852–9 and 1860–1, Cavour was opposed to the populist elements in the *Risorgimento*. He and Napoleon III agreed in 1858 on secretly provoking Austria into war, a course to which Austrian folly contributed. The French played the key military role in 1859 as the Piedmontese force was only about 60,000 men strong. The role of outside powers in crucial moments of Italy's history was also to be seen in 1917–18 and, even more, 1943–5. This was not, however, simply a case with Italian history. It was also, for example, the case with France in 1918 and 1944.

A Mussolini of his own day, Napoleon III's vainglorious posturing and quest for glory were crucial to the cause of Italian unification. Napoleon saw himself as following in what he presented as the benign footsteps of his uncle, Napoleon I. He was also influenced by Piedmont, from 1855, allying with France (and Britain and Turkey) in the Crimean War with Russia in 1854–6 to which it sent 18,000 troops, and by his affair with Virginia Oldoini, Contessa di Castiglione, a cousin of Cavour, who purposefully sent her to Paris in 1858 to that end.

France used steamships alongside railways so as to move its troops into Italy. These served to lessen the problems posed by the Alps and, in particular, the need to move forward in order to prevent Austrian forces advancing from Milan to overrun Piedmont. Rail transported French troops to the ports of Toulon and Marseilles, from which they could use steamships, and move on subsequently by train. Victorious over the Austrians at Magenta and Solferino on 4 May and 24 June 1859 respectively, France benefited from the superiority of its new rifled cannon over its Austrian smooth-bore counterparts. The French cannon destroyed most of the latter with accurate counter-battery fire, and then devastated the Austrian infantry. The battles became attritional in character and fought at close-quarters. French infantry advances with the bayonet were successful against poorly trained and poorly led Austrian infantry, who were unable to draw much benefit from their technically advanced rifles. The Austrians had not been adequately trained in range-finding and sighting and, as a result, the French were able to close and use their bayonets. Tactics were similar to those under Napoleon I, with dense deployments and column formations.

On both sides, there was a lack of adequate planning and of coherence in command. In particular, the doctrine and practice of a systematic process of effective and rapid decision-making was absent. Generals had not yet achieved what was to become the ideal: the implementation of strategic plans in terms of timed operational decisions and interrelated tactical actions. This failure was linked to command practices that were unsystematic and less than taut: such features encouraged incoherent strategies, battles without effective overall plans and piecemeal tactics. These command practices reflected the nature of the commanders, notably the poor military leadership of Napoleon III.

The substantial number of troops deployed increased the problems of transporting, supplying and controlling them. At Solferino, there were about a quarter of a million troops. Such numbers created major problems for command and control, and the high commands of both sides largely lost control of the course of battles that became attritional.

The French, nevertheless, suffered heavy casualties, and the campaign had indicated difficulties with their army, and even more with that of Piedmont. Moreover, the Austrians fought a successful rearguard action at Solferino. Partly for these reasons, the French did not press on to attack the powerful Austrian fortresses of the Quadrilateral and to conquer Venetia. This would have represented a formidable challenge, not least because the Italian-speaking units in the Austrian army had fought well, having very few deserters. There was the danger of an Austrian recovery. Concerned about the Prussian attitude to France's success, as well as about pressure from Catholic circles in France worried about the situation of the papacy, Napoleon III instead negotiated the Armistice of Villafranca in July 1859. This separate peace led Cavour to resign, although he returned to power in 1860.

Venetia was left to Austria, which, in turn, wanted peace because of its concern about the challenge from revolutionary nationalism in case the war continued. Piedmont gained Lombardy and Parma, although in 1860, by the Treaty of Turin of 24 March, it had to cede the duchy of Savoy and the county of Nice to France as its recompense for the war. They also helped maintain the alliance with France, which was a guarantee against Austria. Giuseppe Garibaldi, whose birthplace was Nice, complained bitterly. Under pressure from both governments and the French army, the people of Nice and Savoy were coerced into voting in a plebiscite for annexation. Lombardy was the key gain because of the importance of its industry and agriculture, and also its political prominence as the central stage in northern Italy. Milan had a resonance in, and about, Italy, second only to Rome.

Long possessions of the House of Savoy, the ruler of Piedmont, Savoy and Nice have remained with France since. So also with Corsica, long under Genoa, but bought by France in 1768. There were *revanchist* hopes under Mussolini and Italian occupation after France's defeat in 1940, but they have had no traction since.

After the end of the war, Victor Emmanuel II of Piedmont (r. 1849–61) forbade Garibaldi, the poster-boy of the *Risorgimento*, to advance the cause of unification by attacking the Papal States: as so often, the terms of nationalism divided its supporters, and this was an aspect of the transfer of control over nationalism from Mazzini to Cavour.

Instead, resigning his generalship in the Piedmontese army, Garibaldi and 1,000 red-shirted volunteers sailed from Genoa to Marsala in 1860, landing on 11 May, in order to help a revolt in Sicily against the kingdom of the Two Sicilies (Sicily and southern Italy) of the Neapolitan Bourbons that had broken out in Palermo on 4 April. Garibaldi's advance was a rapid campaign, with battles (at Calatafimi and Milazzo) and street fighting (at Palermo), which led to victory. The role of morale was important. At Milazzo, the Bourbon army lost fewer men, but fell back. The British connived not only by not using the Royal Navy to try to stop the expedition or the subsequent advance to the mainland, but by interposing warships between Garibaldi's steamers and Neapolitan ships, which made it impossible for the latter to attack the steamers.

In 1860, Garibaldi crossed from Sicily to southern Italy, occupied Naples on 7 September, and defeated Francesco II in the battle of Volturno. He then handed over his conquests to Victor Emmanuel, enabling the latter to create the kingdom of Italy in one of the most complete victories of the century. Alongside conquest, there was a revolution by the Neapolitan people, and Garibaldi's rapid victory was due perhaps more to anti-Bourbon sentiment than to Garibaldian republicanism, let alone support for the ruling House of Piedmont. A branch of the Bourbons no longer sat on the French throne, and the cause of the Neapolitan Bourbons enjoyed no effective support in Naples or abroad. Looked at differently, a foreign order had been imposed on Naples, one owing a lot to subversion encouraged by outside intervention. Although expressed then, and since, by some Neapolitans, that was not a view headlined by other Italian commentators. Instead, the emphasis was on the struggle against an external enemy, Austria.

Benefiting from the Austrian withdrawal of their garrisons from Bologna and Ancona in 1859, the Piedmontese army under Victor Emmanuel had exploited the situation, occupying the Romagna, and then marching south to defeat papal and Neapolitan forces and to prevent Garibaldi from determining the future of Italy. Plebiscites in March 1860 were to lead to the Romagna being formally annexed to Piedmont. Papal forces had brutally suppressed a popular uprising in Perugia in 1859, but in 1860, when the Piedmontese troops arrived, the fortress, a symbol of papal authority, was destroyed by the people. A plebiscite led to Umbria becoming part of the new kingdom of Italy. Lombardy was acquired by the kingdom of Sardinia in 1859, followed by Modena, Parma and Tuscany in March 1860, the kingdom of the Two Sicilies that October, and Romagna, the Marches and Umbria in November.

ECONOMIC STRAINS

Disrupted greatly by the French Revolutionary and Napoleonic Wars, the economies of Italy's states continued to struggle thereafter. In part, this was because of the strains created by technological change elsewhere, strains in both agriculture and industry. This situation created a cumulative pressure, as investment capital could not readily be accumulated. Moreover, there were social and political tensions linked to capitalism and to competition over resources. Economic choices were affected accordingly, with the Restoration (post-1815) states seeking to restore aristocratic dominance and thus to limit the middle class, which was more liberal. Capitalist pressures also hit the role of independent peasant families, notably in the plains where large agricultural estates developed. As a result, the move towards landless wage labourers was accentuated. Hostile public responses included attacks on rice fields and strikes.

There was great pressure on the bulk of the population. In 1816, a major subsistence crisis, associated with food shortages and disease, sent death rates up. The general rise in population led to increased pressure on the economic system as more people sought land, employment, food and poor relief. The pressure on the land was a serious problem because of the primitive state of agricultural techniques and technology. Younger sons and poorer sharecroppers were in especially difficult circumstances. Growing rural pauperisation was linked to an increase in the number of day labourers. Poverty was particularly acute in southern Italy, notably Calabria.

As in many countries, undernourishment was the permanent condition of many people. Population growth led to a greater concentration on the production of cereals at a time when, in general, insufficient attention was devoted to the raising of animals, the principal source of manure. It was not only a case of insufficient food, but also of the type available. Pasta and dried beans were the staples. In many areas, such as western and central Sicily, bread was often in short supply and prickly pear was a substitute. Peasants rarely ate meat. Food was often eaten in the form of soup.

The position of women was especially bleak. A disproportionate number of the many children abandoned to be foundlings were girls. Many women worked hard either in agriculture, particularly weeding, or in manufacturing, notably in weaving and spinning. In 1835, it was reported that, in Sicily, most peasant women took part in industrial processes or worked as domestics.

By Western standards, Italy was economically backward, short of capital, had a limited internal market, and showed too little commitment to growth, modernisation and change. This was especially so on the part of the Church. The pressures of globalisation brought home the loss of comparative advantage in many aspects of Italian agriculture and industry. There were resulting losses in markets and employments. This undercut the reliance in the traditional economy on complementary sources of income. Instead, specialisation was now to the fore.

At the same time, regional variation remained central in the response to economic pressures. In Piedmont, unlike in the lower Po valley or Apulia, small peasant proprietors continued to be important, and thus class conflict was more limited and political stability greater than when there were few such individuals and thus a more divided society. Divisions between regions were matched by those within them, a point more generally true in Italian history.

There were significant changes in technology and infrastructure. The first steamship on the Mediterranean was the Neapolitan *Ferdinando I* in 1818. The year 1839 saw the first Italian railway. The first major Italian tunnel, two miles long, was hand-dug in 1851 at the Giovi pass, 472 metres above sea level, between Liguria and Piedmont, and was opened to rail traffic in 1852. Cavour borrowed heavily to develop a rail system in Piedmont. In 1866, the entire peninsula was connected by rail. Electric telegraphs started in 1847 and by 1851 both covered the peninsula and linked Italy to France and Austria, and thence to Britain and Germany. Italy was certainly changing.

CHAPTER NINE

United Country?: 1861–1918

The creation of the kingdom of Italy on 17 March 1861, with Victor Emmanuel II of Piedmont (r. 1849–61) now King of Italy (r. 1861–78) and Cavour as Prime Minister, left the peninsula in flux. Austria still ruled significant areas, notably Venetia, but also territories, Istria, Dalmatia and the Trentino, that some nationalists regarded as truly Italian. Moreover, in the centre of Italy, the Papal States were opposed to the new political order. Pius IX (r. 1846–78) proved a leading opponent of both Italian unification and liberalism. In 1861, religious freedom was established by the new state, a policy that Pius deplored because it affected the position of the Catholic Church.

Attempts by Garibaldi to liberate Rome failed in both 1862 and 1867. In 1862, at Aspromonte, Garibaldi's march on Rome was bloodily blocked by Italian troops. The Pope's position was protected by Napoleon III who had wanted an Italian confederation and not a unitary state. This protection was more significant than the 'crusaders', armed by the Pope, who came from across Catholic Europe and Canada. In 1867, after Garibaldi's men had defeated papal troops at Monterotondo, French forces joined papal units in defeating Garibaldi at the battle of Mentana in 1867. Garibaldi, who received scant support in the Papal States, had become an embarrassment to the Italian government, even if he was possibly acting in agreement with at least some of the authorities. Moreover, Mazzini's quest for democracy, let alone revolutionary republicanism, had failed.

In 1866, encouraged by Napoleon III, Italy joined Prussia in a war with Austria. The Austrians defeated the Italians at Custoza (24 June), also winning a naval battle at Lissa (20 July) in the Adriatic. Alongside conquering Venetia, the Italian government was interested in seizing the territories of Istria and Dalmatia on the other side of the Adriatic. It first planned to seize the island of Lissa, but its fleet was attacked by a smaller and less heavily armed Austrian fleet. The battle became a confused melee of ship-to-ship actions in which Italian unpreparedness and lack of command skills played a role in leading to heavier losses. In the battle, Venetian sailors fought for the Austrians against the Piedmontese and Lombards. The Italian fleet remained in control of the waters round Lissa, but the press pronounced the battle a disaster.

However, the Prussians inflicted a crushing blow on the Austrians at Sadowa in the modern Czech Republic on 3 July, and pressed on towards Vienna. With Austrian civilian determination collapsing, and the Italians now also advancing towards Trieste and Trent, Austria sued for peace. In the resulting peace settlement, Italy gained Venetia, in large part because the Prussians wanted the Austrians weakened. This was a major gain, which it is difficult to see how Italy would otherwise have obtained. Having benefited from France, it now did so from Prussia. Italy had diverted Austrian troops from the war with Prussia.

Had Venetia remained under Austria, then this might have caused war between Austria and Italy over the issue, whether deliberately or inadvertently. Moreover, had this war not arisen, then Italy might have engaged on the Allied side in the First World War at an earlier stage. However, any war that began with Venetia as part of Austria would have posed serious problems for the Italians, and notably so if the Austrians had concentrated on this challenge: Austrian forces would have been based near Milan.

In 1870, Italy again benefited from Prussian success. Napoleon III withdrew his troops from Rome as conflict with Germany neared. In a new power vacuum, Italian forces attacked Rome, which surrendered after a nominal and short resistance. The Papal States were annexed in a major blow to traditional Catholicism. Rome became the capital of Italy. Its political significance in 1849–70 in the struggle for, and definition of, Italian independence and statement helped ensure that Rome would have to be the capital. The legacy of the Roman republic of 1849, as well as of the Rome of antiquity, were thus annexed to the new state.

Pius IX retreated to the Vatican Palace from where he excommunicated Victor Emmanuel II and rejected the new order, as did his successors until the Lateran Pacts of 1929. In turn, the papal role in opposing the *Risorgimento* ensured that liberal nationalism was directed against it. It was symbolic that Galileo became an Italian national hero. When in 1887 a marble column commemorating Galileo was inaugurated in Rome, the event was applauded by the anti-clerical press and sharply criticised by the official Vatican newspaper. Bologna gained a *Piazza Galileo*. Indeed, as in France under the Third Republic (1871–1940), Liberalism, as a political movement in Italy, was in part an anti-clerical movement. The *Teatro Nuovo* in Spoleto, built over the remains of a monastery and opened in 1864, was typical of the values of the period.

Again as in France, this political culture proved highly divisive in a strong Catholic country, not least creating crises of political affiliation and religious conscience, and thus weakened the republic. The situation was even more serious in Italy because the state had weaker roots. As a result of the treatment of the papacy, the ability of the *Risorgimento* to act as a unifying national myth was compromised. By many, it was understood as a civil war but not, as in some countries, for example Japan confronting the legacy of the Meiji Restoration of 1868 and the Satsuma rebellion of 1877, as one the verdict of which could be readily accepted, even welcomed, by most. Moreover, the period saw a marked Catholic revival in terms of the energy of lay devotional cults.

Opposition by the papacy was not the only form of resistance to both the new state and to nation building. In Romagna, clerical elements opposed the new state, as did radicals. In southern Italy, widespread brigandage was an aspect of the transformation of the agrarian order, including the decline of old landowning families, and the emergence of new élites staking out their property and position. In the face of continued large-scale brigandage, much of it political in character, as well as a lack of local support, which culminated in a full-scale rebellion in Palermo in 1866, the new government replaced a civilian justice system it did not trust, in part due to witness intimidation, and enforced the new order with troops. There was much army brutality including the shooting of civilians.

The immediate area, not the distant state, remained the source of identity, interest and loyalty. To some, the *Risorgimento* appeared like a foreign conquest. Mazzini's democratic nationalism had only patchy appeal. Moreover, while average per capita income across Italy did not grow, it faced particular problems in the south, not least due to over-population. As with Iraq in 2003, the new order had also been crass in its treatment of the Neapolitan army: most ex-soldiers were left unpaid and unemployed, and some were imprisoned.

Another response was large-scale emigration, notably, but not only, from Sicily and Naples. Such emigration was triggered by the economic war with France that began with the import taxes imposed on iron and steel when, after 1873, Italy decided to increase its steel production in order to provide rails for the railways and armour for the navy. France reacted by imposing import taxes on food from Italy, mainly from the south. Subsequently, when cheaper American sulphur appeared on the international market, it hit the production of Sicilian sulphur, causing a new collapse in employment.

Emigrants sought economic advantage in the New World, especially in Argentina, Brazil and the United States, in each of which there were large Italian settlements as part of a more general diaspora. Nationalist commentators in Italy regretted the loss of manpower but had no solution, other than to suggest the foundation of Italian colonies in order to provide land and markets. Emigration, both then and thereafter, was to be a major strand in Italian history, one encouraged by the development of steamship services and by the establishment of familial and other links that provided support for new emigrants. An Italian Atlantic developed. Genoa proved particularly important as its maritime centre. Naples was also significant.

Boston, New York and Rio de Janeiro became part of the history of Italy. In Brazil, politicians and employers encouraged Italian immigration in order to reduce the economy's dependence on those of African descent, whether slaves or not. The situation was less favourable in the United States, with nativist hostility directed in particular towards Italians, as both Catholics and Mediterranean. As a result, the hostility was more pronounced than that towards Irish or Polish immigrants, who were only Catholics. This hostility contributed to the immigration restrictions introduced in the United States in 1924.

Meanwhile, Italy itself was badly hit by the economic development of America, notably of American grain exports. As a result, grain prices in Europe, including Italy, fell from the early 1870s. This affected all agricultural regions, including Umbria, thus further encouraging emigration.

Policies in taxation and public expenditure scarcely contributed to the living standards of the bulk of the population. More than half of tax revenue came from indirect taxes on necessities, notably salt and grist, as well as on duties charged on entering cities. However, relatively little was spent on the working class, in town or country. Instead, money went into the military and into new urban townscapes suited for the middle class and the state, for example the *Corso Vittorio Emanuele* and *Corso Umberto I* in Naples, a city which suffered a terrible cholera epidemic in 1884.

Economic policies benefited the industrial north, where Cavour in the 1850s had supported industrialisation. A relatively liberal tariff policy hit attempts to develop industry beyond the artisanal level in the south. Moreover, unification led to a free entry of northern goods into the south, affecting employment levels. In addition, faced by two areas of major steel production – in Genoa and in Pietrarsa near Naples – a parliamentary committee decided that there should be a focus of production on Genoa, a decision reached as a result of more effective lobbying.

Absentee landlords were a particular problem in the south. Frequent peasant riots in Sicily in the 1890s were met by the declaration of martial law, by the deportation of peasant leaders to penal islands and, in contrast, by a land reform policy that, however, was thwarted by the landowners. Living conditions were often poor. Leopoldo Franchetti described, in *La Sicilia nel 1876*, approaching a village in the interior: 'At the top of the climb you find faeces spread down the slope, washed and carried by the rain, then a long string of miserable hovels of one story. Through the open door you can see a filthy room, often without a window, the common lair of the entire family of a peasant and his animals when he has any.' These were dark, damp houses. Sicily was 87 per cent illiterate in 1871.

MAKING HISTORY OPERATIC

Verdi and Puccini, the great composers of the period, provided a heroic reading of the past. In *Norma* (1831), Vincenzo Bellini (1801–35) drew a parallel between Gaul under Roman rule and Italy under that of Austria. Deeply committed to the *Risorgimento*, but mindful of the problems posed by Austrian censorship, Giuseppe Verdi (1813–1901) used often distant and indirect references, rather as Rossini had done with *William Tell* (1829). In *Nabucco* (1842), the exiled Hebrew slaves in Mesopotamia (Iraq) offered an allegory for oppressed Italians, while *La battaglia di Legnano* (1849) employed the defeat of the (German) Emperor Barbarossa by the Lombard League in 1176 as a rallying call for the present. Set in Mantua, *Rigoletto* (1851) depicted a villainous duke, presumably one of the Gonzaga who had ruled from 1328 to 1708. In *La Forza del Destino* (1861), Verdi showed the defeat at Velletri in 1744 of the Austrians by the Neapolitans – in this case perceived as Italians. Verdi supported Garibaldi's expedition in 1860 and served in the Italian parliament.

In *Tosca* (which had its premiere in Rome in 1900 and was based on Victorien Sardou's 1887 play *La Tosca*), Giacomo Puccini (1858–1924) presented papal Rome in 1800 in the grip of counter-revolutionary forces who had suppressed the Roman Republic the previous year, as indeed happened. The heroes, Cavaradossi and Angelotti, are stalwarts of liberty, while the villain, Baron Scarpia, the head of the secret police, is out to suppress all those seeking change. Napoleon's failure or success echoes through the action, as his initial failure in the early stages of the battle of Marengo is greeted with a *Te Deum*, but his eventual success both inspires the captured Cavaradossi, a freethinker living in sin, to sing triumphantly of liberty, and dismays Scarpia. Modern settings of the opera in Fascist Italy do violence to the intensity of the moment it recreates, and reflect a glib, and often misleading, reading from one episode and cultural impulse to another.

Other operas confronted the present, notably the *verismo* of the 1890s with the depiction of peasants, as in Pietro Mascagni's *Cavalleria Rusticana* (1890), and slum dwellers, as in Umberto Giordano's *Mala Vita* (1892). Set in Sicily and Naples respectively, these operas also offered a view of the 'southern problem' for audiences elsewhere in Italy.

THE QUEST TO BE A GREAT POWER

Once united, Italy, despite its multiple social, economic and political problems, sought to be a great power. This ambition was driven by nationalism and by the confidence derived from large-scale industrialisation in the north, notably in Milan and Turin, but also elsewhere, for example with shipbuilding in Genoa. Railways linked the regions of mainland Italy and provided a valuable network in northern Italy.

Nationalism took an aggressive stance, in part due to an intellectual conviction that struggle was a central feature of natural and human existence and development, as well as a cultural belief that struggle expressed and secured masculinity, and thus kept both society and civilisation vital. This was a view that both the nationalists and the Futurists could share in Italy. Belief in war was an expression of a martial spirit and an ideology of masculinity that was sustained by popular literature. Futurism itself was launched in Italy in 1909. Self-consciously dynamic, Futurism wanted to destroy the old. In 1910, its founder, Filippo Tommaso Marinetti, called for the asphalting or paving of the Grand Canal in Venice because it was allegedly a symbol of the past and of past values.

Linked to the belief in struggle and war, the *Risorgimento* was the central narrative in the history of the new state. Francesco Crispi, Prime Minister in 1887–91 and 1893–6, had taken part in the revolutions of 1848 and had joined Garibaldi in invading Sicily in 1860. Success was inscribed in street names and statues across Italy, with streets and squares named after the rulers of the House of Savoy, now kings of Italy, and after the politicians, ministers and military leaders who had furthered the *Risorgimento*, notably Mazzini, Cavour and Garibaldi. Thus, formerly a papal town, Ancona has a *Corso Garibaldi* and a *Corso Mazzini*. Urbino, another former papal town, gained a *Corso Garibaldi*. In Siena, the *Museo Civico* includes a *Sala del Risorgimento* offering the standard frescoes of the period that depicted the narrative of the *Risorgimento*. In Massa Marittima, the *Piazza Duomo* became the *Piazza Garibaldi*. At the local level, there were many Mazzinian associations, but they did not seek to undermine the political system.

The powerful position of the kings under the constitution introduced in 1848 made them major figures. The monarch had the right to appoint and dismiss the prime minister, nominated the Senate, and was central to foreign policy. Ministers were individually answerable to the king, a situation that lessened collective responsibility.

The political situation was complicated by the practice of *trasformismo*, winning votes in Parliament in Rome by conceding power in the regions to the locally dominant, rather as in the South in the United States. This (and a more general) politics of deals, and not of principled compromise, weakened the support for a two-party system on the British model that had been sought in the 1860s and early 1870s, notably by Giovanni Lanza, the able Prime Minister in 1869–73, a system that was also copied by the constitutional monarchy in Spain. Divisions within the Italian parties were a major problem, as was a focus by the deputies on the particular interest of their constituents.

The deputies' understanding of international relations was often poor. This encouraged the quest for colonies as symbols of national prestige. This was seen, for example, from 1876 when the so-called Historical Left, a strong nationalist coalition composed of Garibaldians and Republicans, took power; they wanted what was termed the Third Rome.

From the late 1870s, there was a major deterioration in the public perception of parliamentary conduct, a deterioration that was not eased by the governmental emphasis on a more benign public myth. Politicians sometimes assaulted each other in Parliament, and were also flagrant in their pursuit of personal interest. Only a minority of the male population could vote.

The penal and police codes, which were revised in 1889, were used to oppose Socialism and anarchism, notably by criminalising those held responsible for inciting and condoning political crimes and hatred between the social classes, or for founding associations aimed at committing crimes against public morality, private property and the state. Preventive police practices were widely employed. The prefect served as the provincial chief of police and was able to suppress alleged threats to public order, rig elections and call on the help of the army, which, in 1898, brutally repressed bread riots, killing at least eighty people in Milan. This episode was covered by several painters. That year, the army was also used against agricultural strikers in Emilia-Romagna. King Umberto (r. 1878–1900) was assassinated in 1900 by an anarchist who presented his crime as a retaliation for the 1898 repression. There was a particular sense of crisis in the 1890s as governments responded forcefully to strikes and the developments of mass parties. This underlined a public disillusionment with Liberalism, a disillusionment that was also seen from and with conservatives. Liberals themselves bewailed the impact of conservative assumptions and power groups, notably the impact of clerical views.

In turn, there was a degree of liberalisation in government policy, including in the implementation of the legal code from 1901, under the left-wing Liberal government of Giuseppe Zanardelli in 1901–3, in which Giovanni Giolitti became Interior Minister. This stance, which accorded with the wish of Victor Emmanuel III, whose policies differed from those of his father, Umberto I (r. 1878–1900), reflected an alliance with the reformist leadership of the Socialists. The two groups were united in support of a policy of economic growth without revolution, a policy designed to help the northern working classes but having no traction in the south in which the Liberals, for parliamentary and political reasons, continued an alliance with the landowners who were left in control of the region. The alliance with the Socialists, however, collapsed in 1903, in part due to police violence against strikers and, in 1904, their reformist leadership was overthrown by revolutionaries who pressed for radical action. The first general strike followed that year, and the reaction against this helped Giolitti form a new rightward government and win a general election.

Giolitti, Prime Minister in 1903–5, 1906–9, 1911–14 and 1920–1, then sought to follow a middle path, repressing violent strikes, but also passing social legislation from 1907 to 1914 on medical care for the poor, accident insurance and pension schemes. It was hoped that such measures would preserve the Liberal regime, and Giolitti's policies reflected the fertility of Italian Liberal thought. It is too easy to see the serious problems of these years, and the attitudes of this period, as prefiguring the post-war development of Fascism, as if there was a cursed inevitability in the failure of Italian Liberalism. This approach is mistaken even though the Liberals could, indeed, seek to circumvent Parliament and to rule by decree.

Liberal ideas of liberty, contract and consent had meaning to many, even if their implementation was often flawed. In part, Liberal ideas rested on a determination to replace the Church as the provider, and therefore definer, of social welfare. This had a positive as well as a negative side: anti-clericalism was presented as non-clericalism, an attempt to unify and modernise the state. However, Liberal policies proved difficult to implement, not least due to a widespread lack of support or relevant resources in the localities. The consequence was a haphazard social Liberalism, and one that was less effective than its British counterpart.

Much of the population continued to live in a parlous fashion, notably in the south. In 1915, the official literacy rate among the men mobilised for war was only 37.6 per cent, and was especially bad in the south. Alongside this conservatism, much of it traditionalism, there were elements in the new system, notably an egalitarian legal order and the emergence of political representation, that hit the traditional aristocracy hard. In a changing world, the aristocracy invested in industry and found themselves obliged to mingle with the new commercial interests. Caste barriers declined, particularly with marriages for money.

At the time of the fiftieth anniversary, in 1911, a period of rapid economic growth, the memory of the *Risorgimento* was to the fore under the two Liberal governments of the year, governments which were descendants of those that had secured the *Risorgimento*. The *Risorgimento*, it was argued, had to be secured and completed by further gains. This was a theme judged appropriate for a parliamentary democracy where, in place of an earlier narrow suffrage expanded in 1882, universal male suffrage was introduced in 1913. This introduction was as part of a strategy of accommodating reform Socialism, and also as a response to the Liberals' need to acknowledge their ideology despite their concern about the conservatism of the south. In 1911, Marxists, however, attacked the *Risorgimento* for bringing bourgeois nationalism, not social justice, while Liberalism was condemned on the right for not making Italy strong and great.

Bellicosity was also encouraged by a determination to catch up with those European powers that had already made major colonial gains, notably Britain and France. Competition with the latter was particularly acute, not least after France, in 1881, made Tunisia, a nearby part of the Ottoman (Turkish) Empire in which Italy had strong interests and ambitions, a protectorate. Italy had received no gains from the agreements on the fate of the Balkans and of much of Africa in the congresses of Berlin of 1878 and 1884–5. Colonial rivalry with France helped lead Italy to join, in 1882, in the Triple Alliance, a defensive pact, with Austria and Germany, France's opponents.

France was already in Algeria and Britain in Egypt. War was seen as a way to speed modernisation and progress, and not only by radical nationalists.

With the strong support of Umberto I (r. 1878–1900) and of Francesco Crispi, Prime Minister in 1887–91 and 1893–6, Italy initially pursued territorial ambitions in north-east Africa: in Eritrea, Somalia and, ultimately, Abyssinia (Ethiopia). It was hoped that this expansion would produce land for Italy's peasants and markets for its industry. Eritrea and Somalia proved relatively easy targets, not least as both were open to naval pressure and amphibious attack. In Eritrea, Italy gained the ports of Assab (1882) and Massawa (1885), and then Eritrea (1889) as a whole. Egypt and Turkey were not able to protect their interests in Eritrea. Somalia was also gained in 1889. An Anglo-Italian protocol of 1894 placed Harar in the Italian sphere of influence, treating Abyssinia as an Italian protectorate, a position Italy had claimed from 1889.

Humiliation, however, came to the fore when an Italian army was heavily defeated at Adua (Adowa) in 1896 by Menelik II of Abyssinia, an impressive empire-builder in north-east Africa. France and Russia had provided arms to Menelik, but the key elements were his skill and the incompetence of the Italian commanders who divided their force into advancing columns unable to provide mutual support in the face of a far larger Abyssinian army. Six thousand Italians were killed. A smaller force had already been destroyed at Dogali in 1887. Contemporary stereotyping was captured in a disparaging British military report on Italian army manoeuvres in 1894: 'the evil traits of character generated by despotism and superstition. There is no wholesome spirit of patriotism and religious morality in the country – no sense of duty – nor any adequate infusion of the military virtues which are indispensable to form a solid army.'

The Italians subsequently turned on the Turks. In response to French expansionism in Morocco, Libya, a Turkish colony, was invaded in 1911, although this proved far more difficult than had been anticipated, in large part because the Arabs of Libya fought back hard.

The Italians were the first to use aircraft in war. The war broadened out to include the Italian conquest in 1912 of the Dodecanese islands in the Aegean, of which Rhodes was the most important. The Italians also fought the Turks in the Red Sea, destroying the local Turkish naval forces.

THE MODERN ROME, 1898

In Arthur Conan Doyle's impressive short story 'The New Catacomb' (1898), the 'old Rome' was contrasted with 'the long, double chain of the electric lamps, the brilliantly lighted cafés, the rushing carriages, and the dense throng upon the footpaths'. Although Holmes was never sent to Italy, Doyle visited it several times.

THE FIRST WORLD WAR

When the First World War broke out in 1914, Italy was not obliged to assist its allies, Germany and Austria, because the alliance was a defensive one and both Austria and Germany had launched aggressive wars. Instead, Italy was won over by the Treaty of London, signed on 26 April 1915, by which Britain, France and Russia promised Italy extensive gains from Austria: the Trentino, South Tyrol, Trieste, Gorizia, Istria and northern Dalmatia. This meant, however, that these territories, presented in Italy to the public as the last stage of the war for independence from Austria, had to be conquered. Germany had bullied Austria into offering the Trentino to Italy, but Austria was not willing to match the Allied offer elsewhere. Winning over Italy took it away from Germany's potential alliance system. Moreover, the Central Powers (Germany, Austria) would now have to man a new front along the long common frontier between Italy and Austria, which was the prime strategic benefit for the Allies as opposed to Italy.

In Italy, only the Socialist Party opposed the war when it was voted on by Parliament on 20 May 1915. The rest of the political world wanted to see Italy become a great power, and Antonio Salandra, the conservative Prime Minister in 1914–16, presented Italy's policy as 'sacred selfishness'. Victor Emanuel III (r. 1900–46) was an anglophile, who reflected the strong links between the House of Savoy and Britain. Benito Mussolini (1883–1945), the inflammatory editor of the Socialist Party newspaper *Avanti!*, was expelled from the party because of his support for the war, which he saw as a reconciliation of patriotism and Socialism. Instead, with support from Italian and French industrialists, Mussolini launched the interventionist paper *Il Popolo d'Italia*.

There had been left-wing pacifist activity against the war in Libya that began with the Italian invasion of 1911, when Mussolini and his friend Pietro Nenni lay down on the rails at Forli to prevent the departure of a train carrying troops to Libya. In 1914, there was more left-wing political activity, notably, in 'Red Week' in June, a general strike that triggered widespread disorder, particularly in Emilia, and that led to the deployment of troops. Pacifist views were voiced anew once the First World War broke out. The Socialist Angelo Tasca declared in August 1914, 'Between France and Germany, we choose the International.' Indeed, Italy's move towards war in May 1915 led to hostile large-scale demonstrations and strikes that month, especially in the major industrial city of Turin. However, having opposed the war, the Socialist Party rallied to the flag.

Italy declared war on Austria on 23 May and on Turkey on 21 August 1915, although not on Germany until 27 August 1916 as the government did not wish to provoke the Germans to send troops to the Italian front. This reluctance angered Britain and France as they saw it as a sign that Italy did not want to live up to its commitments. Moreover, the Germans did send troops at once.

Successive Italian attacks on the Austrians on the harsh, rocky terrain on the Isonzo front, designed to open the way to Gorizia, Trieste and Istria, were unsuccessful. On a concentrated front, where there was no way to outflank the Austrians and few opportunities to vary the axis of attack, Austrian defensive firepower prevailed, and, advancing uphill, the Italians in 1915 suffered about 250,000 casualties (compared to about 160,000 for the Austrians) for very few gains. Thanks in large part to the advantages of the terrain, Austrian defensive positions were strong. In 1914, the Italian Chief of Staff had notified the government that the army was not ready for war, and it entered the conflict in 1915 with only 618 machine guns and 132 pieces of heavy artillery. The Italians were unable to open up the battlefield and gain mobility, a situation also seen with the British and the French.

In May 1916, in turn, the Austrians attacked from the Trentino, making significant gains and inflicting heavy casualties, before the Italians, using Fiat lorries and railways to bring up reserves, held the offensive. In August, the Italians captured the city of Gorizia in yet another Isonzo offensive, but again there was no breakthrough, although this was also repeatedly true of the British, French and Germans on the Western Front. Thus, the unimaginative emphasis by Luigi Cadorna, the Chief of Staff, on successive attacks represented one of the instances of a more general failure to rethink goals and methods. In June 1916, the government had lost a vote of confidence in Parliament and resigned, victim of a lack of victory and of disagreements over control of the war effort.

Italy appeared to be a precarious member of the alliance. Austria had been hit very hard and sought German help, but had not collapsed, while in Libya the Italians were affected by strong opposition by Senussi tribesmen, opposition supported by Turkey. However, worse was to come. On 24 October 1917, the Germans and Austrians hit the Italians hard in the Caporetto offensive. The emphasis was on surprise and speed, not attrition. Benefiting from the cover of fog, the Germans and Austrians moved rapidly with machine guns and light artillery on lorries, avoiding Italian strongpoints as they advanced, and destroyed the coherence and communications of the Italian defence. Italy's forces were pushed back eighty miles, a formidable contrast with earlier gains, and lost 20,000 dead, 40,000 wounded and 350,000 prisoners, as well as 3,152 pieces of artillery. The prisoners were to suffer badly from both Austrian and Italian neglect.

This military disaster was linked to a slower-moving political and social crisis, one that led to concern that Italy would collapse, rather as Russia had done earlier in 1917, Austria and Germany were to do in 1918, and as France was to do in 1940. In August 1917, there had been demonstrations against the war in Turin, with crowds calling for peace and bread. This was another iteration of the urban concern expressed prior to the outbreak of the war and was particularly significant as Turin was a major producer of war supplies.

However, Caporetto also focused a fear that much of the peasantry did not want to fight for the state, and raised questions about Italy's regional cohesion: there was concern, in particular, about southern support for the war, revisiting a fear raised when Italy last attacked Austria, in 1866. Indeed, there were demonstrations in the south in 1917–18, with calls for peace and bread focusing on the men absent at the front and thus unable to bring in the crops. Catholic criticism of the war was linked to this peasant opposition. Yet, desertion from the army also affected troops from central and northern Italy, as did a reluctance to be conscripted. Unwilling to accept responsibility, Cadorna blamed the failure of parts of the army to fight, a situation also seen in France and, far more, Russia in 1917. Italian society as a whole appeared alienated, causing a political crisis. Italy's allies feared that it would collapse. Very differently, but with some links, this situation looked towards the weakness the Liberal political order was to face when challenged by Mussolini.

In the event, a new government, under Vittorio Orlando, was formed in October 1917, with Orlando, a skilful politician, making the dismissal by the King of Cadorna a condition of taking office. Victor Emmanuel was happy to get rid of him, and the French also pressed for his departure. In November 1917, a new front line on the River Piave was shored up.

In the face of the invasion of Italy, there was a rallying, a strong sense of unity and of belonging to a mutual heritage and culture, and to one nation and a country. This kept resistance going. In Friuli, the return of the Austrians, who had lost power in 1866, was unpopular with all bar a few, and was followed by the seizure of food, wood, animals and church bells, such that the population started starving. In Italy, pacifism was defeated by parliamentary means. Mussolini's call for a war-dictatorship was ignored. Italy's version of Britain's David Lloyd George and France's Georges Clemenceau, Orlando proved an effective Prime Minister and steps were taken to deal with serious shortages of food, coal and money. Italy's deficit was covered in large part by American and British loans. Price controls were toughened. Bread was more strongly rationed and civilian train services greatly reduced in order to save coal.

In June–July 1918, in the battle of the Solstice, the Austrians tried to repeat their 1917 success, only to be thwarted. They crossed the Piave, but could not secure their position on the western bank. Instead, under pressure on their supply routes from air attacks and a rain-swollen river, and affected by the Italian ability to deploy reserves and by the destructive strength of the Italian artillery, the Austrians, their morale low, withdrew their troops.

As Austria (the Austro-Hungarian Empire) disintegrated that autumn, in the face of nationalist uprisings, the Italian government became worried that they would miss the boat and that their territorial claims would be sidelined in a peace agreement accepting the thesis of national self-determination, and more specifically, the formation of Yugoslavia, both of which would limit Italian gains. Armando Diaz, the Italian commander, was ordered to attack by the government. He did so on 24 October 1918, launching the battle of Vittorio Veneto. The Italian attack on Austrian positions near Mount Grappa was a dismal failure: linear advances into Austrian firepower led to no gains and nearly 25,000 casualties in six days. However, further east, the Piave was crossed from the night of 26 October. The bridgehead was held until 30 October, when the Austrians were ordered to withdraw. Then, and then only, they collapsed due to the retreat of their demoralised troops. The Austrians began to withdraw from Italy, losing many prisoners to the pursuing Allied forces.

On 3 November, Austria agreed to the non-negotiable Allied terms for the armistice. Trieste and Trent were occupied by the Italians the same day. The battle of Vittorio Veneto came to an end, with hundreds of thousands of Austrian prisoners, the armistice taking effect on 4 November. The Italians then began planning an offensive against Bavaria via the Brenner Pass and Austria. This threat affected German decision-making. At this juncture, the Germans were still holding most of Belgium and part of France but were now newly vulnerable.

Victory, however, was grim. Out of a population of 35 million, Italy suffered nearly 600,000 dead and 2.5 million wounded, including half a million permanently disabled, while there was much stress among survivors. There was also the civilian loss caused by the destruction, disruption and disease brought by war, including large-scale flight in 1917 in the face of the Austro-German advance. Higher taxation and borrowing had hit the entire economy, and the budget deficit rose greatly. Whereas Spain's economy had benefited greatly from neutrality, and those of Japan and the United States from wartime growth, Italy's had been hit hard by war. The borrowing was inflationary, as was the shortage of resources and labour caused by the shift to a war economy accompanied by conscription. The national debt rose by 500 per cent in 1915–18, and inflation by over 300 per cent. Giolitti was to see the war as 'the greatest disaster for Humanity after the Great Flood'.

That the pre-war Liberal system and the war were to be followed, in 1922, by a Fascist takeover has conditioned the assessment of both. However, the course of events was far from preordained. Indeed, in the November 1919 elections, the Fascists did not do well, failing to gain a single one of the 508 seats contested. In contrast, the Socialists won 156, compared to 52 in 1913, with the Catholics, now the Popular Party backed by Benedict XV (r. 1914–22), gaining 100 (29 in 1913), and the old Liberal and democratic groups gaining 252, a major collapse from 427 in 1913, and one that indicated that the significant changes linked to the war had created a serious challenge for Liberalism. There was a pronounced regional dimension, with 113 of the Socialists from constituencies north of the Apennines and only 10 from those south of Rome. The Popular Party had won a lot of the former Liberal middle-class vote, but also had reduced the Socialist lead in the countryside, indeed serving there as a peasant party.

The Socialist rural leagues and unions that were becoming more active, notably in the Po valley, suggested a very different outcome for Italy to that which was to occur in 1922. Volatility owed much to the changes brought by the war, but was also a continuance of pre-war developments, particularly the challenges posed by economic disruption, the rise of a mass society, the introduction of universal male suffrage and the re-entry of the Catholics into electoral politics.

CHAPTER TEN

From War to Peace via Peace and War: 1918–45

THE RISE OF FASCISM

The First World War left Italy, like most of Europe, in a febrile state, as reflected in the 1919 elections. There was widespread dissatisfaction with Italy's territorial gains, which were far less than Italy had been promised and far less than Britain and France gained, and Vittorio Orlando, who had failed to prevail in the Versailles peace negotiations, lost power. This dissatisfaction led in 1919 to the occupation of the town of Fiume at the eastern side of Istria, by a volunteer force under Gabriele D'Annunzio (1863–1938), an exuberant, selfish and egocentric poet, who was, as was the norm with his generation in all countries, intoxicated on nationalism. A brave veteran of the war on land and in the air, he referred to a 'mutilated peace'. Fiume, the population of which was overwhelmingly Italian, had voted to join Italy in October 1918. This attempt, which led to clashes with American and French troops and was eventually brought to an end, undermined the authority of the Italian state. The Liberal government earlier in the year had already registered its fury with a peace settlement that allocated to Yugoslavia territories, such as Fiume, it considered to be rightly Italian and that it regarded as promised to Italy under the 1915 Treaty of London. Mussolini took forward nationalist complaints that Italy had been deprived of gains it should have received. D'Annunzio was to be a strong supporter of his.

There was considerable logic to the Italian argument that their allies' emphasis on self-determination should have made Fiume Italian. However, President Woodrow Wilson of the United States was pro-Yugoslav, while France backed Greece and Yugoslavia against Italy in order to keep the latter restrained and to establish a French-dominated sphere in the Balkans. French backing for Czechoslovakia, Greece, Yugoslavia and Romania weakened Italy in the Balkans.

Italy's anger with its wartime allies, and notably over their failure to provide promised gains in the Turkish Empire, ensured that, in the post-war occupation of Turkey, it thwarted these allies as they sought to maintain control there. Instead, Italy supplied arms to the nationalists under Kemal Atatürk, which hit both French and Greek occupation forces. Both states were following anti-Italian policies.

In practice, however, Austria's collapse greatly strengthened Italy's regional power. Moreover, Italy had received the Trentino, the South Tyrol, Trieste, Gorizia, Istria and Zara, gains celebrated across Italy in new street names.

The end of the war also produced severe economic problems. Wartime demand for food and goods ended, and demobilisation hit the labour market, sending unemployment up. The two major parties, the Catholics and the Socialists, each a threat to the old Liberalism, could not cooperate. Giovanni Giolitti, the key pre-war politician and a committed parliamentarian, returned as an elderly Prime Minister in 1920–1, but did not really understand the mass politics of these years, could not control its dynamics and, in particular, failed to contain Fascism. In Italy, some (but far from all) veterans had turned to political extremism, joining the *Squadristi* or Fascist squads founded by Mussolini in 1919 and adopted Fascism. Mussolini himself referred to 'the aristocracy of the trenches'.

Mussolini benefitted greatly from the Red Scare also seen in other countries. In 1919, a group of Socialist intellectuals in opposition to the majority in the party founded a journal, *L'ordine nuovo*, and called for the transformation of the party into one of the revolutionary proletariat. They pressed for factory councils, but failed to persuade the Socialist Party to back a general strike in 1920 and, instead, with Lenin's encouragement, established the Communist Party of Italy in January 1921. Mussolini's squads battled left-wing agricultural workers, notably in Tuscany and the Po valley, and overcame the Communist occupation of factories, such that many Liberals were willing to turn to him as a bulwark against Socialism and Communism. The Socialists and Communists were not violent as a defensive reaction to Fascism, but, instead, were ready to begin violence on their own, such that, at one level, Fascism was the armed reaction of part of the middle class to Socialism. It was a very sad and violent period, and violence spread from both sides.

Fascism had varied meanings for different groups and regions, which helped make it more potent, but also eclectic and confusing. This was a situation that was to be accentuated by the change it experienced through time, not least the exposure to power. A key element was rural Fascism, as it was in the small rural towns that Fascism first developed into a potent mass movement. Fascist apologists were to present it as a 'third force', a corporatist alternative to the divisions between capitalism and labour, and an energetic means to modernisation. However, alongside Mussolini's republican and corporatist approach, one that included Socialist elements, the reality of Fascism was of crude and often violent anti-Socialism and a willingness to ally with élites, old and new, against the assertiveness of labour. This was certainly so in rural areas, for example Tuscany and the provinces of Ferrara and Bologna. The Fascists proved willing to work for the landlords, and the latter came to play a major role in their organisation.

Very differently, Fascism also drew on hostility to Liberalism among intellectuals, Futurists and many others, calling, from before the First World War, as D'Annunzio had done, for renewal and change, but disliking the masses, modernisation and middle-class culture. This élitist disdain for the rationalism of Liberal progressivism, for positivism, parliamentary democracy, Socialism and industrialism, was helped by the crisis of the war. Force was presented as a restorative, and spiritual revolution as a need, an anti-materialist approach that attracted Mussolini. He saw Fascism as a progressive political force.

At the same time, Mussolini lacked a sophisticated political theory. In many respects, he was a Socialist who wanted power and understood the use of force to seize power. He, and the Fascist Party, had a great admiration for technology, which reflected the positivist and materialist basis of nineteenth-century thought. In 1919, nobody knew what Fascism was, and what it could become, because Mussolini also did not know. He went on day by day, step by step, in order to win advantages, but had no long-term policy. Mussolini was against Liberalism because, as a Socialist coming from the working class, he regarded Liberals as oppressors of the working class.

The different tendencies of Fascism, tendencies seen in the architectural styles, old and new, that it sponsored, inherently left it unstable and disorganised, reliant on rhetoric to try to provide a cohesion that was very much lacking. Fascist style was an Italian version of the architectural style found in many other countries, but, being also Fascist, it was the product of a compromise with the middle class: there was much room for architecture according to contemporary preferences, including Art Deco and the imitation of eighteenth-century Piedmontese Baroque.

Mussolini himself saw rhetoric as an aspect of the emotion and enthusiasm that was necessary not only to lead the masses, but also because, as he wrote in 1932, Fascism was 'a religious conception'. In part, this approach was a response to what were seen as the deficiencies of Liberalism and parliamentary democracy, deficiencies that to many commentators were cultural, mythical and aesthetic, as much as political. At the same time, Mussolini's radical nationalism had backing across much of a political spectrum that it sought to supersede in the quest for a broad appeal that could rebase exaggerated (and unfounded) expectations about national power and purpose. These expectations were a product of the weight of the past, the despair of the present and the hope for the future. To be cynical, and Mussolini understandably attracts cynicism, some of the working class was attracted by his Socialist approach, including promises, which were kept, of a welfare state; the middle class was drawn to him by the promises – all kept – about keeping social order and providing benefits to them in terms of social climbing; and the ruling class was assured that nothing would change. This, indeed, proved the case: protectionism was kept, the state provided much money for the industrial system, and no landowner was deprived of his agricultural properties.

MUSSOLINI TO POWER

Lacking popularity, and even apparently purpose, the government succumbed to Mussolini's seizure of power in 1922. Armed Fascists occupied major positions, leading Victor Emmanuel III (r. 1900–46) to ask Mussolini to form a cabinet, rather than enforcing martial law as the existing government wanted. Mussolini's 'March on Rome' (he himself, like many other Fascists, went by train) was certainly preventable, but the political order lacked supporters willing to fight for it. In particular, the military, which was under Victor Emmanuel, was not deployed against the Fascists, as it could have been. There was no equivalent to the deadly and successful use of armed police against the smaller-scale Nazi attempt to stage a coup in Munich in 1923. The Fascist Blackshirts were not supposed to exceed 25,000 men, nor to be well armed. The garrison of Rome, 28,000 strong, was in arms and organised effective checkpoints on roads and railways at a distance from the city. Trains were stopped at stations such as Orvieto. Other military units, for example in Florence, imposed martial law as the government ordered. Therefore, the King's instruction to the military to let the Blackshirts pass was necessary for the latter to succeed. The King's willingness to welcome, and then work with, Mussolini counted against him in 1944–6 and, in particular, played a major role in Italy becoming a republic in 1946.

MUSSOLINI AS POLITICAL ARTIST

In a speech delivered in 1926 on the opening of the *Novocento* art exhibition, Mussolini declared: 'Politics is an art . . . in politics there is a lot of intuition . . . At a certain moment the artist creates with inspiration, and the politician with decision.'

MUSSOLINI IN POWER

Initially, Mussolini included many non-Fascists in the cabinet in order to try to make it more palatable: there were only three Fascists in the first cabinet. However, once in power, Mussolini took control of much of the state, although the armed forces were not circumvented. The Fascist programme of 1919 had called for the creation of a national militia, which was to have been the basis of a popular army under party control, but the programme was not implemented and the Fascists, despite the concern of military commanders, did not create a parallel military force. Indeed, Mussolini made the militia, established in 1923, subordinate to the army, and sought to develop the existing professional armed forces.

This won him support among them, as did his commitment to a national mobilisation of resources and energy that the democratic system had allegedly lacked. In 1923, a Supreme Defence Commission and a Subcommittee for the Preparation of National Mobilisation were established. Nevertheless, whatever Mussolini's ambitions for power, the consolidation of the Fascist regime took time and was still limited in 1922–4. A crisis occurred in 1924 after Giacomo Matteotti, a parliamentary deputy, the Secretary of the Unitary Socialist Party, issued a speech denouncing Fascist violence and electoral manipulation, which, indeed, were serious. He was kidnapped and murdered by *squadristi*.

This murder led to a political crisis, but Mussolini won a vote of confidence in the Senate, and Victor Emmanuel refused to dismiss him. This was the real start of the dictatorship. Mussolini then pushed through increased control in 1925–6. In 1928, elections were abolished. Giolitti, who died in 1928, refused to denounce Liberalism, but most other Liberals accepted Mussolini.

In order to make Mussolini's task easier, much of society was depoliticised and earlier forms of political association were abolished or transformed. Ironically, the Fascist Party was also given only a modest formal role, as were Fascist trade unions. So also, to a degree, in Franco's Spain with the fate of the Falange Party. However, whereas

Franco's control rested on the military, Mussolini needed the Fascist Party because it provided loyal men he could trust. The party was everywhere, controlled everything and reported everything. Those who joined the party could work and go forward in their career, but those who did not faced problems in their jobs and their daily life. The party ensured widespread control over the civil service and daily life. Mussolini was the party, and there was no room for internal elections. In a version of divide and rule, Mussolini played the party chiefs against each other. Moreover, as soon as he thought one was gaining too much power or popularity, there was a change of the guard or a promotion to powerlessness. Thus, when Mussolini decided that Italo Balbo had become too popular, he was promoted to be Governor-General of Libya, and thus removed from influence in Rome.

There was a continuous change of ministers, and every change was unexpected and unpredictable. This pushed everybody to be disciplined and loyal, hoping for a ministerial seat as a reward, or not to lose what they already had. And the party provided Mussolini with people whose career was carefully assessed in advance in order to see whether they could be considered reliable or not.

There was an attempt to develop industry and agriculture in order to make Italy self-sufficient, notably in wheat, although the regime found rural hostility to innovation a major issue. There was also pressure to raise the population. Mussolini, who saw Fascism as a masculine process of assertion (something also true of his boorish and predatory personal attitudes to women), regarded emigration and declining fertility as challenges to his vision of a strong Italy, and this led him to oppose emigration and to adopt pro-natalist policies: Mussolini wanted more men for the military and more colonists for the empire. He sought not only a new generation of Italians, but also more of them.

Women were to be treated primarily not as workers, but as sources of children, an approach that also suited the Catholic Church. The medicalisation of breastfeeding was taken further under Fascism, with feeding times tied to a strict schedule. In his Ascension Day

Speech in 1927, Mussolini announced that Italy's ability to 'count for something in the world' was linked to an ability to reach a population of sixty million by the second half of the century. Films, literature, the radio and advertisements were directed to repeat such a message, while the *Opera Nazionale Maternità e Infanzia* was established to protect mothers and children. The roles women should take were redefined in films. The regime was chauvinistic and sought to restrict the rights of women. In 1927, women's salaries were fixed at half of those of male counterparts, and in 1938 the percentage of company jobs that could be held by women was pegged at 10 per cent. In 1936, birth control became a 'crime against the purity and health of the race'. Abortion, already a crime, was regarded in the same light.

The attitude to women suggests that any tendency to see continuity between Liberalism and Fascism requires qualification. Social welfare as state-building was pushed further and harder by Mussolini but, in part, by means of an authoritarianism that was not so characteristic of Liberalism, and more particularly in cultural matters. In his 1930 speech 'Women and Machines', Mussolini claimed that women's work was 'the root of all political and moral illnesses . . . Eliminating women and children from the workplace not only gives the work back to the father of the family, but it also defends the physical integrity of the race.' His frequent reference to the racial theme was unusual among Italian politicians.

By the Lateran Pacts of February 1929, Mussolini negotiated a settlement of issues between Italy and the papacy, including of the status of the Vatican City which, at 0.44 square kilometres, became the world's smallest sovereign state. The Vatican recognised the Italian state, which paid 750 million lire compensation for the seizure of the Papal States in 1860–70, promised that Catholicism would be the only state religion, that marriage would be regulated by canon law, that religious instruction be given in schools and that bishops be Vatican appointments, albeit taking an oath of loyalty to the king. The Vatican was promised protection from offensive occurrences in Rome.

These agreements were a key moment of Fascism's legitimation. They helped Mussolini's position with much of the public, and were an aspect of a broader anti-Communism and of a wish to control society. Such attitudes and policies were seen in the reform of the educational system, which provided a curriculum focused on vocational employment and Catholic values for working-class students who were streamed separately to the middle class. Pius XI (r. 1922–39) had condemned the proposed alliance of the Reformist Socialists and the Catholic Popular Party in the Matteotti crisis, an alliance directed against Mussolini. Describing Mussolini as 'a man whom Providence has sent us', he sought to use shared values of authority, order and family, only to realise eventually that Mussolini was unreliable. Indeed, in his 1931 encyclical *Non abbiamo bisogno*, Pius condemned pagan worship of the state and Fascist violence against the Church. His criticism, however, was sidelined in 1939 by his successor Pius XII (r. 1939–58), his former Secretary of State, who launched a reconciliation with Mussolini's regime, in large part in order to protect the Church. Pius XII was well aware of Fascist methods.

There was much opposition to Fascism, but it was suppressed by a control of the media, and by intimidation, imprisonment and violence. An authoritarian presence, Mussolini was the *Duce* of Fascism and the head of government. Ministers answered to him, and not to Parliament, while Mussolini nominated the members of the Fascist Grand Council. The only political party allowed was the Fascist one, and local administration was controlled from above. Institutions were affected by Fascist controls. Scientific and cultural organisations were brought under governmental control with the establishment of the *Reale Accademia d'Italia* in 1926. Teachers and university professors were made to take an oath of loyalty in 1931 (only 13 professors out of 1,200 refused), while censorship of books was introduced in 1938. Mussolini saw education as a way to help make society Fascist, and para-educational organisations were established accordingly. Intellectual, educational and social mobilisation were designed to produce not only model citizens but also a technology able to help modernise Italy and make it a strong power. A youth movement, *Gioventú Italiana del Littorio* ('Italian Youth of the Lictor' – the Lictor was a Roman magisterial bodyguard who would hold the fasces, a bound bundle of rods that symbolised authority and power), covering boys from six to twenty-one and girls from nine to seventeen, sought to direct the young, as did control over leisure activities. Jazz was banned. Mussolini sought to improve the lot of the working class, in part to fulfil promises, in part because it was something he really wanted to do, and in part because he could thus modify the existing ruling class, which was not Fascist, by inserting in key positions people who had risen thanks to the party.

The death penalty was reintroduced. The OVRA (*Organizzazione per la Vigilanza e la Repressione dell'Antifascismo*, a secret branch of the regular police) was a major presence and was responsible for the 1937 murder of the Rosselli brothers, political opponents who had left Italy. Fascist bully boys would also attack others, punching the composer Arturo Toscanini in the face when he refused to play the national anthem at a concert in Bologna in 1931. He later went to the United States. Opponents were imprisoned for their opinions. Antonio Gramsci (1891–1937), who had helped found the Communist Party in 1921, becoming its Secretary, was imprisoned from 1926 until just before his death. He had been convicted of subversion.

Unexpectedly, this was also a culturally fruitful period. In music, Puccini was still active, as well as other composers such as Mascagni, Respighi and Wolf-Ferrari. Writers included Pirandello, Deledda, Moravia and Gadda, and poets Ungaretti, Quasimodo and Montale. International recognition included Nobel Prizes. Painters included de Chirico, Carrà, Morandi, Sironi and Balla, as well as new painters, notably Guttuso and Annigoni. Manzù was important in sculpture. Architects included Piacentini, the regime's architect, who introduced reinforced concrete, Ponti, Terragni and Libera. Many of the above-mentioned were not Fascist at all, or, as with Ungaretti, started as Fascist, and then left the party, but they were not persecuted. The regime focused on those who were openly anti-Fascist.

The economy was hit hard by the Great Depression that began in 1929 and, by 1934, about 10.7 per cent of the male workforce was unemployed. Due to fewer opportunities elsewhere, emigration became more difficult during the Depression and incomes did not improve, which helped deprive Fascism of appeal, although the partial rearmament that began in 1935 assisted employment and income figures. This was so in industry, but was not the case with agriculture, which remained parlous. Mussolini's 'battle for grain', which focused on the south, was not bloody, unlike contemporary Soviet policies, but suffered from the usual problems posed by state direction of the economy.

Moreover, Mussolini offered the south, which he disliked, little: Fascism was not popular there. Launched in 1925, the campaign against the Mafia involved an indiscriminate and harsh policing of Sicily that did little for the popularity of the regime. Success was proclaimed but, as in contemporary accounts of Sardinia, this apparent success was a matter of suppressing unwelcome reality, which included terrible poverty. Not surprisingly, there was considerable alienation from the government, a situation described in Carlo Levi's account of the Basilicata region in southern Italy: *Christ Stopped at Eboli* (1945). For anti-Fascist politics, Levi was 'confined' to Lucania in the south in the mid-1930s.

As an anti-Communist, Mussolini's international reception was generally favourable. Nevertheless, Mussolini's belief in the inherently competitive nature of international relations, and in the central role of force in this competition, affected the full range of his policies, cultural, economic, financial and social. Like many politicians and commentators of the 1920s and 1930s, Mussolini was fascinated by new technology, seeing a focus on machines as an analogue for the powerful authoritarian progressivism he intended to introduce. Fascists were particularly obsessed with aircraft, and Mussolini sponsored the dispatch abroad of Italian military aircraft to show the flag, notably in South America where his political model was especially popular in Argentina and Brazil. It was also important in the Balkans. Aside from selling aircraft this way, Mussolini was keen to export his ideological dominance.

International competition was presented as the necessary focus for national effort and as a way to supersede social conflict. Such a policy required the dissemination of a grandiose image of great achievement. So in domestic policy with, for example, the draining of the Pontine marshes near Rome in order to end malaria, alongside the outlawing of strikes and keeping down workers' wages. Making the trains run on time, one of the more famous achievements that were claimed, involved the beginning of electrification, but was in part a matter of breaking the relevant unions, which were particularly left wing. Police were put on trains. Employers benefited from the suppression of unions, although Fascism had far less influence on individual attitudes. The turning of the Pontine marshes into a model settled future was seen as a template for Fascist expansion abroad, and was taken as a model of state intervention by President Franklin Delano Roosevelt in establishing the Tennessee Valley Authority in 1933.

Mussolini readily used his military to support his goals, in large part because his refashioning of the Italian nationalist dream was, while essentially opportunistic, especially bellicose. In 1923, the Greek island of Corfu was occupied in a successful attempt to make Greece back down in a quarrel over Albania caused by Greek expansionism. This use of force pleased the military.

Employing great brutality against civilians, of whom over 50,000 were probably killed, Libya was subdued in 1928–32, a process driven forward to establish that Mussolini was more effective than earlier governments had been. Wells were blocked, flocks slaughtered, and the population forcibly and harshly resettled. Much savagery, including the large-scale use of poison gas (in breach of the 1925 Geneva Gas Protocol), was employed in the conquest of Ethiopia in 1935–6; gas had been used in the 1920s in Morocco by France and Spain. The Italians deployed 557,000 men, including colonial troops, in the campaign.

The League of Nations found Italy an aggressor, but there were no serious consequences.

On the evening of 9 May 1936, Mussolini gave one of his dramatic, stage-managed speeches in Rome, announcing the 'reappearance' of the old Roman Empire. Once established, Italian rule in Ethiopia proved harsh, a harshness that, on the general imperial pattern, owed much to racism. The resulting resistance movement was met with savage and very murderous repression in large part because the Italians did not wish to be defeated. Most of the troops garrisoning Ethiopia came from other African colonies, and could be very harsh: Eritreans had a history of bitter conflict with Ethiopia, while Libyan troops considered themselves white Arabs closer to Italians than to black Ethiopians. The idea that Italy was necessarily more benign (as opposed to simply weaker) than Germany appears very questionable from the perspective of Libya or Ethiopia, and was not true of the army, although there was no equivalent to the Wehrmacht's involvement in the Holocaust.

The war was accompanied by a mobilisation of Italian opinion, which was coordinated by a propaganda ministry established in 1935. This ministry sponsored favourable accounts, hindered unfavourable ones, and sought to manage the flow of information. The war was also used to make the Fascist system seem necessary and superior, and to legitimate both Mussolini and militarisation. The serious financial drain of the conflict was ignored. Support for a citizen soldiery became central to Fascism as a political religion. These emphases meant that the social welfare side of social policy was marginalised.

In practice, Italy could not readily afford its heavy military commitments to Ethiopia and to the Francoist side in the Spanish Civil War (1936–9), and its general military build-up. In the Spanish Civil War, the Italians sent 73,000 troops to Franco's assistance, far more men than Hitler did, their aircraft bombed Republican cities, such as Barcelona and Malaga, and their submarines attacked Soviet ships en route to Republican ports. Mussolini wished to shape the Francoist regime, but Franco was not interested in compromising his independence. As a reminder of the variety of Italian commitment, the Italian Garibaldi Battalion fought as volunteers for the Republicans against Italian forces in the battle of the Guadalajara in 1937. The choice of name for the battalion was powerfully symbolic.

There was also a broader diplomacy and geopolitics of confrontation. Mussolini employed a mixture of professionals and Fascist Party figures as envoys. Diplomats were expected to conform to Mussolini's anti-liberal ideology and to his contempt for Britain and France. The use of Fascist diplomats who held such views, such as Dino Grandi, envoy in London from 1932 to 1939, led to a failure to note British strengths or to probe the possibilities for cooperation. Similarly, there was an unwillingness on Mussolini's part to appreciate warnings from Italian diplomats about the risks of cooperation with Hitler. In 1933, Mussolini proposed a 'European Directorate', based on a Pact of Four of Britain, France, Germany and Italy, that could agree on a revision of the Paris peace treaties of 1919. The idea did not fly.

The Italians supported a major naval build-up designed to contest the position of Britain and France in the Mediterranean. Moreover, whereas in 1934 Mussolini had moved troops to the Brenner Pass in response to an ultimately unsuccessful attempt by Austrian Nazis to seize control of Austria, by 1938 he was aligned with Hitler when he mounted a successful takeover. Long seeing Hitler as a rival in Austria and the Balkans, Mussolini was repeatedly regarded by Britain as a possible ally. However, he shared both Hitler's contempt for the democracies and his opposition to Britain and France. These views became more important to him in the late 1930s, and Germany ceased to be presented as a barbarian state beyond the Alps. Political and economic links between the two powers increased.

There was a linkage to measures against Italian Jews. In 1938, all Jewish children were expelled from state schools, Jews were banned from teaching (over 200 were sacked), the civil service, the military, and much else. Marriage between Jews and non-Jews was prohibited, as was 'excessive' wealth. These measure were readily enforced, with scant criticism from the Church hierarchy with very few honourable exceptions. Compared to Germany and Austria, there was less anti-Semitic feeling among the population, and far less support for deportation and mass murder. At the same time, alongside sympathy on the part of some for those Jews they knew, there was an unwillingness to extend this sympathy to others, let alone to protest on their behalf. A new government body, the *Demorazza*, instructed to enforce the laws did so with vigour. The courts proved readily compliant and tended to decide close cases against Jews. In many respects, the Racial Laws represented a reimposition of past norms, notably those in papal Rome until 1870. Furthermore, there were to be many people involved in the Italian dimension of the Holocaust, not least in seeking to profit from a despoliation of Jews.

A major war had seemed possible over Ethiopia in 1935–6, and Britain and France had drawn up plans, including for the closing of the Suez Canal and the bombing of northern Italian cities. In the event, there had been no conflict, which further encouraged Mussolini, who actively intrigued with the opponents of Britain and France, including Arab nationalists, as in Palestine. Arms were supplied to Afghanistan and Yemen. There was also support for anti-British nationalists in Malta, some of whom suggested unification with Italy.

Mussolini was not interested in limits. The range of Italian commitments was exhausting. Potential international opponents failed to appreciate that, alongside Italian strengths, there were weaknesses. In the late 1930s, as Mussolini planned an invasion of Egypt, the British anxiously considered how best to defend their position there. In November 1938, the Italian Chamber of Deputies echoed to calls for acquiring 'Tunisia, Corsica, Nice, Savoy', all French possessions. The following April, the Italians successfully invaded Albania, a former client state. The invasion enabled Mussolini to show that Italy was making gains as Hitler had recently done with Czechoslovakia. Victor Emmanuel III added King of Albania to his titles of King of Italy and Emperor of Abyssinia.

INVASION OF ALBANIA, 7 APRIL 1939

The badly managed invasion of Albania, one conducted against a nearby and vulnerable target, but planned by an incompetent High Command, was successful in part because there was little resistance from the outnumbered and divided Albanians. The political decision for the invasion came unexpectedly, largely in response to the German occupation of Bohemia and Moravia and the determination to make a move to bring Italy benefits. The armed forces knew of the assignment only shortly before the invasion: orders were issued from 31 March. The suddenness affected the resources available, including merchant shipping, and the planning was inadequate, as were long-term preparations for amphibious operations. The depth of the water in the inshore waters was not factored into the planning. The first ship of the Italian convoy entered the bay at Durazzo by 4.50 a.m. and the garrison there had been swept away by 9 a.m. The Italians lost twelve dead and eighty-one wounded in the entire operation and the 50,500 men in the Albanian military dispersed, most subsequently joining the Italians. As a result of fog, the ship carrying the army landing parties was late, whereas the army units that were intended as the garrison when Durazzo was seized were landed as the first wave. A lack of wharves made it difficult to unload the ships. The next day, a motorised column advanced on the capital, the inland city of Tirana, although they were delayed because, in the darkness of night-time preparations, they had been provided with diesel instead of the necessary gasoline.

The column reached the city when the first aircraft of the airlift from Grottaglie airport in Apulia in Italy was landing in Tirana airport. The airlift worked well and carried an entire regiment, but could not carry mortars or artillery. A lack of air transports meant that the troops were carried in ninety bombers, with emergency floors of wooden planks added. King Zog fled.

> Official Italian accounts presented the operation as a well-organised triumph, a process aided by the ability to report brilliant moves by non-existent units.

In 1939, nevertheless, Italy did not join its ally, Germany, in war with Britain and France, instead declaring non-belligerence. Mussolini's forceful report on 4 February 1939 to the Fascist Grand Council showed a clear opposition to France. However, even though relations with Hitler improved, notably with the Pact of Steel signed on 22 May, this depended on a verbal understanding that neither Germany nor Italy would provoke war before 1943. Mussolini's son-in-law and Foreign Minister from 1936 to 1943, Count Galeazzo Ciano, opposed this alignment and claimed that Mussolini was furious with Hitler for not consulting him about the invasion of Poland, which launched the war. Mussolini, who appreciated that Hitler, rather than being his equal, was becoming more prominent, had doubts, alongside his bombast, about the sophistication of the Italian military.

ITALY ENTERS THE SECOND WORLD WAR

German success in 1940 at the expense of Denmark, Norway, the Netherlands, France and Britain led Mussolini to declare war on Britain and France that June, ignoring the caution of the military. The results were eventually devastating for Italy, bringing it to defeat, invasion, occupation and civil war.

Initially, however, there had been optimism. On 10 June, after the French had been clearly defeated and the British forces had withdrawn from Dunkirk, Mussolini joined in because he feared that he would otherwise lose the opportunity to gain glory and territories in what looked like being a short war. He hoped to benefit from, and match, earlier German successes. Feeling that Italian greatness required domination of the Mediterranean and, therefore, British defeat, Mussolini sought gains from the British Empire and from France, and more power in the Balkans, where he had long supported Croatian separatists at the expense of Yugoslavia and had opposed Greece.

German victory brought to a head Mussolini's ideological affinity with Hitler, his contempt for the democracies, his sense that Italy was only semi-independent due to Britain's powerful role in the Mediterranean, and the inherent violence and aggressive expansionism of his regime. These factors overcame his awareness of the poor financial and military situation of Italy and his realisation that there was scant support for the war. Little enthusiasm was shown by the Italian public. Indeed, privately, Mussolini frequently expressed very disparaging views about the Italian people.

Mussolini's policy entailed overcoming the pronounced pessimism of the service chiefs, and destroyed the conviction in the British Foreign Office that Italy would remain neutral and the linked illusion that Mussolini could be a moderating 'back-channel' to Hitler. This had been hoped for by those in Britain keen to see a negotiated end to the war with Germany.

The Italian attacks were held in the Alps by far smaller French forces. Casualties on both sides were light, but the Italians suffered more losses, and also the humiliation of being unable to defeat an already clearly beaten opponent. In part, this reflected the nature of the Alpine frontier, where the French had prepared first-rate defences to cover the few routes of advance. Prepared themselves for defensive warfare, there was no opportunity for the Italians to emulate the mobile warfare of the Germans, nor indeed for them to use effectively their greater numbers. From the war, Italy got back the losses of 1860: Nice and Savoy, but not more. Hitler's concern to bolster Vichy France was important to the terms, but so, even more, was the absence of success by seizure, a form of success Hitler understood. Corsica was not to be occupied until November 1942, at the same time that German forces occupied Vichy France.

Germany and Italy also clashed over relations with Britain. Hitler was ready to have Britain keep its empire if it accepted his dominance of the Continent, but Mussolini wanted part of this empire. Prior to

Italy's entry into the war, Italo Balbo, an Air Marshal and the Governor-General of Libya, proposed opening hostilities with a surprise assault on Malta. An initial landing by airborne troops and naval infantry was to be followed up by the landing of a division that had been trained for a proposed landing on the Greek island of Corfu. Mussolini decided that the operation was not necessary because, given the imminent fall of France, the war, he wrongly felt, was already as good as over.

Mussolini's ambitions and the views of his supporters were not based on a reasonable assessment of the capabilities of the Italian military machine; and this failure, a mistaking of rhetoric and illusion for reality, was to lead to a series of disasters. In order to offset a German approach to Romania and to ensure that the Balkans remained clearly in the Italian zone of influence, Greece was invaded from the Italian dominion of Albania in October 1940. However, the invasion was repelled and the Greeks, in turn, advanced into southern Albania. Mussolini's conviction that Italy would easily win was cruelly punctured. In harsh terrain, the outnumbered, poorly trained and inadequately supplied Italians were outfought by more numerous, more resilient, better-trained and more motivated troops. The division intended for Malta ended up supporting the forces in Albania.

An invasion of Egypt from the neighbouring Italian colony of Libya was designed to win Italy a major role in securing victory and gains from the British Empire. Mounted by far greater forces (215,000 to 31,000 defenders), this poorly prepared and badly commanded invasion was spectacularly routed in December 1940 by the British, a term that includes imperial forces, notably Australians. In a brilliant counter-offensive, the British went on to conquer eastern Libya, taking large numbers of prisoners. That many Italian families therefore had male members as British prisoners gravely sapped confidence in the war within Italy. These prisoners were better fed than troops that remained in the Italian army.

The British also defeated the Italians in East Africa, regaining British Somaliland in March 1941, and, from January 1941, conquering Italian Somaliland, Eritrea and Ethiopia, a substantial area, although in northern Ethiopia the Italians held out until late 1941. This was a formidable achievement for the British, and the Italians again lost about a quarter of a million prisoners. However, the subsequent passing of the age of empire, as well as the extent to which the war is remembered in Britain as a struggle with Germany, have ensured that the achievement has been largely forgotten.

Successful British attacks on the Italian fleet in the Mediterranean in 1940–1, notably in the air attack on the fleet in Taranto, and in the battle of Cape Matapan on the night of 28–9 March 1941, helped lead the Germans to send help. British plans for amphibious attacks on Italian islands in the Mediterranean – Pantelleria or the Dodecanese – were now impossible or redundant. The British defeat of Italian forces in Libya led Hitler, on 11 January 1941, to order the movement of troops to aid in the defence of western Libya. The following month, they were named the Afrika Korps. German aircraft and submarines made a major difference in the central Mediterranean, while Germany came to play a key role in areas of Italian interest: North Africa and the Balkans. Italian forces took part in the conquest of Yugoslavia and Greece launched on 6 April 1941, including in the invasion of Crete in May, but the Germans took the principal part. Moreover, although the eventual territorial settlement of Yugoslavia and Greece benefited Italy, with the occupation of one-time possessions such as the Ionian Islands, it was essentially arranged at Germany's behest.

Entry into the war led to an accentuation of the discriminatory treatment of Jews, but, again, not at the German level. At the Ferramonti concentration camp that began operating, in June 1940, with 160 Jews from Rome and contained, when it was liberated by the British in 1943, 1,604 Jews and 412 non-Jews, there were no killings or deportations to German-controlled Europe. At this stage, conditions were relatively humane, and death rates by natural causes were low. The camp included two synagogues. The Italians refused to deport foreign Jews from Italy, the forced labour of Jews was not lethal, and there were Jewish army and naval officers who remained hidden 'behind desks' for years after 1938.

Starting from a far weaker industrial base, with a very low production of lignite and steel, Italy was less able than Germany to create an effective military-industrial supply system that met its needs. This contributed to Italian failure and a general sense that the war had gone adrift. In the First World War, Italy had relied heavily on Britain and France for materials, but this recourse was now closed. Moreover, Italy, despite Mussolini's bombast and the theories of authoritarian efficiency, was unable, unlike under his predecessors in 1915–18, to introduce an effective mobilisation of resources and to establish a strong war economy. The economy was not militarised. Taxes did not become realistic, there was only limited direction of the large industrial companies, and both weapons and weapons systems were delivered in insufficient quality and quantity. Partly for these reasons, it proved difficult to rebuild the military after serious early losses against Greece and Britain.

For example, the Italians were unable to sustain the relative air strength built up in the 1920s and early 1930s because their industrial base lacked the ability to raise production as well as to keep pace with developments in aircraft technology. Much of the air force in 1940 was obsolete, and newer aircraft were less effective than their British counterparts. By using German engines, the Italians did begin to make effective fighters from 1941, but in insufficient numbers. The year 1941 was the peak of Italian aircraft manufacture, and in 1942 and early 1943 this output fell markedly. There were problems with capital availability, expertise and production facilities.

Public life was hit hard, including with the banning of dancing (1940) and of motor cars (1941). Rationing was introduced in 1939 and then spread, although it was also evaded. Inflation became serious and taxation increased, leading to widespread evasion. Conscription was less readily evaded than in 1915–18.

The more serious Italian problems were strategic and operational, not least poor command on land and a failure to integrate land and sea forces. These, rather than the availability of weapons, led to their failures in East Africa and Libya, and the same was true in the

Mediterranean, where the Italians were outfought, despite their navy including a number of modern warships and submarines. Based in Bordeaux, thirty-two of the latter took part in the battle of the Atlantic from July 1940, although with only limited success, just as the Italians had also provided aircraft to help the Germans in the Blitz on Britain in 1940.

German alliance politics did not amount to coordination. There were no summits equivalent to those of the Allies, intelligence was not shared and there was a general failure to sustain cooperation. Mussolini rejected German dominance of the Axis until after Italy was defeated in Greece and North and East Africa in 1940–1. These defeats coloured Mussolini's view on the strategic situation in 1942 and 1943: he urged Hitler to negotiate with Stalin and to concentrate on defending Western Europe, a policy designed to protect his own position, but one that did not match Hitler's views.

The war involved a brutal Italian occupation policy in the Balkans, a brutality drawing on Fascist ideology, imperial expansionism, racialism and the experience of a deadly and often cruel Resistance, that included war crimes that Italians tend to ignore. Moreover, the Italian forces on the Eastern Front, 60,000 strong in 1941 and 220,000 in 1942, could treat civilians brutally, although certainly not on a German scale. Despite the presence of these forces and of others in the Balkans and North Africa, Italy was not able to contribute greatly to Axis Grand Strategy. Italy had brought new commitments for Germany in North Africa and the Mediterranean, and there were major problems in coordination between the Italians and the Germans. Most notably, there was no cooperation with Japan. In Somalia, Italy had a colony on the Indian Ocean, with a port at Mogadishu, while destroyers were based in the Italian Red Sea port of Massawa, in Eritrea. However, both were conquered by the British (on 25 February and 8 April 1941 respectively), before there was any prospect of cooperation.

Nevertheless, Italian forces still played an important role in North Africa in 1942–3 and in resisting the invasion of Sicily in 1943. There has been a misleading tendency to underrate Italian fighting quality, but it is true that Italy failed to make an effort commensurate with its resources. Nor was it successful. In November 1942, the German-Italian army was broken by the British at El Alamein in Egypt, after which Libya was conquered and the Germans and Italians fell back to Tunisia. The Germans greatly reinforced the Axis position in Tunisia, but this was attacked both by the British advancing via Libya and by American forces that had invaded Morocco and Algeria that November. The Germans and Italians in Tunisia surrendered in May 1943, greatly increasing the number of Italians in captivity. Two months later, Sicily was successfully invaded.

OPERATION HUSKY, 10 JULY 1943

Amphibious power and air support allowed the Allies to seize the initiative and helped ensure a wide-ranging attack on Sicily, the largest island in the Mediterranean, one in which 180,000 Allied troops were initially involved alongside 750 warships, 2,500 transport ships and 400 landing craft. This was to be the second largest amphibious operation of the war in Europe; D-Day in Normandy in 1944 being the first. The landings were more sophisticated than those mounted by the Allies in North Africa in 1942. There were appropriate ship-to-shore techniques, notably amphibious pontoon causeways and trained beach parties. The British landed in south-east Sicily and the Americans further west between Cape Scaramia and Licata.

Once landed, the Allies faced problems from the defenders of the island. The Italian Sixth Army, commanded by General Alfredo Guzzoni, defended Sicily. Including navy and air force personnel, Guzzoni had 315,000 men and 40,000 Germans. His troops were primarily composed of Coastal Divisions – five of the nine – and he had only a few obsolete tanks. After considering options, he concentrated his force in the south-eastern sector, which was the Allied territorial objective. The SIM – Italian

Military Intelligence Service – was sure the Allies were going to land in Sicily, after precise information had been received from its agents in Lisbon, while German intelligence believed the Allies would land in Sardinia or Greece. Albert Kesselring, the German commander, disregarded the Italian intelligence reports and deployed the German tanks of XIV Panzer Corps in central and western Sicily. On 7 July, Guzzoni was warned that a landing was expected within two or three days, but, despite the information from Lisbon and the Allied seizure of the offshore island of Pantelleria on 11 June after heavy bombing, Kesselring kept his troops in the interior and did not defend the coast. In contrast, the Italian troops were deployed there and on 10 July were able to blow up the ports of Gela and Licata to deny them to the Allies.

The Italian forces resisted but were overwhelmed. For example, when the Eighth Army landed, that part of the coast was defended by the 206th Coastal Division, which was scattered along an 82-mile-long line. The British first wave alone outnumbered the Italian defenders three to one. The Italians, who had no tanks, were annihilated. However, when the British then moved on to attack the Italian-defended city of Catania, it took twenty-three days of hard fighting. The Seventh United States Army landed south of Gela. Italian coastal units resisted as best they could, but suffered heavy casualties, the 429th Coastal Battalion losing 45 per cent of its men. The Livorno Division counter-attacked supported by fifty obsolete Italian tanks and by aircraft bombing the beachhead, but the attack failed with the loss of 50 per cent of the troops. German tanks were too far away to offer initial support. When they finally arrived, the attack was resumed with initial success, but, supported by naval firepower, American troops fought bravely and enlarged their beachhead. The Allies benefited from support from the local Mafia. Some Italian officers seeking to organise opposition to the Allies were shot, while some American units were guided by Mafiosi.

Subsequently, with the British held before Catania, George Patton and the Seventh United States Army moved north to Palermo, creating and exploiting opportunities for outflanking opposition. The heavily outnumbered Assietta Infantry Division was unable to stop him and, having taken Palermo, Patton moved east on Messina after fighting off counter-attacks at Troina. The Americans proved far more effective than they had done in Tunisia, and, repeatedly, gained and used mobility. However, the Germans fought well, taking advantage of the terrain, which limited the use of armour. The capture of the island was completed on 16–17 August, and it provided a valuable base from which mainland Italy could be attacked.

THE FALL OF MUSSOLINI

The crisis of the Italian military system became that of Fascism in part because the limits of both were similar and Mussolini could not, and would not, confront this. His determination that Italians would fight, and that to compromise was to degrade Fascism, ignored realities, and reflected the disastrous continuation into wartime of the posturing and concern with appearances seen in his earlier period of power. Mussolini himself blamed everyone else: the King, the Church, the bourgeoisie, the generals, the soldiers and the people, as he was to do until he was killed in 1945.

In 1943, civilian morale was badly affected by Allied bombing. There was anger about the government's inability to protect civilians. The Allies deliberately sought to encourage such attitudes through the bombing and underlined this message through extensive leafleting. The deficiencies of anti-aircraft defences and civilian shelters contributed to this situation. Many fled into the countryside. The home front was close to collapse. There were strikes in Milan and Turin in February.

The invasion of Sicily precipitated a growing crisis of confidence in Mussolini among the Fascist leadership, as well as among other Italian leaders, especially the King. Having promised totalitarian efficiency and national modernisation, the now-demoralised Mussolini had only delivered failure, the third humiliation following Adua in 1896 and Caporetto in 1917, and one that was becoming the most serious.

After the meeting of the Fascist Grand Council on 24 July 1943, the first since 1939, Mussolini was arrested at the King's behest on 25 July and a government was formed by Marshal Pietro Badoglio, a former Chief of Staff, although he was an individual consistently without ability. This government was backed by the army and the Church, and excluded the Fascists. A foolish ditherer, Badoglio sought to reach an agreement with the Allies, while avoiding the need to acknowledge defeat. Meanwhile, the Germans rapidly built up their forces.

An armistice with the Allies, the Armistice of Cassibile, was signed by the new Italian government on 3 September 1943 and was announced five days later. However, the Germans rapidly seized most of Italy, with the new Italian government, which had fled from Rome to Brindisi, unable to organise effective opposition. The army was not given appropriate instructions, although much of the fleet was able to sail to join the British in Malta, albeit under German air attack. The army effectively disintegrated. Units were dissolved by their commanders to avoid coming into conflict with the German army, or were disbanded by private initiative. The units of the regular army that continued officially remained with the King, but some joined the partisans or were arrested by the Germans. Many Italian soldiers who refused subsequently to support Mussolini's Republic of Salò, in German-occupied territory, were deported to German internment camps in Germany and Poland for forced labour, mostly in armament factories. As a separate trajectory, the papacy had moved from being complicit with Fascism, in part due to opposition to liberalism, democracy and Communism, to deciding, in contrast, that Mussolini had to go.

The fall of Mussolini's regime provided opportunities for many Allied prisoners of war to escape. They were generally sheltered by Italians who often took considerable risks to do so.

WAR IN MAINLAND ITALY

British forces invaded Calabria from Sicily on 3 September 1943, meeting no resistance, with fresh landings on 4 and 8 September, while, further north, the major port of Taranto was occupied by a British amphibious force on 9 September. From there, the British advanced to capture the ports of Brindisi and Bari, the latter falling on 14 September. These operations in Apulia were greatly eased by the Italian armistice as there were no German forces there.

The main invasion force was landed on 9 September in the Gulf of Salerno, south of Naples, in Operation Avalanche. However, the German response to the over-extended Salerno landing proved more rapid and determined than had been anticipated, not least in preventing the Allies from using Montecorvino airfield, which they had captured on landing day. The shallow beachhead was only consolidated and expanded with considerable difficulty, which made it impossible to use the ports of Salerno and Vietri once they had been captured. The Germans proved able to build up their forces faster than the Allies. On 12 September, a German counter-attack tested the Allies hard, exhausting their reserves and leading to the dropping of American airborne forces into the beachhead. Blocked, the Germans began to withdraw to north of Naples on 16 September, while on that day there was the first link-up between patrols from Salerno and British troops advancing overland from Calabria.

The Allies pressed on to enter Naples on 1 October. The Germans had earlier withdrawn in the face of a popular rising there that they could not crush, as well as of the Allied advance. The Allies were left in control of southern Italy, but the Germans had established a strong line across the peninsula, making plentiful use of the mountainous terrain to create effective defensive positions, from which they were to fight ably and cause heavy casualties for the attacking Allies.

The Germans in Sardinia reached an agreement with the local Italian authorities on 9 September to evacuate the island unopposed. The Allies, in the shape of American parachutists, arrived on Sardinia unopposed on 14 September. The Germans withdrew northwards to

Corsica, but the local Italian garrison there resisted them. Germans from Sardinia took the Corsican port of Bastia, but Italian armoured units seized it and forced the Germans to leave by sea. Other German units on the island fled when the Allies landed. The Allies made the Italians withdraw from Corsica to Sardinia, leaving their heavy weapons and vehicles behind.

The new Italian government declared war on Germany in October 1943. Although that made little difference to the course of the conflict, it eased Allied occupation issues and helped ensure that Italy was not occupied after the war and was treated better than Austria.

In a daring airborne operation on 11 September, the Germans had rescued Mussolini from captivity. They put him in charge of a puppet state in northern Italy, the Italian Social Republic, or Republic of Salò, established on 23 September, but he was now of limited importance, shuttling between his wife and his mistress. The Germans essentially ran what was left of Axis Italy, while Mussolini proclaimed that Fascism was really a revolutionary ideology. Italy and the Italian state had fallen apart.

Italian culpability in the Holocaust was seen with the Republic of Salò, which did not need to be coerced into arresting and deporting Jews to slaughter in the extermination camps. Mussolini's attitude was ambivalent. Although not anti-Semitic himself, he did not prevent article I from being included in the Verona Manifesto of 14 November 1943, which stipulated that those 'belonging to the Jewish race were foreigners and enemy'. In March 1944, Giovanni Preziosi was allowed to organise a Department for Demography and Race, followed by an Inspectorate for Race. Well over 8,000 Jews were deported, mainly to Auschwitz, of whom only about 1,000 survived. About 7,750 were killed in Italy by the Germans, often with the help of Italian officials. In the former ghetto in Venice, the list of names of those killed is a poignant memorial. However, about 35,000 Jews avoided being arrested and/or deported. Of these, some 29,000 hid in cities and the country, often under false names, and were frequently helped by the local population. Others escaped to the Allied-occupied south and to

Switzerland, or found shelter in church buildings, including in the Vatican. About 2,000 Jews joined the partisan Resistance. Not all ordinary people followed the policy of the authorities, and many Jews survived because of the generosity and bravery of such people.

The war in Italy was hard fought, and Allied landings at Salerno (1943) and Anzio (1944), designed to open up the conflict, failed to produce expected outcomes. In July–August 1943, it had seemed that Italy might be swiftly seized by the Allies, but Rome did not fall until June 1944. The campaign involved formidable Allied resources. In the eventually successful fourth battle of Montecassino in May 1944, 25 divisions, 2,000 tanks and over 3,000 aircraft were committed by the Allies. The monastery, founded by St Benedict in 529 CE, was destroyed in the bombing.

The Germans still held northern Italy at the end of the 1944 campaigning season. Moreover, they did so with a relatively modest amount of troops. In part, Hitler held on because he wanted to limit Allied air attacks on southern Germany from Italian bases.

Italy, instead, moved into the front line of the air war, with Allied air attacks as part of the process of conquest. These contributed to the devastation and social breakdown of the war. Already by 1943, Anglo-American bombing had wrecked 60 per cent of Italy's industrial capacity and badly undermined morale. Bombing focused on industrial centres and ports, notably Milan, Turin, Genoa and Naples. Rome was also bombed. There was far less bombing of other cities, such as Venice. Towns that found themselves near the front line were heavily shelled, as Rimini was in 1944.

The social fabric that was damaged and the social capital that was lost were to prove difficult to replace in the post-war decades. In large part, this was a legacy of Mussolini's divisiveness under the further strain of a defeat he totally failed to anticipate. There was no Allied breakout into northern Italy until April 1945. This breakout helped revive the Italian Resistance, which had been bloodily suppressed by the Germans the previous autumn and, in particular, winter. Genoa, Milan and Venice were liberated by the partisans ahead of the advancing Allied army. Mussolini was shot by partisans on 28 April while trying to flee to Switzerland, and then his body was hung up in Milan. Separately, and due to the Anglo-American advance, the German forces in Italy unconditionally surrendered.

Mussolini was the most conspicuous casualty in the civil war between the Resistance and the Republic of Salò, each of which raised roughly comparable numbers of fighters, while neither enjoyed mass support, and understandably so given the brutality shown by both to those they suspected and captured. The need of the people in very harsh circumstances to support themselves also discouraged commitment. In 1943–5, there had been, at the same time, a patriotic war against the Germans, a civil war between Fascists and anti-Fascists, and a class war, as well as a disinclination to commit, for example, to serve in the forces. The Resistance itself had been seriously divided between the Communists and the non-Communists. The former, who dominated the actual fighting, very much took directions from Moscow and these were for the 'Popular Front' approach seen with Committees of National Liberation. The combination of these conflicts contributed to a disintegration of beliefs, and of faith in institutions, and resulted in violence that had profound effects in the post-war period. Enduring family and neighbourhood ties correspondingly became even more important.

Repeated military failures from 1915, and a tendency to underplay successes, possibly also contributed to what has been presented as a crisis of 'performative masculinity' on the part of Italian men, or, more simply, to a society in which 'feminine' values, such as religious observance and family links, are to the fore. However, there is no clear gender segregation on this point, or on the sentimentality that has also been discerned. Moreover, the most significant legacy has been a comprehensive pacifism. This interacted with taking all the benefits of NATO without casualties, especially during the Cold War.

REFIGHTING THE WAR

As with other countries, post-war politics rapidly came to the fore and led to a determination to overcome the past. In this case, it meant excusing it. Thus, in 1946, there was a general amnesty for those charged with Fascist crimes, an amnesty proclaimed by the Minister of Justice, a Communist. In contrast to Germany, it later, notably from the 1990s, became possible in Italy for some mainstream politicians to offer a positive approach to the wartime regime. More particularly, the contest over the reputation of Mussolini, and not least over the popularity of his Republic of Salò in northern Italy in 1943–5, was directly linked to the legitimacy of political groupings across the spectrum from Communists to neo-Fascists. These groupings looked back to the 1940s and earlier for evidence of their probity and of the iniquity of their opponents. As a result, the reputation of Mussolini had (and has) a greater resonance in Italian politics than that of Hitler in Germany.

In Italy, the left sought a praiseworthy origin in terms of its wartime and earlier hostility to Mussolini, but, more generally, the emphasis in Italian public culture was not on alliance with Germany in 1940–3, but rather, very much, on opposition in 1943–5. Thus, the focus was on a war of liberation, with the Resistance presented in a heroic light, not least as a redemption from Fascism. This provided an appropriate lineage for the post-war democracy, and, separately, shifted attention from the Italian imperial role, both pre-war in Libya and Ethiopia as well as in Greece and Yugoslavia in 1941–3. In all of these cases, opposition had been harshly treated, and ignoring this helped the Italians in their self-presentation as victims of the war. Indeed, Italian troops were frequently contrasted with their German allies and seen as *brava gente* who had not been involved in war crimes, and this contrast was more generally applied by Italians to wartime occupation by the two powers.

There were also competing attempts by the different political parties to annex the positive reputation of the Resistance to their benefit. Thus, on the model of Gaullists in France, the Christian Democrats challenged the Communists' effort to present the Resistance as their movement. In turn, the radicals of the 1968 generation criticised the Christian Democrats' usage of the Resistance by arguing that the true radicalism of the Resistance was thus neglected. For example, Church participation in the Resistance was limited, although in some areas, such as Lucca where many priests were as a result shot, this was not the case. Radicals also claimed that the extent to which the post-war government, although dominated by the Christian Democrats, owed much to the practice of Fascist government was downplayed, and they criticised the 'Establishment' and the Church for backing Fascism. This argument was taken to vindicate radical opposition to the existing system in the 1960s and '70s.

From another direction, from the right, there was a widespread (although far from universal) positive re-evaluation by some of Mussolini and Fascism. He was treated as a far more benign figure than Hitler. Mussolini indeed was, but that was scarcely a comparison of which to be proud. In particular, it was claimed that, in a self-sacrificing fashion, he had agreed to head the Republic of Salò in order to protect northern Italy from harsh German rule, a claim, typical of the later neo-Fascist attempts to justify themselves, that research in the German archives has failed to substantiate.

The decline in the reputation of the Italian Communists in the 1980s was a factor in the positive re-evaluation of Mussolini, and one that gathered pace following the end of the Cold War, with Italy sharing in what was a general development in Europe, one seen for example in Romania and Hungary. In part as a result of this decline, there was a reduced stress on the role of the Resistance in Italy. Moreover, the Resistance itself was called into question by some commentators arguing that part of it had been compromised by its Communism. Large numbers of Italians had supported the Republic of Salò and fought the Resistance in a low-level, counter-insurgency conflict in 1943-5, and their history came to be more favourably treated by some. Already, during the Cold War, the pressures of Italian politics, and the anti-Communist position of the Italian state, had ensured a degree of acceptance by some for those termed the *bravi ragazzi di Salò*.

After the War: 1945–90

POST-WAR REORGANISATION

The post-war world brought an Italy settled in the West after initial uncertainties as to whether its large Communist Party would help take it into the Soviet bloc alongside Eastern Europe as a whole, bar Greece and Finland. A country in ruins, as parts of it, notably Palermo, long remained, with its overseas empire entirely gone, and with Italian communities elsewhere expelled, particularly by the French from Corsica and Tunisia and by the Yugoslavs from Istria, Italy faced a period of renewed turmoil after the Second World War. This was in part because it was on the front line of the Cold War with a Communist bloc that included Yugoslavia, and because of a bitter territorial dispute over Trieste that lasted until settled by the United States in 1954. The liberation/conquest of Italy by Anglo-American forces in 1943–5 played a key role in placing Italy in the Western bloc, as did post-war intervention in Italian politics by the Americans in order to stop a Communist takeover.

Meanwhile, the old order was rejected when Italy voted in 1946 in a referendum for a republic in what was a close result. That year, Victor Emmanuel III had abdicated in favour of his son, Umberto II, but this did not sway the result. America supported the end of the monarchy, and Britain, the traditional ally of the House of Savoy, was from 1945 under Labour. The House of Savoy went into exile. Moreover, the title 'Your Excellency', one much employed by officials during the Fascist period, was abolished. There were trials of a few Fascist leaders, and the killing of many Fascists.

Italian culture celebrated myths of a good, anti-Fascist majority, one that brought together Communist and Christian Democrats, with virtually all victims under Fascism. These myths were seen in 'neorealist' films, notably Roberto Rossellini's *Roma città aperta* (*Rome:*

Open City, 1945), Luchino Visconti's *La terra trema* (*The Earth Trembles*, 1948), a film about the fishermen of Acitrezza, and Vittorio de Sica's *Ladri di biciclette* (*Bicycle Thieves*, 1948), as well as in literature, for example works by Italo Calvino, author of *Il Sentiero dei Nidi di Ragno* (*The Path to the Nest of Spiders*, 1947). Street names were altered to proclaim the new political orthodoxy. Like many other towns, Ancona got a *Via Giacomo Matteotti*. Nationalism was reconceptualised, while the idea of Italy as a Great Power and an empire was discarded. The legacy of ancient Rome was largely put aside, as also, separately, was the earlier presentation of the *Risorgimento*.

Expressing the values of the anti-Fascist opposition, the new constitution came into force in 1948, but, by then, divisiveness was to the fore, including over films. Only parts of the left tried to portray the majority as anti-Fascist, a view that enjoyed little support in the south and from the Church, let alone the unrepentant Fascists.

Since then, the battle over Italian history has ensured that conservative historians and commentators can be apt to trace the ills of the 1980s onwards to the late 1940s. The counterpart was the critical search on the left for continuities between Fascist Italy and the Christian Democratic system that dominated the new republic from 1948 until the 1990s. The criticism of continuity, which was certainly the case with the incorporation of the Lateran Pacts of 1929 into the new constitution, as the Christian Democrats wished, neglected pressure for a degree of reconciliation. If there was only limited 'defascistisation', that in part reflected not only the wishes of the Christian Democrats but also of the Communist leadership.

In 1943, the *Democrazia Cristiana* was founded as a successor to the People's Party. In the 1948 election, the Christian Democrats defeated the Communists and their Socialist allies. American intervention played a role, but a vote for democratic reconstruction was more significant. Continuing the pattern of the 1919 election, the Liberals had already done very badly in the election of 1946, an election in which the Christian Democrats, Communist and Socialists gained an overwhelming majority of the seats. The Christian Democrats benefited from the enfranchisement of women (as also was the earlier case with the British Conservatives), and also from the electoral support of the Catholics. The Vatican made vast propaganda efforts while America provided money. The 1946 election had supported the coalition government that had followed the war, with 86 per cent of the voters opting for parties produced by the resistance to Mussolini.

However, this government was brought down by the Prime Minister, Alcide De Gasperi, the skilful Christian Democrat leader, who, in 1948, won nearly half the vote. He was Prime Minister from 1945 to 1953. De Gasperi had started his political activity when elected a Catholic Party deputy from Trentino to the Austrian Parliament in 1911–18. After the First World War, he was elected to the Italian Parliament in 1921 as a member of the Popular Party, which later evolved into Christian Democracy, and sat in Parliament until 1927, when the Fascist authorities arrested him. Sentenced to four years in jail, he was released in 1928 and, in 1929, became a Vatican librarian, a post he held until 1944 when, as a consequence of his clandestine political activity, he was appointed as a representative of Christian Democracy in the National Liberation Committee.

Italy joining NATO as a founder member in 1949 (as occupied West Germany could not do until 1955) was a key event. America established major bases, notably at Naples, for its Mediterranean fleet and for its air force. The new economic order, however, was not that sought by America. Much the Americans proposed, Italian governments, business and agriculture resisted, in large part by remaining wedded to corporatist solutions. Only Fiat really bought into the American vision. It made a big difference, but the new economic order that emerged after 1949 did not look like what the Americans sought.

Italy benefited from the 'Long Boom', a period of rapid economic development that saw an average annual growth rate of nearly 6 per cent between 1951 and 1968 and that lasted until the oil-price crisis hit in 1973. Economic growth owed much to the application of advanced, mostly American, technology and production methods, as well as to American investment. In agriculture, mechanisation led to productivity gains and to a movement of workers from the land, mostly to the cities where wage rates therefore remained low. The country developed a mixed economy that included much state planning and nationalisation. It benefited greatly from Italy staying out of wars and spending relatively little on defence. Unlike for Britain, France, the Netherlands, Belgium, Portugal and Spain, there were no colonies to protect.

There was a pronounced regional dimension to economic development. The relative failure of southern Italy was seen in the mirror of the role of the north, the economic and political powerhouse of the country centred on Milan and Turin. Northern Italy saw new purpose-built manufacturing plants that permitted a more effective introduction of new technology and organisational methods. Southern Italy was regarded and treated by Italian governments and by the EEC (European Economic Community), of which Italy was a founding member in 1958, in terms of failure, being identified, on the pattern of the pre-First World War Liberals, more as a problem society than as a zone of economic underperformance.

Partly as a result of the agrarian reform introduced with American encouragement in 1950, a reform intended to keep people on the land, average farm sizes in southern Italy were too small to generate much profit, and this hit living standards, and thus the domestic market for manufactured goods and services. The independent peasantry that had been sought (as also by the Americans when introducing land reform in occupied Japan) were in practice just differently poor. As a key aspect of structural reform, attempts were subsequently made to encourage consolidation, both among individual landholdings, which were often highly fragmented, and between them. However, farm size affected the potential for mechanisation by limiting investment capital. The loss of people from the land, many to shanty towns in northern Italy, notably outside Milan, was concentrated among the young, many of whom did not find the terms of agricultural work attractive: much of Italian agriculture was not really competitive with other EEC economies, especially that of France, a situation that has continued to the present, with the additional complication of competition from new members: first from Spain, and, subsequently, from Eastern Europe. The loss of people from the land greatly affected the character of rural and small-town life. Many small towns became apparent ghost settlements with few young people on the streets.

Emigration from southern Italy worked as a safety-valve since it lowered unemployment, and so decreased social tensions. Further, remittances from the workers to their families remaining behind helped the latter increase their incomes and living standards. Emigration was within Western Europe and to traditional destinations, notably the United States, but also to largely new destinations such as Australia and Canada.

The war had discredited Fascism, although a general amnesty was issued in 1946. In an atmosphere of moral and political conservatism, the right was reborn in the different form of Christian Democracy: many former supporters of Liberalism and then Fascism backed the Christian Democrats. This became a continuing tradition that, in its corporatism and clericalism, contrasted greatly with those of British Conservatism and American Republicanism, being more similar to the Christian Democrats in Germany. The Christian Democratic Party sought to anchor Italian democracy in European unification. In 1951, Italy was one of the six founder members of the European Coal and Steel Community, albeit the poorest. The same six established the EEC with Italy playing a key result in the Messina Conferences of 1955 and 1956 and the Treaty of Rome of 1957. Despite the arguments of the enthusiastic federalists of the period, few Italian leaders saw the EEC as likely to replace the nation state. However, for an Italy still suffering from devastation and political dislocation, the EEC offered a means to create space for Italian economic development. In particular, it provided a way to organise the huge boom in intra-European exports that had taken place in the 1950s, a boom that was an aspect of post-war recovery and was part of the post-imperial adjustment in Europe. The fall, and then removal, of internal tariffs led to a further rapid growth of trade within the EEC. Membership of the EEC was also a rejection of the Communist bloc, and a substitute for former hopes of empire.

In the 'Italian miracle', growth enhanced profitability and encouraged investment, resulting in renewed expansion – Italian industrial exports boomed, while car ownership in Italy rose markedly as an important part of the Americanisation of Italian life and culture, one also seen in the rise of television culture. Fiat by 1967 was Europe's leading car manufacturer, while its owners, the Agnelli family, played a role in Italian politics. Films such as the very many of Alberto Sordi, as actor and later director, depicted Italy during the boom. As a result of car ownership, oil imports became more significant, which led Italy to develop interests in the Middle East, notably Libya. Average real-consumption expenditure doubled between 1956 and 1970, although this was far more to the profit of the middle class than of their working-class counterparts whose standard of living remained far lower than in Britain, France or Germany. Nevertheless, there was a major rebound from the privations of Fascist autarkic self-sufficiency and then the war.

Industrial expansion benefited the north, whereas, particularly in the south, the EEC's Common Agricultural Policy (CAP), finally agreed in 1962, provided price guarantees and income support, reducing the rate of rural depopulation. Less positively, the CAP was associated with large-scale corruption in Italy, as farmers refused to stick to the rules, Italian government refused to pay the subsequent fines and some agricultural statistics were faked. The protectionism involved also led to a higher cost for food, which hit urban workers and the poor, although exchange rates were more significant. Italian monetary policy encouraged competitive devaluation, which pushed up import prices. The foundation of the EEC was encouraged by the USA as a way to stabilise Western Europe in the non-Communist world.

Although, albeit with ten prime ministers in 1953–63 between Alcide de Gasperi and Aldo Moro, two figures of greater stability, the Christian Democrats remained dominant, and thus able to develop a system of complacent corruption and jobbery. Politics was far from static. Moreover, the context of regional and social divisions, and the gulf between state and civil society, remained prominent. In 1960, there were large public demonstrations in opposition to a tactical alliance by Fernando Tambroni, the Christian Democrat leader and Prime Minister, between the Christian Democrats, the neo-Fascists and the Monarchists. This led to its abandonment, and, under Moro, the Christian Democrats, investing in the ideology of anti-Fascism, instead followed a model of 'Opening to the Left'. An alternative 'Third Force' of the secular centre, an attempt to create a viable alternative to the Christian Democrats and Communists, did not win electoral support when it arose in the 1950s. The duality of Christian Democrats and Communists proved too strong. Each benefited from widespread corruption, notably of, and through, local government.

CRISIS IN THE 1970S

Although the causes were separate, however, the serious economic problems of the 1970s brought much disruption to Italy, following on the student activism that had begun in 1967 and led to the closure of the University of Turin. Student activists claimed that Fascism was still strong in Italy and was inherent in the bureaucracy of the state and the structures of the system. The display of authority was treated as if Fascist. In practice, there was a contradiction between the conservatism of institutions and the aspirations of some of the young, and a rejection of the ideologies of the previous generation by a new one, some of whom appeared dissatisfied with an affluence and democracy rejected as unfair and bland. By treating a society that had a stated opposition to Fascism as Fascist, the young claimed that its ideology was inherently conservative and empty. In response, in March 1968, Paolo Emilio Taviani, the Minister of the Interior, arguing that Mussolini's seizure of power in 1922 was the product of police weakness, warned students that the same would not happen again. Crises of student and worker disaffection or *contestazione* persisted into 1969, with the 'hot autumn' leading to major concessions to the trade unions in 1970.

Violence by right-wing extremists in the shape of bombings and by left-wing anarchists in the form of assassinations became more sinister, each aiming to use what was termed 'a strategy of tension' in order to overthrow a democracy they despised. Economic pressures did not lead to an authoritarian regime nor to governmental direction of national resources. Economic difficulties did encourage the rise of the far-right *Alleanza Nazionale*, but neither they nor the radical left were able to gain power. The far-right did not come into any government coalition in the 1970s, as it (in a much less extreme form) was to do in the 2000s.

Nevertheless, there were three far-right coup preparations, notably in 1964 by General Giovanni De Lorenzo, head of the *Carabinieri* and formerly of one of the intelligence services, and, more clearly, in 1969 by Prince Junio Valerio Borghese, as well as extreme-left street terrorism. The far-right plans looked to elements in the military and the Borghese plans involved elements in the CIA. He also sought Mafia help.

The key group on the extreme left, the *Brigate Rosse* (Red Brigades), active from 1970, and defining itself as the 'New Resistance', drew on a degree of support from the fractured left that owed much to the illusions of former students as well as to the disillusionment seen in films such as Nanni Moretti's *Ecce Bombo* (1978). Attacks on industrialists, presented as exponents of the 'multinational imperialist state', did not create the way for the worker-democracy of which revolutionaries dreamed, but were followed by assassinations of politicians. These assassinations became an important factor in the political system and helped ensure that the period from 1969 to 1983 became known from 1981 as the *anni di piombo* (leaden years). Atrocities, over 14,000 in total, committed by both left-wing and right-wing terrorists, led to 374 deaths and over 1,170 injuries. The revolutionaries were more middle than working class. The left-wing terrorists were killed or imprisoned, but no senior figure among the right-wing terrorists was ever jailed.

The Communists in Italy had attempted to go for what was termed the 'historic compromise' between Communism and the established

Christian Democrat-dominated political system. This was an aspect of the détente more generally seen in Europe, notably with the Helsinki Accords of 1975 and of what was termed as Euro-Communism, and contrasted with the fervent earlier support of the Italian Communist Party for Stalin and its willingness to back the Soviet invasion of Hungary in 1956.

A pact was negotiated in 1976, with the Communist Party agreeing not to try to overthrow the Christian Democratic government and to support Italy's continued membership of NATO. In 1978, this pact brought the kidnapping and death of one of the most prominent Italian politicians, Aldo Moro, and the murder of his five bodyguards. Prime Minister in 1963–8 and 1974–6, and leader of the Christian Democrats from 1976, Moro had played a key role in constructing this compromise.

However, to the *Brigate Rosse*, the compromise was an aspect of control by the *Stato Imperialista delle Multinazionali* (Imperial State of Multinationals) and the USA. Moro was subject to 'trial by people', a process far harsher than that to which terrorists were exposed, and his body was symbolically abandoned halfway between the offices of the Communist and Christian Democrat parties in Rome. The *Brigate Rosse* hoped that by exposing the conspiracy that Moro allegedly represented they would inspire popular anger, paving the way for a proletarian revolution; an unrealistic aspiration.

Left-wing terrorism has continued, notably with the assassination in 1999 and 2002 of Massimo D'Antona and Marco Biagi, government economic advisors, but it has become less significant. Emergency anti-terrorist laws, mass arrests and persuading some to turn state's witness hit far-left terrorism hard, although there was no comparable treatment of the far-right. Those responsible for Biagi's murder were killed or jailed. The key element was the end of the Cold War.

Films such as Stefano Vanzina's *La Polizia Ringrazia* (*The Law Enforcers*, 1972) and Francesco Rosi's *Cadaveri Eccellenti* (*Illustrious Corpses*, 1976) made much of plotting by the far-right. The citizenry emerge in such films as victims. In Elio Petri's *Indagine su un*

Cittadino al di sopra di ogni sospetto (*Investigation of a Citizen Above Suspicion*, 1970), internal political disorder provides the background to a presentation of police corruption. Fiction also looked to the impact of terrorism, as in Loriano Macchiavelli's detective stories.

Other alleged conspiracies also excited interest. Relations between aspects of the government establishment, criminal networks and political extremists, in this and other cases, were unclear, but led to widespread suspicions that sapped confidence in the entire system. Although statements by the *Brigate Rosse* provided no evidence for such allegations, it was alleged that the Moro case was linked to the USA, the Masonic lodge Propaganda Due (P2) and the ambitions of Giulio Andreotti, the Prime Minister in 1972–3, 1976–9 and 1989–92, and a rival of Moro within the dominant Christian Democratic Party. Relations between Andreotti, a sinister figure, and the Mafia were repeatedly alleged and seem to have been well founded, certainly in the case of indirect links. The miasma of corruption encompassing crime, business and politics included, and drew on, the secret services, and focused for a while on P2, the extensive membership of which included leading members of the military, the secret services, the judiciary, and the business and political communities. The P2 lodge, a 1970s phenomenon mostly neutralised by the end of the 1980s, sought to spread its power within Italy deliberately in order to increase its political influence.

Related networks played a prominent role in the Vatican, and the death of Roberto Calvi encouraged fresh speculation. The head of the *Banco Ambrosiano*, he was convicted in 1981 of financial offences and released pending an appeal. In 1982, Calvi was found dead in London. Initially presented as a suicide, there were many reports, especially in Italy, of Mafia involvement in his murder. The suicide of another banker, Michele Sindona, in 1986 was also seen as a murder. Italy continues to be a Catholic society, but with limited respect for the Church. Reports of misgovernment and corruption in the Vatican continue to be prominent to the present day. However, Pope Francis is seeking to introduce reforms to the Curia and has publicly spoken of the Vatican's commitment to fighting against corruption and the Mafia.

The late 1970s also saw an upsurge in Mafia activity as heroin brought new levels of profitability. Indeed, it was said that the Mafia could touch the sky. This led to an assault on the state, notably with the killing in 1979 of Cesare Terranova, the Secretary of the new Anti-Mafia Commission, and in 1982 of Carlo Dalla Chiesa, the newly appointed Prefect for Palermo.

Domestic crises were accentuated in the 1970s by concern about Italy's stability in the event of the Cold War flaring up. Via the secret-services, P2 was linked to the CIA, which played a major role in anti-Communist activities, for example in the Gladio system. Designed to organise resistance in the event of Soviet occupation, this system proved a basis for secret political action. The Vatican was also probably an important part of the equation. Although there is no evidence to suggest that the Vatican actively supported Gladio, it remains likely that it knew of its existence. If this was the case, neither the Vatican nor the Church in general would have avoided backing the organisation in case of a Soviet invasion, which the Vatican, with its fundamental ideology of Christian democracy, vehemently opposed.

There was a possibility that international and internal discontent would coincide and indeed interact, and that Italian radicals would be strongly encouraged by the Soviet Union, as opposed simply to receiving the secret service funds that were provided in order to sow disruption. However, this possibility was lessened by the hostility between radicals and both the Soviet Union and its Communist allies in Western Europe. The radicals were not seeking a goal that accorded with Communist objectives, and these funds were far smaller than Soviet payments to the Italian Communist Party. From the Soviet point of view, the radicals were undisciplined and descendants of the Trotskyites.

Indeed, the Italian Communist Party, the most powerful one in Western Europe, not only publicly dissociated itself from the *Brigate Rosse*, which, in 1976, had urged 'Don't vote, shoot', but also pressed for action against them. The official Communist commitment, under the able Party Secretary, from 1972 until his death in 1984, Enrico Berlinguer, to the existing democratic system in 1973 reflected a sense not only of democracy under challenge, but also of society jointly assailed by the extreme left and the extreme right, which was indeed the case.

The latter was very likely responsible for the bloodiest episode of the period in Italy, the bombing of the railway station in the Communist stronghold of Bologna in 1980. Eighty-five people were slaughtered in an atrocity that was even more troubling because of well-founded suspicions of complicity between the far-right and anti-democratic elements in the establishment, including in the secret services. In some matters, there was certainly cooperation between the two. Other atrocities considered as staged by the far-right included the first major one, the bombing of a bank in the *Piazza Fontana* in Milan in 1969 (sixteen killed), and the bombing of a train in 1984. These were attacks on public spaces that were intended to spread fear and confusion and perhaps to discredit the extreme left by having them blamed.

With the Communists scoring 34.4 per cent of the votes cast at their peak, in the elections of June 1976, there was unease on the right and in the USA that they might be able to gain a role in government; even though the Communists sought to lessen anxiety by defining themselves as Euro-Communists. In 1976, however, the Communists had wanted a *sorpasso*, an overtaking of the Christian Democrats, only to fail. Furthermore, the united left of Communists, Socialists and various minor parties had failed to win the predicted half of the vote. There appeared to be no absolute majority for the left, one that reflected its inability to win the working-class vote to the degree it anticipated.

However, at the time, Berlinguer declared that the election was the end of an era and the failure of anti-Communism. The triumph of the left was proclaimed in 1976 in Bernardo Bertolucci's sprawling and self-indulgent film *Novecento*, an account of twentieth-century Italian history, and in the new daily newspaper *La Repubblica*. Intellectuals convinced themselves that Antonio Gramsci's dictum of a hegemony in ideas, their hegemony, would be followed by one in society. In practice, although the left was more prominent in some areas of the arts, the more conservative Catholics were dominant from the late 1940s in the ministries responsible for education and culture, and in the monopoly national television and radio broadcaster. The universities were strongly affected by patronage and factionalism, but there was also pluralism.

The right was scarcely behind the left in turning the public world into a sphere for corruption and self-serving. I can recall the head of a humanities department in a distinguished Italian university expressing his surprise in the early 1980s about how much I taught, and telling me that he did not teach students, but was responsible for keeping his department in line. When I asked what that entailed, he said there were no Communists in that department (and that they should go to Bologna), and that he went down to Rome every week to report at the ministry to an official who, in turn, visited once every two months and was treated to their hospitality. Worthless gossip over an *aperitivo* or a symptom of a corruption followed by at least a few? I do not know. Italians offer both views of this account. At any rate, an expression of cynicism that was fairly normal and that remains notable.

In the event, Communism had reached its level. Moreover, under a new leader from 1976, Bettino Craxi, the Socialists moved away from the Communists and, from 1978, turned their hammer and sickle into a carnation, which undercut the prospect for a Popular Front. In the 1980s, a coalition of the Christian Democrats, the Socialists, the Social Democrats, the Republicans and the Liberals governed, and consigned the Communists to irrelevance. The left as a whole was affected by the murderous nihilism of the Red Brigades because they had connected strongly with many left-wing myths. Nevertheless, Craxi was Prime Minister from 1983 to 1987, the Socialists won 14.3 per cent of the vote in the 1987 general election, and, from 1987 to 1992, participated in government, gaining much benefit as a result.

This was a period in which an excessive budget deficit led to significant governmental borrowing at high rates of interest. The resumption of appreciable economic growth in the 1980s, however, had encouraged consumerism and its capacity for expressing individualism. Already, by 1975, over 90 per cent of households had a television and fridge. Advertisements on the former were important in the spread of consumerism and in the shaping and sharing of consumerist values. Communism, already weakened in the 1980s, was to be hit hard by the developing crises and then, in 1989–91, the collapse of the Soviet bloc. Craxi saw this as his opportunity to remake Italian politics round a Socialist-led, left-wing alliance.

CHAPTER TWELVE

Modern Italy: Post-1990

At a time when West Germany was incorporating the formerly Communist East, the Italian political system was engulfed in a series of crises in the 1990s. In 1992, a very belated anti-corruption drive began under the name of *mani pulite* (clean hands). *Tangentopoli* (Bribe City), the name given to large-scale criminal corruption that the magistrates found centred on Milan, and spanning business, politics and organised crime across the country, led to a collapse in public confidence in the existing system or, rather, in its ability to keep going in its current form.

Legal processes played a key role. Prominent individuals charged included two former prime ministers, the Christian Democrat Giulio Andreotti and the Socialist Bettino Craxi. Andreotti, the political patron of Rome, Lazio and Sicily, the last an area where patronage was especially strongly entrenched, was investigated and then tried for Mafia links, although he was cleared. The particularly corrupt Craxi fled in 1994 to Tunisia, where he died in 2000, having been sentenced in absentia in 1994 to imprisonment. This action hit the patronage structures they had directed. The two men's parties, the Christian Democrats and the Socialists respectively, were badly hit by these scandals, and both were disbanded in 1994, part of what was termed the end of the 'Republic of the Parties'. Craxi claimed that all political parties took money illegally in order to fund their activities, but, even allowing for this, he was personally corrupt and unapologetic.

As a result, other parties became prominent or were founded. In 1993, a government of national unity was established, followed, in 1994, by the election of the untried Silvio Berlusconi, leader of the new *Forza Italia* party, as Prime Minister. Born in 1936 and based in Milan, where he was a friend of Craxi, Berlusconi had made a fortune in business, first in real estate and then in television. He was the anti-Communist candidate. Berlusconi sought to run the country as a big company, but he found the administration far worse than he anticipated, and was hit by the size of the huge national debt.

The sale of state-owned companies reduced liabilities, but his attempt to reduce the major liabilities posed by a very generous pension system lost him political support. Berlusconi's fall and replacement by a government of technocrats in 1995 was followed, in 1996, by a centre-left government under Romano Prodi. This government collapsed in 1998, but was immediately reconstituted by Massimo D'Alema, the former leader of the Communists, only for his coalition to collapse in 2000, and to be replaced by a technocratic government under Giuliano Amato. Keeping Berlusconi from power was a consistent goal.

In 2001, Berlusconi became Prime Minister again, having done well in the elections by promising a job-creation programme he could not fund, and despite his facing criminal charges. He benefited from the unstable recent governments having done badly. In the event, the jobs did not materialise, although in 2001 inheritance tax was abolished, followed in 2008 by the tax on first houses. Like Donald Trump, Berlusconi was a showman-businessman turned politician. He argued for a new start and promised business skills, but, according to his adversaries, the latter were in practice a matter of dubious influence-mongering, and they alleged he transferred these attributes to politics and government, sustaining and developing many bad assumptions and practices, and countering the anti-corruption drive of the 1990s.

An important change under Berlusconi in 2004 was the decision to suspend conscription from 1 January 2005 and to slim down the army as a professional service. The end of conscription was part of a more general global process, one that limited the scope of the state and ended one of the practices that brought a degree of national experience. At present, there is talk of the reintroduction of compulsory military service with the possible alternative of community service.

PERCEPTIONS OF ITALY

A lack of interest in modern Italy was very apparent at the turn of the nineteenth and twentieth centuries, for example in E. M. Forster's novel, *A Room with a View* (1908). Indeed, the reconceptualisation of Italy into a less impressive society, if not a land of the past, which was such a powerful feature of its imaginative treatment by eighteenth-century Grand Tourists, has remained potent and dominant ever since. Apart from the republicanism of Garibaldi, the energy and success of the *Risorgimento*, and, to an extent, the *apparent* 'order and backbone' that Mussolini produced and that aroused contemporary interest in the 1920s and 1930s, Italy has since been regarded, fairly or unfairly, in such a fashion, as indeed less civilised or developed than say Germany, France or Britain. The comparisons were (and remain) frequently seriously flawed but, although post-war Italian achievements in design, fashion, film, food and industrial production, such as luxury yachts, shipbuilding, trains, domestic appliances, furniture and lighting, enhanced Italy's status substantially, this approach can be readily seen in current attitudes. It is less overt than prior to 1945, but modern discussion of Italian politics and crime, notably the Mafia, and the sizeable publishing industry based on guides, travel books and reminiscences of Italy, nevertheless manifest this tendency to see Italy as in some way less developed than other major Western countries. Spain, long regarded as backward, has been more successful of late, striking outside commentators as modern and progressive, although this may be a long-standing British problem rather than an Italian one.

PROBLEMS OF THE PRESENT

There were major structural problems, economic, social, political and constitutional. Although in 1993 the electoral system was reformed in order to produce a strong past-the-post element, this was replaced in 2005 with a proportional correction to the new system. Combined with low thresholds for representation by individual parties, this correction helped move Italy back towards a more unstable political position. In addition, although Italy benefited from membership of the European Union (EU), it was not an easy relationship with Italy hit hard by German (and other) competition and under pressure from the fiscal demands of the euro.

Moreover, there was concern about instability in the Balkans and North Africa. Indeed, Italy served as NATO's airbase. In the 1994-5 NATO air campaign over Bosnia, Italian air bases from Ariano to Gioia del Colle were crucial. In the 1999 NATO campaign over Kosovo and Serbia, Italian air bases, notably Amendola, were again crucial. The 2011 NATO campaign in Libya operated from Italian air bases as well as from Italy's two aircraft carriers. These carriers were used as part of the NATO campaign in Afghanistan. At the same time, Italy stayed out of the 2003 Gulf War.

More generally, Italy was hit by the pitiful performance of the huge and dysfunctional political class, the inefficiency of the institutions, both lay and religious, the character of the south, which requires large and continuing transfers of public funds, and the fact that half of those polled feel that the state should guarantee everyone a job. There was both dependency on, and dislike of, the state. The same year that Italy won the World Cup (2006), there was a huge corruption scandal in Italian league football, a combination that appeared typical to many commentators, although there was also corruption in other national football systems. Limited confidence in Italy in institutional forms, and a strong role for tax evasion, were suggested by the percentage of total personal consumer expenditure spent in cash in 2007: 38, compared to 18 for Britain and 22 for France; although the unwillingness to use a credit card is not necessarily due to tax evasion. Indeed, there is considerable distrust of electronic currency. However, the place of organised crime also encouraged a cash economy.

The weight of the past and of the Church has helped make Italians unresponsive to a sense of collectivity necessary to make secular institutions work for the common benefit. Instead, an anarchic atomism prevails, often in the form of kinship groups. Personal links, and the related patronage, are important in business and politics.

The Italian right has failed to produce a decent governing élite, and the left to offer a convincing reforming one. Counter-cultural ideas, such as the Slow Food movement, founded in 1986, command support on the left for what are, to a degree, reactionary, anti-scientific and impractical ideas. The country punches well below its weight on the international scene, and growth rates have declined, notably as compared with Germany but also with reference to the euro area as a whole. Within Europe, the lead Italy had maintained over Spain lessened. The fiscal crisis of the late 2000s and 2010s exposed major and persistent weaknesses in the Italian banking system, although most banks are usually quite careful in giving loans. Italy also ranked poorly in the Economic Freedom Index and in corruption indices. The violent anti-globalisation protests at the international summit held at Genoa in 2001 were beaten back by the police, but some of their ideas were close to mainstream attitudes, as the Five Star Movement (*Movimento 5 Stelle*, M5S) was to reveal.

A combination of globalisation and corruption was offered by organised crime. Italian criminal syndicates developed links with the wider world, especially in illegal trading in drugs, prostitution, migrants and arms. The Mafia (Cosa Nostra) of Sicily, the Camorra of Campania, the 'Ndràngheta (a term from a Calabrian dialect derived from ancient Greek) of Calabria, and the Sacra Corona Unita of Apulia, all proved highly successful. Thus, the 'Ndràngheta moved from kidnapping to drug smuggling. In each case, and more generally, politics, crime and business all interacted and much to the harm of the local population. State action against the Mafia in the 1990s, stemming from the decline of the Christian Democratic Party that had long protected it, provided opportunities in the drug trade for the Camorra, which was also close to the Christian Democrats. This action against the Mafia was encouraged by the murder in 1992 of two key anti-Mafia prosecutors, Giovanni Falcone and Paolo Borsellino (as well as Falcone's wife and the police escorts), murders which, like an explosion in 1993 that destroyed part of the Uffizi Gallery, were a clear and powerful defiance of the state. These prosecutors had been responsible for a mass-trial in Palermo, drawing on the revelations of a 'super-grass', Tommaso Buscetta, which resulted in the conviction and imprisonment of 360 defendants between 1986 and 1992. The murders led to the deployment of troops in Sicily.

By 2016, it was estimated that the wealth of the 'Ndràngheta stood at 44 billion euros and that its revenue, and that of the Mafia and Camorra together was 9.5 per cent of Italy's GDP. The following year, the statue of Falcone in Palermo was decapitated, while killings by the Foggia crime syndicate, an offshoot of the Camorra, led to new concerns. Italian detective novels offered what was generally a broader critique of Italian society, one well grounded in particular regional and urban environment. This was also true of foreign novelists, as in Michael Dibdin's *End Games* (2007), in which his detective protagonist, Aurelio Zen, moved from Venice, and finds in the south a harsh landscape, banditry and a wall of silence.

The character of national humour and confidence suggests a perception that this was, indeed still is, a very bad period. The sense of national pride and identity comes not from military power, political leadership, public institutions or scientific inventions, but from sport, food and lifestyle, and, to a degree, past economic and cultural achievements. At the individual and family level, a loss of hope, optimism and expectations was seen in high unemployment rates and emigration, and in the large numbers of the young who continued to live with their parents, including well into their thirties. This practice was linked to the small size of families, a marked contrast with the past and with national clichés.

This situation ensured that indigenous population growth was limited. By 2006, 26 per cent of the population was over sixty and the median age was forty-two, figures comparable with Germany, but less favourable than in Britain, France or Spain. The fall in infant mortality that was particularly steep in the 1970s discouraged the need for 'insurance' babies to cover possible deaths by other children, while the fall in the agricultural workforce ensured less of a need for male babies, as did changing social assumptions about family structure and inheritance. Despite the strictures of the Catholic Church, an institution that found it difficult to accept the nature of modern society for others let alone itself, contraception became much more common, and the average number of children per woman fell, and especially so in Italy where it fell to 1.18. Female work patterns were important, as was the difficulty of obtaining housing, a difficulty linked to the impact on real incomes of the inflation that accompanied the introduction of the euro. The cost of childcare is also an issue. Emigration from Italy in the early 2000s still amounted to an annual figure of about 50,000.

The age-balance is made more serious by the pension situation. In Italy, most pension provision is by the state and there are relatively few private pensions. As a result of this, the consequences of the combination of greater longevity and generous provision will be borne by the future. That means that the young will pay for the old or the to-be old; and that despite the fact that there will be few of the young to do so, and proportionately fewer with time.

Thus, public finances face particularly serious problems to match those of the banks. The ability of the Italian state to cope with these problems is limited. German economic predominance in the EU means that it is difficult for Italy to achieve an export-led growth that will provide the necessary funds. Indeed, the powerlessness of a situation in which Italy's destiny is so clearly controlled by Germany brings up historical resources not only of the last world war but also of the medieval, and later, control and power wielded by the Holy Roman emperors. There were related echoes of past feelings of powerlessness and related fatalism.

As elsewhere in Europe and also Japan and China, the financial penalty of supporting the past, in the sense of the elderly, stands as a major burden on the young alongside the difficulties of obtaining homes, jobs and promotion. It is no surprise that this leads to a sense of defeat that discourages some from having children.

NATIONAL HUMOUR: DARIO FO AND MODERN SATIRE

Awarded the Nobel Prize for Literature in 1997, Dario Fo (1926–2016) was a playwright and actor who sought to be a provocateur on behalf of the people against the powerful through his concept of *Il Popolo Contro i Potenti* (The People against the Authorities in Church and State). Fo's plays focused on the corruption of power as in *Accidental Death of an Anarchist* (1970), which dealt with the real death of a detainee in police hands. *Can't Pay? Won't Pay!* (1974) tackled housewives turning to shoplifting as a result of very high food prices. Fo also took his plays to the people, as in having them performed in factories, rather than in conventional theatres. The Church was a critic of Fo who himself moved from Communism towards a position comparable to the Five Star Movement. Fo was not the sole critic of the Church. In 2006, Emma Dante was attacked as anti-Catholic for her play *La Scimia*.

The low rate of indigenous population growth accentuated the impact of large-scale immigration. The latter rose greatly with the overthrow of Colonel Gaddafi and the breakdown in Libyan stability in 2011, as this meant not only immigration from the former Italian colony, but also the use of the Libya–Italy route as an entrée for immigrants from elsewhere, including in particular the former colonies of Eritrea and Somalia, but, more generally, from Africa and the Middle East. In 2012, the European Court of Human Rights banned the return of migrants to Libya as had happened earlier.

There was a great increase in numbers arriving in Italy. In the 2000s, immigration was above 50,000 a year, and by 2016, with a rapidly increasing rate, 181,000 sailed to Italy from Libya. This became the principal means of entry into Europe after the route from Turkey via Greece was largely closed. In July 2017, the government announced it would add to the four existing centres for processing migrants and asylum seekers, another six, which were to be in Calabria, Sardinia and Sicily. The presence of migrants is readily apparent in these areas, for example in Sassari in Sardinia, but also elsewhere, as in Ventimiglia. In August 2017, it was claimed that up to 700,000 migrants were waiting in Libya. The projected growth in the world population – from 7.6 billion in 2016 to 8.6 billion in 2030, and maybe 10.75 billion, if not more, by 2100, with much of the growth, both numerically and in percentage terms, coming in Africa – will probably drive these pressures further to the fore.

Mass immigration proved highly divisive in Italian society (and in many other countries), as well as a strain on the social fabric. In the municipal elections of 2017, and the general election of 2018, both the Northern League (*Lega Nord*) and the Five Star Movement were very hostile to immigrants, and especially so to Rome where fraud in migrant care was an issue in the 2017 conviction of a major criminal organisation. Many Italians showed great sympathy for refugees, both individually and collectively, but there was also a sense of exhaustion and growing concern about their numbers.

This accentuated tensions within the European Union about what was seen in Italy as the country being ignored by the European Commission and taking a disproportionate share of burdens. This criticism was certainly well founded with respect to France, which devoted much effort to preventing immigrants moving on from Italy, as also did Austria. Popular anger increased. In 2017, the government faced public criticism when it sought to grant citizenship to children born in Italy to migrants if at least one of their parents had lived in the country for five years. The proposal would have allowed about 800,000 minors to apply for citizenship. The ruling Democratic Party withdrew the measure because it feared that it did not have sufficient parliamentary support. The Northern League had campaigned strongly against the measure, its leader, Matteo Salvini, claiming that 'citizenship is not a gift'. A survey published in the newspaper *La Repubblica* in September 2017 revealed that 46 per cent of Italians said that migrants were a 'threat to public order and personal safety', compared to 26 per cent in 2012.

Earlier in 2017, Giusi Nicolini, mayor of the island of Lampedusa since 2012, lost the position in the election, blaming her defeat on hostility to her openness to immigrants and her hostility to uncontrolled development: 'The economic crisis, together with terrorism, means security is getting the upper hand over welcoming migrants . . . The majority of locals were [also] against my campaign for legality and my fight against the cementing over of the island.'

Separately, however, immigrants do much of the work, notably social work, in effect supporting a nation increasingly dominated by the concerns of pensioners. The latter were influential both in the political parties and in the trade unions, which offered scant help to immigrants, who were also criticised by the parties of the right. Due to a mixture of self- and applied segregation, immigrants congregated in particular areas, such as Ballarò in Palermo, including in shanty towns, as did the Roma. They were exploited by criminal groups, notably in making women work as prostitutes.

The extent to which the corrupt nature of political culture was a product and cause of a society that is more generally characterised by a corruption that is possibly inherent to its corporatism is unclear. The willingness to change the law in order to help Berlusconi to avoid trial on false accounting charges underlined the problems of ensuring probity in public life. The corruption widely associated with Berlusconi (Prime Minister in 1994–5, 2001–6 and 2008–11) sapped confidence in politics, contributed to widespread cynicism and became a subject of the arts, as in Nanni Moretti's hostile, albeit confused, film *Il Caimano* (*The Cayman*, 2006), which presents dirty money as the source of his career. In 2017, in the trial of Massimo Carminati, the gangster known as 'the last king of Italy', a telephone intercept revealed that he had compared himself and his associates to inhabitants of a world in which all levels mixed, criminal favours were exchanged, and 'it is even possible that I find myself at dinner with Berlusconi'. That, of course, is proof of nothing.

The key player in commercial television, Berlusconi was blamed, with much reason, for taking it downmarket and, more generally, for debasing Italian culture. In large part, his political career was designed to protect his enormous television profits. He benefited, both financially and politically, from the particularly high rate of average television watching in Italy compared to the rest of Europe, notably from the older, less educated part of the population which watches daytime television. Conversely, Berlusconi can be regarded as successful in creating a good, effective and profitable business that provided a strong competitor to the partisan state-owned television.

Blaming opposition and criticism on Communists, Berlusconi, in 2008, held out the prospect of mass action in order to ensure his right to power: 'if we do not get the vote [in a general election] I believe millions of people will go to Rome to demand it'. His authoritarianism was defended by supporters on the grounds that technocratic governments were undemocratic, and that checks and balances made Italy ungovernable, but these checks and balances were erected to block the chance of another dictator like Mussolini.

However, though seriously flawed, Berlusconi was not a Mussolini. Indeed, the contrasts between the ways in which these two showmen gained and wielded power said much about shifts in Italian politics from the 1920s, more particularly the move away from gaining power through force and intimidation. As an obvious contrast, Berlusconi was overthrown in 2006 as a result of electoral failure. He contested the results, only to have them confirmed by the judiciary. In place of his disjointed coalition, another, from the left, was established under Romano Prodi, who had already been Prime Minister in 1996–8 and President of the European Commission in 1990–2004. However, that government, in turn, was weakened by division and had a precarious existence, not least because attempts at reform exacerbated its divisions. Prodi managed to stabilise the fiscal situation, but at the price of growth.

The Catholic Church was hostile to government policy, notably over the government's support for homosexual civil partnerships, but even more to the government's proposals for partially withdrawing support, especially fiscal relief, from private schools. These are nearly all Catholic, and their academic quality was generally poor. From his election in 2005, Pope Benedict XVI was very supportive of the constant commentary by Italian bishops on Italian politics, commentary that was strongly directed against social liberalism.

In 2008, benefiting from Catholic activism against the Prodi government elected in 2006, Berlusconi returned to power after victory in new elections caused by a rebellion in Prodi's coalition. Berlusconi devoted his period in office to protecting himself and his many business interests from serious charges of tax evasion and bribery, none of which resulted in condemnation. In 2011, Berlusconi stood trial on charges of abuse of power and of paying for sex with an underage Moroccan dancer. He was to be acquitted of the latter, but ejected from Parliament over a tax-fraud conviction, which at the time of writing was pending an appeal to the European Court of Human Rights. Also under pressure from the scale of government debt, and unwilling to back German plans over Greek indebtedness, Berlusconi was obliged to resign in 2011. His alleged links with the Mafia remain alleged. Berlusconi has always denied any involvement.

The sleazy Berlusconi was replaced by an entirely unelected government of technocrats headed by the economist Mario Monti, a government acceptable to the financial markets and thus to Germany, which, under Chancellor Angela Merkel, was consistently opposed to Berlusconi. This held power until an inconclusive election in 2013 led to a weak left–right coalition under Enrico Letta. In turn, this coalition was replaced in 2014 after the centre-left took power under Matteo Renzi and with the support of Berlusconi. Renzi, a Tuscan known as 'The Demolition Man', had become leader of the centre-left Democratic Party in 2013, a party that was the successor to the Communist Party.

The more significant development was the rise of an explicit and vocal anti-politics in the shape of the Five Star Movement, directed by

Beppe Grillo, a former comedian. It won a quarter of the votes in the 2013 election and subsequently had candidates elected as mayors of Rome and Turin. A populist and utopian movement, Five Star stands for a post-ideological transformation in politics, including overcoming the conventional distinction of right and left, and introducing rule by plebiscite in order to replace representative democracy by the popular will. Five Star also involves an attack on corruption and on officeholders serving for more than a term, and criticism of the EU, notably of the euro. In practice, Italy's membership of the latter depended, and depends, on German support, and on the 'quantitative easing', which provided stability in the euro area, supported by Mario Draghi, the Italian economist and banker who has served as President of the European Central Bank from 2011. The colourful Five Star party, despite successes in some municipal governments, is thought by some to be only partly plausible if looked at through a glass darkly, and then if kept from power. In February 2018, nearly 28 per cent of those polled backed the party.

In 2016, a popular referendum rejected the government's proposal for constitutional reform in order to strengthen its position. The government proposed that the party winning the largest number of votes would gain the absolute majority of the Chamber of Deputies, while there was not to be a directly elected senate. Presented as a means to ensure political stability, many Italians saw this as a dictatorial system. This failure led to the resignation in 2017 of the Prime Minister, Matteo Renzi. The south had voted solidly against the proposed changes, and Berlusconi opposed them. Renzi was replaced in December 2016 by Paolo Gentiloni, also from the Democratic Party, who announced that his priorities would be creating jobs and tackling the damage made by the deadly earthquakes that hit central Italy in 2016. In practice, political and fiscal measures were a key need. Gentiloni is a count who was active on the left from his early days.

Berlusconi remains a force, head of *Forza Italia*, despite his conviction for tax fraud in 2013. He appears to be seen by some as a kingmaker, although, from 2015, *Forza Italia* was overtaken in the polls by the Northern League, which in 2017 was allegedly planning to lead the right in part by changing to a more nationwide name and policy.

There were particular regional dimensions to corruption. This was especially seen in a series of scandals related to rubbish collection, scandals that reflected greater affluence, the transformation of material culture, and political breakdown. The resulting pressure on local government provided a topic for politics, notably in Rome, where corruption and intimidation served in the award of public contracts. A Five Star mayor was unable to overcome the crisis of public life in Rome in the mid-2010s, but the faults were from across the entire political system and much was due to rule of the city by left-wing coalitions for most of the period between 1976 and 2008.

The situation was more dramatic in Campania, the region around Naples. By late 2007, the local rubbish dumps there were all full, and rubbish collection had ceased. If the role of organised crime, the Camorra, in Campania in rubbish-related racketeering was relatively unusual, this crisis also reflected more widespread pressures, not least opposition to incinerators and to rubbish dumps near settlements. In turn, such opposition is a product of greater knowledge of, and concern about, toxic emissions and run-off, as well as of the risks posed by some of the garbage. In Campania, the criminals created space in their dumps for fresh rubbish by paying boys to set light to it, although this produced highly dangerous fumes.

Research published by the University of Pisa in 2008 suggested that pollution, especially dioxins, from Campania dumps was an aspect of a wider pollution-linked crisis in the sperm levels of Italian males, with sperm counts dropping from the 1970s, most notably in urban areas and least in remote rural ones such as Apulia. This pollution also seriously affected cheese production in Campania in 2008. The crisis continues to the present. The dominance of the Camorra was also seen in the burning down of Naples's science museum in 2013. Given that the Camorra had benefited from the government money allocated after the 1980 earthquake near Naples, it is scarcely surprising that they have continued their theft of the future. The 'Ndràngheta are involved in the traffic in toxic waste and radioactive material.

At the same time, Italy is affected by more general changes, including climate change. Conversations readily register this and form part of the experience and memory of individuals and communities. Rome had tropical-style rainfall in the spring of 2001, but visiting the valleys of the Adda and the Po in northern Italy in October 2005, when the water levels were unseasonably low, the conversation was on how there was far less snow on the Alps, on how it was not so cold in the autumn, on change. There was a sense of unease: water is of life and change seemed out of control. Indeed, the drought that hit water levels in 2005–6 had serious consequences for agriculture, while that in 2017 led to the declaration of a state of emergency.

Water shortages also caused environmental degradation. Increased extraction of water from rivers ensured that river levels, notably of the Po, Italy's most important river, dropped and, as a result, the volume of fresh water reaching the sea declined. The greatly increased pollution of the Adriatic was a related issue. Rising consumption of water also led to the depletion of natural aquifers and to the movement of salt to the surface, which greatly affected soil quality and agricultural productivity. The decline in snowfall was also a factor, as water availability from snow-melt is more consistent than if it falls as rain when much becomes run-off.

Despite complaints in the Veneto in the mid-2010s, the quality of drinking water remains high. There are strict rules about quality, the water is regularly tested, and the results are publicly available. Travellers used to complain about the water. They have little reason to do so now. However, in 2017, against a background of a very hot summer, and the driest spring in sixty years and maybe since 1800, there were serious problems with water supplies in Rome in part because nearly 44 per cent of the city's water was lost to its notoriously leaky network of supply pipes. Ageing pumping systems were also a major problem. The city government has long failed to carry out promised reforms. Many public fountains were switched off and the water pressure in the pipes was reduced for eight hours during the night.

As with most countries, each year brought an additional crisis. Whereas, in 2005–6, it was water shortages, in 2007, in contrast, the focus was on the collapse of social cohesion reflected in the role of arsonists in causing forest fires. In Italy, as in Greece, this was given an added twist by claims that the arsonists were working for property developers determined to see land cleared for development whatever the attitude of officials. Such action was of a pattern with the more general assault on the landscape seen since the Second World War. The tatty sprawl of much of northern Italy was more than matched by illegal building in the south and Sicily, and notably on the coast. Corruption was part of the process.

In 2012, the *Costa Concordia*, a massive cruise ship, ran aground on the west coast of Italy due to incompetence and thirty-two people died. By 2016, the focus was on the banks, with Italy's third largest (and the world's oldest), the *Monte dei Paschi di Siena*, facing particularly grave problems. It had been used to help raise money for its indirect owners, the Democratic Party. The largest, UniCredit, had to raise over 20 billion euros from shareholders, but did so easily. In 2017, the Italian government was unhappy with the plans of the European Central Bank to oblige lenders to increase provisions for non-performing loans. This was seen as likely to hit Italy, not least as many bankruptcy cases remained unresolved there for a long period of time.

Poor economic performance and dud loans have posed very serious issues. In 2017, at 1.5 per cent, Italy had the lowest growth of the major world and euro-area economies. Unemployment in December 2017 was 10.8 per cent, which was higher than the euro-area average. Juvenile unemployment was 35.5 per cent in July 2017. Italian manufacturing has been hit hard by the growth of East Asian exports. In 2017, Alitalia, the Italian flag carrier, went into bankruptcy protection as, with 3 billion euros of debt, it was no longer a going concern. Ryanair, which claimed to have 28 per cent of the Italian market, filed a non-binding offer. At the end of 2016, Italy's massive public debt came to 132.6 per cent of GDP, one of the highest percentages in the EU, although that depends on how the debt is calculated. This level of debt greatly limited the options for government stimulus of the economy.

At the same time, Italy is the third largest annual contributor to the EU, after Germany and France. Expenditure is not the sole issue: Italy spends a little less than Britain on health, but the results are much better. Life expectancy is high, higher than the United States or Britain. Rates of death by cancer are lower than in Britain, France and Germany, and cancer survival rates are higher than the EU average for both men and women. Obesity rates are lower than in Britain, Spain and Germany. Rates of chronic illnesses are lower than in Britain, Spain, Germany and France.

SOUTHERN DEVELOPMENT

In his novel *Il Ladro di Merendine* (*The Snack Thief*, 1996), Andrea Camilleri provided a grim account of the corrupt and debasing process of environmental change, locating it in Sicily:

> Until thirty years ago, Villaseta consisted of some twenty houses . . . In the boom years, however, the frenzy of construction (which seemed to be the constitutional foundation of our country: 'Italy is a Republic founded on construction work') was accompanied by a road-building fever, and Villaseta thus found itself at the intersection of three high-speed routes, one super-highway, one so-called link, two provincial roads, and two inter-provincial roads. Several of these roads, after a few miles of picturesque landscape with guard rails appropriately painted red where judges, policemen, carabinieri, financiers and even prison guards had been

killed, often surprised the unwary traveller by suddenly
ending inexplicably (or all too explicably) against a hill-
side . . . Villaseta thus rapidly turned into a sprawling,
labyrinthine town.

In his *La forma dell'acqua* (*The Shape of Water*, 1994) he
wrote that, nearby, there were 'the ruins of a large chemical
works inaugurated . . . when it seemed the magnificent winds of
progress were blowing strong . . . leaving a shamble of compensation benefits and unemployment.'

The failures of government are linked to those of politics and
of the court system. It is no surprise that Italy is particularly bad
at complying with EU laws. A dysfunctional political system
encourages this contempt. At the same time, it is the contradictory
nature of Italy's contemporary evolution that requires discussion.
Alongside criminal networks and political dysfunctions, there are
the world-beating industries in technology, transport, fashion, food
and drink, and tourism that take Italy to be the seventh economic
power in the world, and provide high standards of living in the
north. Alongside the collapse of Alitalia, there is a fully functioning
and expanding high-speed rail network as well as the success of the
World's Fair in Milan in 2016.

Histories on Offer

History was again part of politics. By 1961, the centenary of bringing
Naples and Sicily into the state, the anniversary was handled very
differently to 1911. Italy was a republic in 1961 and, unlike in 1911,
the role of the House of Savoy was scarcely to the fore. Moreover,
the left, notably in the person of Antonio Gramsci, had denounced
the *Risorgimento* as a Liberal movement that had neither sought,
nor brought, social justice. Instead, the emphasis in 1961 on the left
was on the resistance to Germany and Italian Fascism in 1943–5,

a resistance in which the left, notably the Communists, had been prominent. In 1961, the commemoration of the *Risorgimento* was pushed by the Christian Democrats who then dominated the Italian government. Emphasising the *Risorgimento* meant countering the view of the left, and also affirming an honourable tradition of, and for, Italian nationalism.

As so often, political developments in Italy interacted with the handling of its past, and notably as the political system was reformulated in the context of the serious crisis of the early 1990s. In particular, the right reformed, with the *Movimento Sociale Italiano* (Italian Social Movement, MSI), the Fascist Party, moving from the political margins. As late as 1992, the MSI marked the seventieth anniversary of Mussolini's seizure of power by donning black shirts and giving the Fascist salute. However, in 1994–5, the leader, Gianfranco Fini, as part of a reconstruction of the right linked to the decline of the Christian Democrats and to the formation in 1994 of the first Berlusconi government, changed the MSI into the more moderate, post-Fascist *Alleanza Nazionale* (National Alliance). The latter kept some aspects of Fascist social thinking, but sought acceptance, not least by a rejection of anti-Semitism. Distancing himself from the party's legacy, Fini, who made repeated trips to Israel, declared in 1996 that the verdict on Mussolini was 'best left to the historians'. This was a rejection of his 1994 claim that Mussolini was 'the greatest statesman of the twentieth century', on which he commented in 2009, 'If I still took that view I would be a schizophrenic, given everything I have done in the past fifteen years.' Also in 2009, Fini (from 2008 until 2013 President of the Chamber of Deputies) declared, 'We have come to terms with our past, we have said clear words of condemnation on Italian history between the two wars.'

Moving Fascism from the margins as Fini did made it more difficult to use the resistance to Fascism in 1943–5 as a convincing national myth for present purposes, although it is still the founding myth of the Republic, notably on the left where the role of Britain and the United States in the liberation is downplayed, if not ignored, in favour of the idea of a spontaneous, national, left-wing Resistance that liberated Italy.

An unwillingness to let well alone was shown by Berlusconi, the erratic head of *Forza Italia*, and, as such, the leader of the Italian right in the 1990s, 2000s and early 2010s, as he sought to defend the Fascist era from attacks. For a long time, Berlusconi, who saw historical revisionism as a means to provide unity to his coalition of support, refused to take part in the annual 25 April commemoration of liberation from Fascism. His defence of the Fascist era indicated the degree to which totems had changed in Italian politics, with Mussolini now more broadly semi-acceptable to a wide current in Italian opinion. In 2009, *Forza Italia* and the *Alleanza Nazionale* were merged into the new and misnamed People of Freedom or Party of Liberty movement under the leadership of Berlusconi, although in 2010 Fini became a leading critic of Berlusconi and launched a centrist 'third pole', only for his new parliamentary group *Futuro e libertà per l'Italia* (Future and Freedom for Italy) to do very badly in the 2013 general election, winning no seats. Aside from defending the Fascist era from attack, Berlusconi introduced legislation in 2009 that would have given pensions and honours to those who fought in the war, whether for the Resistance or for the Republic of Salò. The proposal, which, in effect, equalised the two, was not approved.

The Berlusconi government also offered compensation to Libya, a colony from 1911 to 1942, in large part because it wanted and needed to retain the supply of Libyan oil, but also to help persuade Colonel Gaddafi to restrict migration to Italy, and to provide indirect state support to Italian enterprises, because all the compensation had to be used to pay for work for Italian companies. However, the government generally displayed the tendency of the far-right to underplay or ignore Italian atrocities abroad, while also calling for acknowledgement of those that Italians had suffered. In 2004, Italian television addressed the brutal treatment by advancing Communist Yugoslav forces of the 250,000 Italian civilians in Istria in 1945, as the Yugoslavs sought to secure control of a region that Italy itself had gained from the

Austro-Hungarian Empire after the First World War. The slaughter of 11,000, with many thrown to their death into the *foibe*, limestone chasms, was a key aspect of the memorialisation by Istrian exiles whose views became influential in the 2000s. There had been no such massacres when Italian forces arrived in Istria in late 1918. Readier than its predecessors to express or channel xenophobic sentiments, the Berlusconi government was more prepared to advance the issue. In 2005, a new national day of remembrance was introduced for Italians slaughtered in Istria. There were ceremonies in every commune, flags at half-mast and extensive coverage. A linkage was drawn to the post-war border settlement. In 2009, Fini declared in a speech in Trieste, the nearest Italian city: 'Istria was Roman and then Venetian, which means it is Italian.'

In Ethiopia, where tens of thousands were slaughtered from 1936 in reprisals for resistance to Italian rule, large numbers of civilians were killed, including pregnant women and children, and a particular effort was made to slaughter intellectuals. It was entirely in keeping with Italian revisionism that Marshal Rodolfo Graziani, a brutal figure in Libya, Governor-General in Ethiopia in 1936–8, and Defence Minister and Chief of Staff of the Republic of Salò, who was convicted of collaboration and imprisoned after the war, was released in 1950 and, in 2012, celebrated in a monument built with public funds at Affile near Rome. The Italian government and army have never accepted the true nature of their murderous rule of Libya and Ethiopia.

As with 1961, domestic politics also affected the 2011 (150th) anniversary of the conquest of Naples and Sicily. A left in which Communism was far weaker was ready now to embrace the *Risorgimento* as a progressive nationalism. Conversely, Berlusconi's government was somewhat embarrassed by the anniversary. In large part, this was because the governing coalition included the Northern League, a separatist movement for which union with the south was a mistake and which often expressed critical views about southerners.

These and other differences also affected more specific episodes, such as the popular revolt in the Sicilian town of Bronte in 1860, one in which local notables were killed only for order to be restored by one of Garibaldi's generals, who executed five radicals. Used from the 1950s by Marxist historians as a symbol of a popular revolution crushed by the incomplete *Risorgimento*, this episode served in 2011 to enable attacks on the *Risorgimento* from the opposite side of the spectrum, not least as an instance of northern oppression of the south.

With strong support in such centres as Verona, Pavia and Treviso, the Northern League, founded in 1989, has pushed separatism hard. It did well in the 1992, 1994, 1996, 2001 and 2008 elections with its call for an end to the subsidising of the south. In the 2008 election, it won 8.3 per cent of the vote, but in 2013 only 4.1 per cent. The Northern League has sponsored its own history involving an emphasis on northern Italian distinctiveness. Its full title is *Lega Nord per l'Indipendenza della Padania* (Northern League for the Independence of Padania). At times, this history was highly problematic, as in attempts to argue that there was a northern Italian political identity prior to the Roman conquest. Nevertheless, this was a connection made by many.

History has possibly become more significant as a form of identity because of the decline in religious devotion – church attendance rates were below 20 per cent by the 2000s. However, the traditional history focused on the *Risorgimento* was increasingly lacking in popular appeal, much to the open regret of Carlo Ciampi, President from 1999 to 2006, and a moderate political figure.

Where Italy is going is unclear, but the same is true for the world as a whole. Indeed, Italy's crisis is that of the modern West. Yet, that is also a cop-out. Italy has done so much worse than Germany since unification, and than Germany, Japan and Austria since defeat in the Second World War, even though the last three faced occupation. Moreover, the parlous state of modern Italian politics, and the failure to create a viable nation state, contrasts greatly with that of Germany, Japan and Austria, and, indeed, with France. Having done very well in terms of economic growth in the 1960s, Italy has become a basket case, seemingly unable to adopt and implement policies able to provide economic renewal and government reform. The causes of the Italian dilemma are many, but a broken political system is probably foremost. How different, though, is Britain?

CHAPTER THIRTEEN

The North

ENTERING ITALY

To turn briefly to the history of individual regions, it is instructive to retrace the route of tourists from the past. Their views serve alongside the experience of the present to throw light on perceptions of the particular historical character of parts of Italy. The most prominent tourist experience in the past was that of travellers on the Grand Tour in the eighteenth century. The end of the Wars of Religion, with the Peace of Westphalia in 1648, made travel newly possible and, from across Europe and notably by Protestants to Catholic Europe, Italy was the prime destination. The newly wealthy, the Americans of their day, were the British, and their views came to define the experience of Italy.

Today, the prime way for the British to reach Italy is by air, a process recently eased by the growth of scheduled services by budget airlines and by the expansion in the number of Italian airports with direct services from abroad. In place of an Italy in which most tourists arrived at a small number of major airports, notably Milan and Rome, there are now direct flights to smaller airports such as Alghero, Bari, Bologna, Catania, Cuneo, Florence, Foggia, Genoa, Lamezia Terme, Lecce, Olbia, Palermo, Parma, Perugia, Pescara, Pisa, Rimini, Treviso, Turin and Verona. Areas such as Apulia, Calabria, Sicily and Sardinia have been opened up for tourism.

Arrival by air succeeded the age of train, which developed once routes through the Alps in the late nineteenth century linked the Italian system to the more general European one. I can recall the Paris-to-Milan night sleeper in the early 1960s and my younger brother, Stephen, falling out of his bunk with a heavy clunk in the middle of the night. When I first visited Turin to do archival research, in 1979, it was by means of train from London, ferry across the English Channel, train to Paris, metro across Paris, train to Turin. That in essence was the modernisation of an earlier, and far slower and more unpredictable, world of carriages and boats. Italy was framed for tourists by the experience of travelling to and from it. These difficulties make it easy to appreciate the sense of achievement felt on arrival.

There was no set route for tourists in the age before trains and steamships. It was possible to sail from Britain to Italy, but that was uncommon. Instead, the usual route was via France, although travel overland could be via the Low Countries and Germany. The Alps had to be crossed, or, alternatively, bypassed by sea, and there was no good road from France along the Mediterranean coast until the Napoleonic period.

Most tourists preferred the Alpine route. In the days before steamships, this was less hazardous and unpredictable than travelling by sea, and there were opportunities to break the journey. The most common route was from Paris via Lyons over the Mont Cenis pass to Susa (a pass in which tourists were carried across in the equivalent of a sedan chair by barefooted porters), and then on to Turin. As Savoy, like Nice, was part of Italy until ceded to Napoleon III of France in 1860, the frontier was at Pont-de-Beauvoisin.

TURIN

Tourists today tend to rush through Piedmont or, focusing further south, to miss it out, which is a mistake as it has much to offer, not least the wine. Destroyed by Hannibal in 218 BCE, *Taurisia* was refounded in 27 BCE as the Roman colony of *Augusta Taurinorum*. It became prominent when the House of Savoy moved the capital from Chambéry in Savoy in 1563. The royal palace was built in 1658. The city's centre very much bears the imprint of the architect Filippo Juvarra in the early eighteenth century and of the House of Savoy. Indeed, it is the most royal of Italian cities, as well as the most rectilinear in its street plan. In 1861, Turin became the first capital of Italy, only for the capital to be moved to Florence in 1865. Turin then developed as a major centre of industry, notably, from the end of the century, with the Fiat Company, which can be appreciated in the impressive *Museo Nazionale dell'Automobile*.

Many eighteenth-century tourists liked the city, its rectilinear street plan, and the spectacular new buildings erected under Victor Amadeus II (r. 1675–1730). Richard Pococke thought that the 'great part of this small city is exceedingly well built, wide straight streets, fine palaces'. William Freeman found Turin 'an handsome large town, the streets wide and the houses finely built . . . the Duke's palace is large and richly furnished and the apartments lie well together'. In 1763, Margaret, Viscountess Spencer noted:

> The chief things thought worth seeing at Turin were, the King's Palace, the great Theatre, a hunting house of the King's, and the Church of the Superga from whence there is a glorious view, bounded on one side by the Alps.

All can still be visited. In the mid-eighteenth century, Savoy-Piedmont had a population of 1,774,000, but only two towns, Turin and Alessandria, had more than 20,000 people.

GENOA

From Turin, there were several routes for tourists going into Italy: east to Milan or to Parma, or south to Genoa. There was no set course for the Italian section of the Grand Tour. Tourists were influenced by their point of arrival and of expected departure; the season of the year, which was important because of summer heat and due to the onset of malaria near Rome; the inclinations of their travelling companions; their desire to meet and accompany friends; and their wish to attend specific events. These were notably the opera in Reggio (in Emilia, not Calabria), Bologna and Milan, the carnivals in Naples and Venice, and religious, especially Easter, ceremonies in Rome.

From Turin, tourists travelled, via Asti and Alessandria, to reach the Mediterranean at Genoa. This was a city very different to Turin. There was no royal court to serve as a focus for activities, but Genoa had a richer history and more artistic treasures.

Founded in the fourth century BCE, Genoa was a major Roman

port. An independent city-state in the Middle Ages, Genoa, having contested the position with Pisa, the navy of which it defeated at sea at Meloria in 1284, became the major maritime power in the western Mediterranean. It also traded as far as Crimea. However, Genoa did not match its rival, Venice, in its gains, wealth, reputation or multiculturalism. Hit by the Black Death, Genoa was in decline until the sixteenth century, losing control of Sardinia and its Aegean possessions, and being controlled by the Visconti of Milan for a while.

In the sixteenth century, in response to the expansion of Turkish naval power, Genoa attached itself to the Spanish system and benefited accordingly, not least in its economic and fiscal penetration of the Spanish world, including the kingdom of Naples. Many palaces were built, including the *Palazzo Ducale* (the seat of government) and those along the *Strada Nuova* (now *Via Garibaldi*), as well as the Jesuit Church. These repay the attention of tourists today. An edict in 1576 consolidated the power of the oligarchy, suppressing the Assembly of the People.

The city slumbered in the seventeenth century and declined in the eighteenth, although the wealth existed to repair the city after it was damaged by a French naval bombardment in 1684 and in fighting in the War of the Austrian Succession in 1746–8. Corsica was sold to France in 1768. Annexed by France under Napoleon I and awarded to Piedmont by the Congress of Vienna, Genoa became important in the nineteenth as the port for Piedmont and a centre for shipbuilding. These elements became more important in the 'Long Boom' after 1945, only for the city's economy to hit serious problems in the 1970s recession.

Arriving in 1788, Charles Abbot, a lawyer, praised 'the magnificence of the natural situation of Genoa and the great abundance of immense palaces constructed upon a scale of grandeur unknown in other cities'. However, in 1729, the liberties of married women with their *cicisbei* (male companions not their husbands) caused surprise, while, in 1778, Philip Yorke was unimpressed by the police: 'murderers are frequently left to escape with impunity'.

MILAN

Many tourists went east from Turin to Milan, although they tended to find the countryside flat and uninteresting. Much of Lombardy belonged to the duchy of Milan, which was held by the Habsburg family from 1540 and, even more, from 1559 to 1859 with only short intervals. As elsewhere in Italy, crossing a frontier made it possible to make contrasts. John Mitford, a lawyer who was later an MP, Speaker of the House of Commons and 1st Baron Redesdale, readily discerned in 1776:

> the change of government. The Sardinian monarch, supporting with difficulty a large military establishment, and a numerous royal family, draws from the hands of the peasant every farthing which the ingenuity of the farmers of the revenue can find means to extort. The imperial family, supporting their state with less difficulty, do not bear so hard upon the inhabitants of the Milanese. A traveller soon perceives a labour bestowed upon the cultivation of the lands, a neatness in the various habitations, and a comfortableness in the appearance of the peasants which he does not meet with in Piedmont.

A major Roman centre, called *Mediolanum*, notably under the later empire (see the third-century frescoed Ansperto Tower), Milan had become newly prominent again in the Middle Ages. A leading industrial centre, Milan was one of the independent communes, but was brought under the rule of a series of families, particularly the Visconti and, after a brief republican interlude in 1447–50, the Sforza, before becoming first Spanish and then Austrian. Of the 1.1 million inhabitants of Lombardy in the 1700s, 130,000 lived in Milan, whereas the next three largest towns had a combined population of only 54,000.

Milanese society was regarded by British tourists as particularly agreeable and welcoming, but the city as lacking in great sights to rank with other major destinations. The comments of tourists are always interesting, but they do not generally capture political change.

This can be seen in their comments in the eighteenth century. Tourists and others understandably tended to focus on change from the French invasion of 1792 on, and, correspondingly, minimised that in earlier periods. In fact, there were important developments then. After replacing the Spanish Habsburgs, the Austrian Habsburgs dominated Italy from the 1700s to the mid-1730s, and northern Italy from the late 1730s to the mid-1790s. That, however, did not mean that there was a constant policy, however much later Italian nationalists were to suggest otherwise. The Emperor Charles VI (r. 1711–40) claimed to have inherited his Italian dominions as Charles III, his view of himself as the rightful king of Spain, and not to rule them by right of conquest. Partly as a result, he administered these dominions through the traditional Spanish Council of Italy, now based in Vienna, but still with Spanish and Italian members. His financial demands, however, were unpopular and may have contributed to the general support of the Milanese nobility and senior clergy for the administration of the duchy in 1733–6 on behalf of its conqueror, Charles Emmanuel III of Sardinia, ruler of Savoy-Piedmont. Indeed, the general absence of local assistance in Italy for Charles VI during the War of the Polish Succession (1733–5) was striking.

Under Charles VI's daughter, Maria Theresa (r. 1740–80), in contrast, a major attempt was made to increase government power in the Milanese. This reflected her financial problems, the widespread interest in reform in Vienna and, possibly, the greater prospect of successful change in Habsburg Italy after the loss to Spanish reconquest in 1734–5 of Naples and Sicily with their strongly entrenched nobility. In 1747, Gabriele Verri redrafted the Milanese laws. In 1749, the sale of offices was forbidden, and payments were fixed for services performed by officials. In 1755, the criterion for membership of municipal administrations was changed from noble status to wealth. The land survey of the Milanese was completed, and in 1760 the system of self-assessment for taxation was replaced by that of official assessment. Under the plenipotentiary ministers Count Giovanni Luca Pallavicini (1744–7 and 1750–4), Count Ferdinando Bonaventura von Harrach

(1747–50), Count Beltramo Cristiani (1754–8) and Count Carlo Giuseppe di Firmian (1758–71), who came from nearby Trent, the power and ambitions of the central government increased appreciably. Although local government was left in the hands of local citizens, a measure of uniformity and centralisation was introduced. The Council of Italy was abolished in 1757. Milanese revenues appear to have doubled between 1749 and 1783.

Although Maria Theresa's eldest son, Joseph II (the Holy Roman Emperor who was ruler of the Habsburg dominions in 1780–90), alienated the patrician reformers in Milan by replacing the traditional administrative and judicial system in 1786 with new administrative units and courts and a new code of law, these changes were accepted without violence. In 1784, Joseph noted, 'I have ordered the government [in Lombardy] to see in what manner they can adapt the principles established in the German provinces to local circumstances. The most important aim is certainly to improve and accelerate the administration of justice.'

After conquest by the French in 1796, the Austrians regained Lombardy in 1814, holding it until defeated by the French and Piedmontese in 1859. In the twentieth century, Milan strengthened its role as Italy's financial and industrial capital, as well as the centre of design and fashion. One testimony was Manchester's claim to be the 'Milan of the North', a view very few Milanese share.

FOOD AND THE TRAVELLER

The Italians pride themselves on their food, its quality and their preparation of it. Today, visitors to Italy know what to expect. This is not because Italy is noted for providing international cuisine. Indeed, it is far less affected by it than Britain or even France. Instead, foreigners are familiar with Italian food. Growing up in suburban London, 'going Italian' was the alternative to Chinese or Indian. Italian food is also favoured elsewhere. The first day

I visited Japan, I was taken to lunch in a provincial town, in an Italian restaurant.

Such an experience, of course, no more captures the variety, depth and quality of Italian cuisine than of its Chinese or Indian counterparts, although it provides familiarity. Moreover, this familiarity is encouraged by the degree to which in most (but by no means all) modern Italian restaurants, there is considerable continuity in what is provided, as well as far less 'fusion cooking' than in Britain or the United States.

In the past, however, travellers faced a far less predictable experience. Alongside shortages of food, there was variety. This was imposed by the seasons (still an element today) and by the difficulties in storing and transporting food and drink. Linked to this, there was also greater variety in methods of preparation and cooking. The absence of Italian restaurants abroad meant that this was new to travellers. Most had not, for example, encountered pasta. In 1788, Charles Abbot discovered ravioli in Genoa: 'It looks like boiled tripe.' John Swinton, who, in 1731, also first ate ravioli in Genoa, was more positive. Although a number of shops in London in the late seventeenth and early eighteenth centuries specialised in Italian food and drink, there were not the equivalent to French cooks in certain aristocratic households.

Travellers faced two food regimes. In rural areas, there was a lack of variety, and often a shortage of food. In towns, quantity and variety were less of a problem for those who could pay. In both cases for travellers, the use of olive oil and garlic was particularly different, and olive oil was greatly disliked. Moreover, travellers needed certificates to eat meat in Lent. The extent of regional variations was such that advice to eat particular local dishes was very helpful. Andrew Mitchell was very impressed by the mutton at Spoleto, John Swinton by the beef and veal at Genoa, Norton Nicholls by the veal and butter in Sorrento, and Sir John Fleming Leicester by the cream and butter in Turin.

Travelling East

From Milan, there were two major routes further into Italy in the eighteenth century. Tourists could go east, via Brescia, Verona, Vicenza and Padua, to Venice, or south-east, via Piacenza, Parma, Reggio and Modena, to Bologna. From Bologna, they could continue to Pesaro and the Adriatic coast, or, far more commonly, turn south across the Apennines, to Florence. Many of the cities of Lombardy, the Veneto and, in particular, Emilia-Romagna offered much to see. Parma and Modena were the capitals of duchies, and Bologna a major centre of artistic treasures. William Freeman found 'many palaces of Palladios' in Vicenza, while Henry, 2nd Viscount Palmerston was impressed by the amphitheatre at Verona, but Sarah Bentham was more critical about the latter: 'The want of sewers make the streets often very offensive from the stench of the filth.' At Padua, in 1793, she dined on 'some excellent small birds roasted for dinner, which they called thrushes – and sheeps brains fried in small pieces . . . sorrel generally made a side dish and meat pounded in a mortar and baked in a mould often appeared like a pudding and macaroni in a variety of forms'.

Paintings attracted much attention and tourists felt able to make critical judgements. In 1755, George, Viscount Villiers visited Cento specifically to see the Guercinos in the artist's birthplace: 'The Appearance of our Saviour to the Virgin after his Resurrection: the colouring is good, but the countenances want the proper expressions, and the drapery is very indifferent.' In 1788, James Robson condemned Giulio Romano's *Fall of the Giants* in the *Palazzo Te* in Mantua,

> which though esteemed an inestimable composition amongst the connoisseurs, I think loses all its grandeur and majesty in so small a room, by bringing such monstrous figures of human form, down to a level with the eye, nay even to the floor you walk upon. For want of height and distance, they lose much of their dignity of character, and so does the scenery that accompanies them.

He thus missed the point of the frescoes, which were designed to make the spectator feel involved in the giants' fate.

Some of the cities preceded the Romans, notably, as with Mantua, because this was an area of Etruscan settlement. These cities were transformed during the long centuries of Roman rule, while more were founded by the Romans, for example Pavia, Reggio and Verona. Cities that were capitals, Parma and Modena, benefited at the expense of those that lacked such power, notably Piacenza and Reggio. Parma gained a major palace under the Bourbons, but it tends today to be overlooked in favour of older sights, a pattern more generally true of the modern tourist experience of the Italian eighteenth-century. Other tourists today are more interested in car museums such as the Ferrari museums in Modena and Maranello.

Whatever the governmental structure, the cities of the region tended to be (and often still tend to be) where the notables lived. Taxes, rents and tithes supported manufacturing and trade in bringing wealth to the cities. The region suffered greatly from French conquest in the 1790s.

VENICE

Unlike most Italian cities, Venice was not a Roman city. Moreover, it did not have a propitious start as the city was founded in a malarial swamp. However, the ravages of the 'barbarian' invasions, first Hun (453 CE) and then Lombard (568), meant that refuge was a key element. Authority was ultimately wielded by Byzantium, but local assertiveness increased. In 697, Venice elected its first Doge, while, in 828, St Mark's corpse was smuggled out of Egypt becoming the basis for a basilica. St Mark replaced the Byzantine patron saint. For a long time thereafter, Venice was in the shadow of mainland powers, but naval strength and trade brought wealth and power. Helping Byzantium against Norman expansion led, in 1082, to the Golden Bull, under which Venetians were exempt from tolls and taxes in the Byzantine Empire. This was the basis of great wealth. The exemption and Venice's maritime ascendancy had to be maintained in the face of

Genoese opposition, but, after major struggles in the thirteenth and fourteenth century, success was obtained.

In 1297, the Venetian constitution was formalised with a largely fixed oligarchy protected by the Council of Ten, established in 1310 to maintain security. In 1355, a planned absolutist coup by Marin Falier, the Doge himself, was quashed and he was executed on the steps of the *Palazzo Ducale*. The city was run by its nobility who were divided between the dominant wealthy and their more numerous poor colleagues. Overseas territories provided poor Venetian nobles with posts and opportunities to plunder the local population. As a result, the loss of Venice's possessions in southern Greece to the far more numerous Turkish invading army in 1715 was blamed for an increase in noble crime and vice in Venice. There were too few ennoblements to keep the nobility open to merit and mobility. The decline of the Venetian nobility has been variously explained by historians, for example due in part to the infertility produced by gonorrhoea, for which there was no reliable cure, and/or to the marital strategies of the nobility: the stress on obligations to the family over individual inclination, a stress common to the nobility throughout Europe, produced in this context a pressure for younger brothers and sisters to remain unmarried, in order to avoid a spreading of family resources.

Public discussion of politics was banned, and notably with foreigners. Over many centuries, Venice was able to establish an empire at once overseas and on the *terraferma*. It centred on the *Palazzo Ducale* with the Doge's Apartments, *Collegio* (Council Room) and *Sala del Maggior Consiglio* (Grand Council Hall), which today hold paintings by Tiepolo, Tintoretto, Titian, Veronese and others.

Venice was noted as a centre of sexual activity. In *Much Ado About Nothing*, Shakespeare refers to Cupid spending 'all his quiver in Venice' (Act I, sc. i). Sacheverell Stevens wrote of the courtesans: 'the most insinuating, and have the most alluring arts of any in all Christendom'. Algernon, Earl of Hertford found 'beauties without numbers' in 1706.

A strong tradition of independence led to clashes with other authorities and, in 1606–7, Venice was placed under a papal interdict, while in 1618 a Spanish conspiracy to seize the city was quashed. In 1797, angry that it had refused to back him against Austria, Napoleon delivered on his promise, 'I shall be an Attila to the state of Venice.' Its independence was ended for good. After rule by Austria, France and, from 1814, Austria again, Venice became part of Italy in 1866.

Tourists continue to be impressed, as their forbears were, by its splendid treasures and spectacles. Lacking the spectacular sites of Rome and many other cities, Venice was not a city where tourists could commune with Classical civilisation. A medieval city, greatly embellished with the products of sixteenth-century Italian culture, Venice offered a different set of perceptions and, in many respects, was a distinct civilisation, certainly compared to the Classical-Baroque interaction of Rome. Leaving in 1793, Sarah Bentham presented a contrast that other tourists also noted: 'The day was calm and serene and the city of Venice looked beautiful rising from the sea, but there appears a great measure of meanness with magnificence in the buildings.'

Venice's alternative is Trieste, the capital today of the region of Friuli-Venezia Giulia. Part of this region was Austrian until captured by Italian forces at the very end of the First World War, and Trieste was Austria's Adriatic port, and a major centre. It did not look to Italy. In 1754, George, Viscount Villiers, George, Viscount Nuneham and William Whitehead travelled from Vienna via Graz to Trieste. From Trieste they found that 'The road is very mountainous along the shore of the Adriatic, and as rough and rocky as can possibly be conceived' until it entered Venetian territories.

Long cosmopolitan and dynamic, Trieste has not benefited from being a fag end of Italy. It suffers from huge economic problems that separate the once flourishing city from the rest of northern Italy. However, Trieste retains a café culture and cuisine that speaks to a more interesting recent past than that of most Italian cities.

CHAPTER FOURTEEN

Central Italy

To the south of the Lombard plain, the Apennine mountain chain long posed a major problem for travellers seeking to enter Tuscany or, further south, to move between the east coast and Rome. There were few passable routes across it, and these could be blocked by winter snows. The usual crossing was the road from Bologna to Florence. In 1792, Samuel Drew, a doctor, complained: 'I was much dissatisfied with these Apennines, a long lingering ascent up barren sandhills . . . dreary, barren and worthless.'

FLORENCE

Florence to eighteenth-century tourists stood for art. Indeed, for William Lee in 1752, it was 'a most agreeable place abounding in every species of virtue that one can wish to see, sculpture, painting and the arts carrying to the greatest perfection'. The Renaissance treasures of the Uffizi were regarded as the single most important artistic site in Italy. George, Viscount Nuneham went repeatedly to the gallery in 1756. Florentine married women were regarded as particularly accommodating. Anne Miller noted: 'The ladies in general of easy virtue, and their expenses light.' Tourists did not tend to note such features as the 'popolo' outside the Pitti Palace crying out for 'Bread and Work' and singing menacing songs, or the military precautions taken in the 1720s against the threat of trouble over high taxes.

'CICISBESHIP'

'The Princess Borghese [Agnese Colonna] was so kind as to put him a little upon his haunches, by putting him frequently upon her own. Nothing dresses a young fellow more than having been between such pillars, with an experienced mistress of that kind of manège.' Philip, 4th Earl of Chesterfield was clear of a value of travel for his illegitimate son, Philip Stanhope. Horace Mann, the long-standing envoy in Florence, commented on how 'an English traveller frequently deranges the whole harmony of "cicisbeship"', by which a married woman had a male companion, a 'cavalier servente', who accompanied her to social gatherings, and was sometimes her lover. The system provided opportunities for a relationship that was in accordance with local customs. Thomas Pelham of Stanmer (1728–1805), later 1st Earl of Chichester, had a long affair in Florence in 1750 with the married Countess Acciaioli, who then took another British lover. Her married friend Maria Serristori had had a relationship with Charles, 2nd Marquess of Rockingham in 1748–9, while Francis, 10th Earl of Huntingdon (1729–89) was in 1755 reputed to be the lover of Marchesa Capponi, 'the flower of Florentine nobility and, as I've heard, lewdness'. 'Cicisbeship' contributed to the idea that Italian women were highly sexed. Francis Drake saw the practice as a way to learn the language.

Probably founded as an Etruscan village, Florence was also allegedly established by Julius Caesar. A relatively minor settlement for a long time, Florence became a self-governing free town in the twelfth century while conscious of the need to compete in historical myth with older, nearby Fiesole. In 1434, Cosimo de'Medici, from a family that acted as bankers including to the popes, took power, a situation sustained by his successors in the face of much local opposition. In 1497, however, the city fell under the sway of Girolamo Savonarola, a puritanical Dominican monk, although his call for repentance proved of limited traction. Savonarola was executed in 1498, and, after a republican interlude, the Medici returned, ruling continually from 1530 (from 1549 residing in the Pitti Palace) until 1737 when the line ran out.

The Grand Duchy of Tuscany then passed to Francis Stephen of Lorraine, the husband of the Habsburg heiress Maria Theresa. He sought to modernise Tuscany, although that did not have the same meaning as today. For example, an edict of 1748 greatly cut back the ceremonies to be observed in burials and mourning, an example of the determination of many governments to control religious practices and to limit expenditure on them. Nobles who had died were to be exposed in churches upon a pall with twelve wax candles around their corpse, citizens being permitted only six candles. Non-citizen commoners were denied funeral ceremonies and were to be carried to their graves with four flambeaux only. Pope Benedict XIV (r. 1740–58) condemned the edict for infringing clerical jurisdiction.

Francis Stephen's second son, Leopold, made major changes in Tuscany where he was Grand Duke from 1765 to 1790. The ideas of Cesare Beccaria proved particularly influential. In his *Dei Delitti e delle Pene* (*Of Crimes and Punishments*, 1764), Beccaria attacked the death penalty and torture, emphasised the value of prevention, and called for consistency in sentencing and a rational and utilitarian approach to justice. In Tuscany, where an attempt in the 1740s to revise the legal code had been rejected, there were major changes. The appointment of judges was reformed, the imprisonment of debtors abolished, the publication of judgments instituted, and precise regulations for sentencing and the conduct of cases introduced. In 1786, the death sentence was abolished and the right of the accused to a defence was recognised.

After the Napoleonic interlude, the Habsburg family lost Tuscany to the new kingdom of Italy in 1860. Florence served as its capital from 1865 until Rome gained the position in 1871.

SIENA

To the south, the city of Siena was Florence's main rival and a setting of archaeological difference, with Siena characteristically Gothic and Florence Renaissance. Probably of Etruscan origin, Siena developed as a Roman city and flourished in the Middle Ages as a manufacturing centre. The Council of Nine dominated the city in the Middle

Ages, and their role is commemorated in the museum in the *Palazzo Comunale*, with Ambrogio Lorenzetti's fresco cycles, *Allegories of Good and Bad Government* (c. 1338–40). These depict the results of such governments in terms of city environments, and are relevant for Italy today. Siena, however, lost out repeatedly to Florence, becoming its possession, a verdict settled in 1559: the Sienese do not see this as a verdict settled for today. The *Palio* (silk banner), a series of parades and horse races, brings medieval traditions into the present.

Pisa

Pisa, a major port under Rome, was another independent state, which flourished in the Middle Ages only to be defeated by the Genoese in 1284 and brought low by Florence, which annexed it in 1406. John Mitford wrote in 1776 of reaching

> the decayed town of Pisa . . . The buildings erected as receptacles for the victorious galleys of the republic, are now made the stables of the prince. The loss of liberty has reduced this once flourishing town from one hundred and sixty thousand inhabitants to about fifteen thousand.

In contrast, the wealth and independence of medieval Pisa left impressive works from that period, notably the large cathedral begun in 1064 with the fruits of a successful attack on an Arab fleet off Palermo the previous year. The main facade was not completed until the thirteenth century, while the elliptical dome was added in 1380. Construction of the Baptistery, an unusual round one, started in 1152, while that of what became, due to poor foundations, the Leaning Tower next door began in 1173. Pisa was sufficiently significant to have a distinctive Pisan-Romanesque architectural style.

Lucca

Founded by the Etruscans, Lucca had a conventional trajectory via Roman town to a self-governing city in the twelfth century. Despite coming under the control of Pisa in 1314, the city regained and, behind its still-impressive wall, kept its independence from 1370, fighting off Florentine attack in 1429. Relations were often difficult. For example, the outbreak of animal disease in Lucca in 1715 led Florentine troops to close the border to livestock traders. In 1805 Napoleon put Lucca under his sister, Elisa. Hilaire Belloc described Lucca as 'the most fly-in-amber little town in the world'. The city wall around the old city remains in excellent condition and there is a tree-lined footpath along the top that gives fine views.

The old city reflects the reused nature of many such places. In the *Piazza Anfiteatro*, named after the Roman amphitheatre, can be seen parts of that structure that were used for the walls of medieval houses. The Roman forum became the site of an eighth-century church that, in turn, was replaced by a Romanesque one built from the eleventh to the fourteenth centuries.

To Rome

Pressing south many tourists felt that they had entered another Italy. Charles Abbot commented in 1788: 'The hills grow scabrous and dingy. The soil is brown and stony and the mean olive tree and stinted vine give it an appearance of poverty.' The approach to Rome across the Campagna in what is now the region of Lazio dismayed many, Abbot writing: 'Wretched, barren, sandy country all the way to the very gates of Rome – hardly an attempt to cultivate. . . We were repeatedly exclaiming all the way upon the miserable appearance of the country.' To Sarah Bentham, the city 'appeared to be situated in a desert'. Abbot also noted a change in the wildlife, with lizards appearing frequently upon the walls. There was, moreover, a border to cross, and one that helped define a very different realm: the Papal States. This was the only Church state in Italy as the prince-bishopric of Trent was part of the Holy Roman Empire, but it was a very large one.

ROME

Rome was the goal of many tourists, the furthest point of numerous tours, and both reality and symbol of what was desirable about foreign travel. In a culture dominated by the Classics, Rome was the focus of interest. Charles Cadogan, who visited the city in 1784, thought:

> it is as impossible for a person to dash through it, as it is for him to fly. I stayed a full fortnight there, and only had time to get just such a general idea of the numberless wonders both of modern and ancient times, as to determine me to spend 2 or 3 months there before my return to England.

One of the major attractions of Rome was that it was readily possible to find such edification. Like Paris, Rome had the facilities a tourist could wish for, but the greater importance of tourists to the economy of the city helped ensure that they played a more central role than in Paris. Tourists purchased paintings and antiquities, hired antiquarians and sought artistic advice. Rome's cosmopolitan artistic colony made the city's marvels readily accessible to the tourist, and the range that it had to show increased the city's appeal. Rome offered Classical and Baroque sculpture, architecture and painting, and many tourists treated it as the cultural goal of their travels. As artistic and cultural interests and appreciation shifted, this helped ensure that Rome was culturally recreated. Rated with Michelangelo and the Classical world at the beginning of the eighteenth century, the works of Bernini declined in reputation, while the excavation of Classical sites in and near Rome in the second half contributed to a major re-evaluation of taste.

Interest in ancient Rome did not contribute to the reputation of modern Italy. Henry, 2nd Viscount Palmerston commented in 1764: 'It is deplorable to see what havoc has been made by barbarians and bigots. Little has escaped but what by its vast solidity had withstood their efforts or by being converted to some use has served the purposes of avarice.'

Rome's ecclesiastical character, including its role as a pilgrimage centre, did not provide the British (with the exception of Jacobite residents and Catholic tourists) with many points of access, and the activities of the papal court were less interesting to them than those of lay courts elsewhere. Rome, however, offered a range of secular entertainments, including the carnival and the annual fireworks, fired from a *girandola* (revolving wheel) that created the impression that St Peter's was glowing red.

Rome was also the base for trips into the surrounding countryside, notably to visit Classical sites, for example along the Appian Way, or scenic towns in the hills, particularly Frascati and Tivoli. Tivoli reflected the levels of antiquity Italy can offer. The hilltop town, a retreat from summer heat, holds the Villa Adriana, the summer residence of the Roman Emperor Hadrian where he had some buildings constructed on the model of foreign works that had impressed him, and the Villa d'Este, a convent turned into a pleasure palace by the wealthy Cardinal Ippolito d'Este, a would-be pope and the second son of Alfonso I, Duke of Ferrara, in 1550. The volcanic crater-lakes of Albano and Nemi in the Alban hills were another attraction. The appeal of the region in part stemmed from the lustre of the paintings of Claude Gellée, better known as Claude Le Lorrain (1600–82), who provided golden blues in sky and water and golden stone to light his landscapes with their timeless pastoral scenes. In contrast, few then, or now, go to visit Etruscan remains although there are important seventh to sixth century BCE necropolises that can be visited, notably at Cerveteri and Tarquinia.

Less attractively, Rome has been the centre of state power. The consequence has been periodic town-clearing for the benefit of a new political order. Mussolini was to get much of the blame, but he was scarcely the first. Under his Liberal predecessors, the *Vittoriano*, popularly known as the Wedding Cake, built in memory of Victor Emmanuel II, was built too large in order to dominate existing skylines, as well as using marble from northern Italy that clashed with the local stone. The Palace of Justice was another disproportionate work.

Mussolini declared in 1934: 'After the Rome of the Caesars, that of the Popes, there is today a Rome, the Fascist Rome, which, simultaneously ancient and modern, demands the adoration of the world.' He wanted the city to be a parade ground for Fascism. Much destruction took place to create new perspectives such as the *Via della Conciliazione*. One of the most known and popular meeting points in Rome is still 'in *Piazza Venezia* under the Duce's balcony', not least due to the number of buses from different lines that stop there.

In contrast to that of Mussolini, the first two Romes had each lasted for many centuries. Imperial Rome had moved its centre of power to Constantinople and had been unable to see off the 'barbarians', but the papacy proved able to take over the secular reins in Rome, and that position gave them the basis for ecclesiastical independence from Byzantium. Yet, that process was periodically hindered by the intervention by powerful rulers, and often with dire consequences. From 1309 until 1377, the papacy was under French control in Avignon, a papal possession in southern France, and the subsequent 'Great Schism' ended only in 1417, and Pope Martin V (r. 1417–31) did not enter Rome until 1420. He had to restore much of the infrastructure. The early sixteenth century brought both the permanent loss of part of the Catholic world in the Reformation and the brutal sack of Rome in 1527. The French Revolutionaries and Napoleon were to bring fresh turmoil.

The city itself suffered differing forms of neglect. Papal administration in the nineteenth century did not deal with floods and malaria; the Liberal regime (as in Naples) moved the poor away from central areas in order to build grandiloquence; and Fascism, with its own grandiloquence, followed before a new system, with its own social claims, and corruption, notably in building permissions, but also in much else, began. As with imperial and papal Rome, Rome as the capital of independent Italy saw massive building. The population, under 200,000 in 1870, rose to about 460,000 by 1900. The new state required a large bureaucracy and Rome was its centre. Under Mussolini, ceremonial architecture was crucial, notably Classicism in the centre and the more modernist building for the *Esposizione Universale di Roma* (EUR) planned in the suburbs for the twentieth anniversary of Fascism coming to power, a plan that fell victim to the collapse of Mussolini's dreams. Moreover, public housing was built to house the workers on the site of older neighbourhoods. Much of Rome was built or rebuilt from the late 1940s, notably with the hasty expansion of the suburbs in the 1950s and '60s. There has been some improvement over the last two decades, but there has also been the inability to cope with the city's rubbish problem and its incessant corruption.

CHAPTER FIFTEEN

The *Mezzogiorno* (Land of the Midday Sun, or South)

NAPLES

The history of southern Italy has been dominated by Naples and its region, and the same is true of the tourist experience. Legend claims that the city was founded by traders from the Greek island of Rhodes in about 680 BCE. In turn, *Neapolis*, founded by Greeks from Cumae (Cuma) in 474 BCE, became the settlement, only for the Romans to take over in 326. The underground remains of the Roman city are both extensive and dramatic.

After the fall of Rome, Naples became a duchy, under Byzantium and then independent, only to be captured by the Normans in 1138. Having been ruled by the Hohenstaufens, the city was captured by the Angevins in 1266 and the Aragonese in 1442. The latter led to rule by Spain. Naples was the most populous city in Western Europe in the early seventeenth century, and one expanding physically with the new *Quartieri Spagnoli* (Spanish Quarters).

However, by then, there was a major gulf between the development and prosperity of the northern Italian economy and the situation in the south. Northern Italian economic development was pronounced after *c.* 1100, with a relative decline of the southern economy especially after 1282. The degree and chronology of southern relative decline is controversial, especially with regard to Sicily, but the mainland kingdom of Naples was in freefall politically, and to an extent economically, during the fourteenth century, and increasingly an economic colony of the north. Northern merchants controlled its trade, and the south became a source of raw materials and foodstuffs for the north. The origins of the *Mezzogiorno* problem certainly go back to the later Middle Ages. The problem was readily apparent in the sixteenth and seventeenth centuries, and thereafter.

As a reaction to foreign rule, whether by Angevins, Aragonese or Spaniards, public ritual was designed to build up cohesion and community. Public ritual was also an expression of identity intended in part to supersede serious divisions, as with the 1585 bread riot. The number of patron saints rose and their celebrations helped structure the year. Founding myths also played a role, not least in order to demonstrate greater longevity than Rome. The Masaniello rebellion in 1647 against Spanish rule was crushed the following year.

Naples had an Austrian interlude in 1707–34. Charles VI recognised the privileges of Naples in 1713, 1717 and 1720, and did little to alter the administration or to limit noble privileges, both there and elsewhere in Italy. However, Austrian rule was swept aside by war. Naples had a French Revolutionary interlude in 1799, and a Napoleonic one in 1806–15, but was ruled by a cadet branch of the Spanish Bourbons from 1734, before being conquered in 1860 and thus forcibly taken into the new kingdom of Italy in 1861.

Naples has been a political, social and economic challenge to the Italian state ever since. Reform initiatives repeatedly go nowhere as was amply seen earlier in the eighteenth century. An attempted reform of the law courts failed in 1735, as did moves towards legal codification in the 1740s. Popular clamour greeted an edict of 1777 announcing the cutting of subsidies on olive oil for the citizens of Naples, and, fearing riots, the authorities suppressed the edict. Unwilling for political reasons to increase urban taxes or to cut urban subsidies, such as those on bread in Naples, many of the eighteenth-century governments pushed up rural taxes. The inability of the Neapolitan government to supervise local customs offices led to their corruption and domination by local interests. The government operated in an information vacuum. For example, it found itself unable to procure an accurate notion of the state of its woods because of unreliable and contradictory reports.

The lively sun-drenched harbour views that eighteenth-century tourists purchased from painters, especially Pietro Fabris and Claude-Joseph Vernet, captured the attraction of the city, which was generally presented as more fluid and sunlit than Venice. In his *Travels through Italy* (1766), John Northall referred to 'the usual method of going to see Naples before the weather grew hot'. Norton Nicholls wrote in July 1772 of a city where 'the nights are so delightful and the days so hot' that no one slept at night: 'I am become a greater friend of the moon than the sun.' Winter visitors found the air delightful.

However, the Neapolitan progressive economist Antonio Genovesi had a very negative view of the city. Although the 1726 estimate of 70,000 licensed prostitutes and 60,000 living by the law in Naples may be questioned, it underlines the role of the city as a service centre. In 1800, of the nineteen cities of the world believed to have had a population of over 300,000, Naples came fourteenth, as the fourth in Europe, behind London, Constantinople and Paris.

The appeal of Naples continues and wandering about the city can be more relaxing than wandering about Rome. However, tourists today may note the troops deployed to maintain a semblance of law and order. Locals sometimes claim that membership of the Camorra reflects poverty and youth unemployment. In reality, the state has devoted much investment to the region, and a more reasonable explanation relates to its ungovernability. This can take many forms, including driving cars at speed through red lights.

NAPLES REGION

Nearby tourist destinations were among the major attractions for tourists, as they continue to be. Vesuvius was one of the great sights. A natural phenomenon close to a city, it was (and is) possible to visit it more easily than other volcanoes. Mary, Lady Palmerston saw an eruption in 1793: 'The mountain continually throwing out red hot stones which resemble the stars of a number of rockets.'

The Classical sites west of Naples, especially Solfatara, Pozzuoli, Posillipo, Baia, Lake Miseno, Cumae and Lake Avernus, had long dominated the attention of travellers, and they continued to do so in the first half of the eighteenth century. In particular, the Phlegraean (Burning) Fields, an area famous from the Classical past as the entrance to Hades, the Underworld, was made exotic and mysterious by the hot springs, steam jets, sulphurous gases, mysterious caves and brooding craters that reflected its volcanic origins. Lord William Mandeville discovered in 1719 that 'the crust of earth upon which one walks, is generally not above a foot thick, and wherever one pierces it, as I did in several places with my sword, there comes out a sulphur-ous vapour, hot enough to burn one's hands or feet, if in the way'. Virgil, who had lived at Naples, and other Classical authors were read as sources by tourists.

In the second half of the eighteenth century, attention shifted to nearby excavated sites, notably Herculaneum, Pompeii and Paestum. The first two were covered as a result of the destructive eruption of Vesuvius in 79 CE, but, by 1738, the theatre of Herculaneum had been excavated while official excavations at Pompeii were begun in 1748. These discoveries of Roman remains played a major role in the development of European taste, in part thanks to the relative inaccess-ibility of Classical remains across much of the Mediterranean. Joseph Spence wrote of Herculaneum, which he visited in 1741: 'I have walked two miles about the streets of it . . . one is obliged to creep almost all the way through narrow passages . . . with two or three smoking flambeaus before you . . . It is a journey fitter for a mole than a man.'

The Greek remains at Paestum on the Gulf of Salerno, south of the Amalfi peninsula, became a major tourist site and were profoundly influential for the formation of neo-Classical taste. Paestum was the Latinisation of *Poseidonia*, a Greek colony founded in about 600 BCE by colonists from Sybaris in Calabria. The town had been abandoned under the Romans because of malaria. The building of a road across the site led to the discovery of the temples there in 1746. Its pastoral setting, with grazing animals, cypresses and oleanders, helped make Paestum seem a real version of the idyllic Classical scenes depicted by painters. Henry, 2nd Viscount Palmerston remarked: 'I was more struck with them than anything I ever saw except the first view of

Rome . . . one is struck with the idea of Palmyra, Baalbeck, or some of those forsaken places' in the Middle East.

Although cost-savings today have affected the extent to which the grounds can be toured, the Royal Palace of Caserta remains a great site, and one that is not sufficiently visited by foreign tourists. Begun in 1752 by Luigi Vanvitelli, this was to be a Neapolitan Versailles and included a dramatic sequence of fountains and basins closing with a monumental cascade. There was nothing to equal the palace in Britain and the cascade could not be matched at Versailles.

FURTHER SOUTH

Much of mainland Italy is south of Paestum, but it tends to this day to receive relatively little attention, although tourism to Apulia has become far more popular of late, being greatly helped by cheap flights to Bari. Italian tourism in the region is long-established, but has led to a lot of ugly and sprawling coastal developments, as in Calabria.

The environment of the far south is particularly bleak, with the mountains more prominent and the plains less significant (other than in Apulia) than elsewhere in much of Italy. Tree cover is less, and the summer heat greater. The natural beauty is starker as in mountainous, but largely deforested, Calabria. A counterpart is the *peperoncino* (chilli) that is important to the local cuisine and that is celebrated in the annual *peperoncini*-eating contest held in the town of Diamante.

Agriculture employs a relatively high percentage of the population, but does not produce much of a surplus and is heavily dependent on the protection regime offered by the European Union's agricultural subsidies. Regional development schemes have brought factories and roads, notably the *Autostrada del Sole*, but have failed to engender significant growth or youth employment. There has certainly not been a convergence with the rest of the country comparable to that of the American south, nor growth to match that of resource-poor Japan. On a long-term pattern, emigration has been considerable. This has led to the abandonment of many houses and of some settlements. They are sometimes sold for very little in order to encourage people to come and live there. Many towns and cities appear down at heel, for example Cosenza.

The south did not benefit from Liberal hegemony after unification, or from the industrial boom in the north during the First World War, nor from a post-1918 protectionism that disproportionately helped the north. The *Cassa per il Mezzogiorno* (Fund for the South), established with state funds in 1950, created scant new employment, but served short-term political concerns. Linked to growth in the north, the relative per capita income of the south (as a percentage of that of Italy as a whole) in fact fell, from 70.14 per cent in 1951 to 65.05 per cent in 1969, and in the 1960s, the percentage of national industrial jobs fell to 15 per cent. By 1970, nearly half the nation's unemployment was in the south. 'Cathedrals in the desert', the large industrial plants that reflect and attract investment, did not bring much benefit for the southern economy, as there were few regional economic linkages and few local jobs generated. The social fabric in the south has been hit hard, which helps in the continual vitality of organised crime. So also with politics, at once often corrupt as well as ineffective. The state-dominated *Cassa* did not allow for autonomous modernisation in southern Italy.

Of the few eighteenth-century tourists who went further south than Paestum, most were interested in Classical architecture and archaeology. Visiting Apulia in the late 1710s, George Berkeley was very impressed by the Baroque architecture of Lecce, a city of great antiquity, with important Roman remains. The city had been extensively renovated, with exuberant Baroque works by Francesco Antonio Zimbalo (1567–1631) and Giuseppe Zimbalo (1620–1710), both of whom were born in Lecce. Giuseppe's works included the *Prefettura*, the facade and altar of the Basilica of Santa Croce, and the bell tower of the cathedral.

One of the most successful novels set in southern Italy, *The Castle of Otranto: A Gothic Story* (1764), a brooding mystery, was written by Horace Walpole, who visited Naples in 1740 as part of his tour, but did not in fact travel on to Otranto. Indeed, in 1786, when Lady Elizabeth Craven gave Walpole a drawing of the castle there, now the

Castello Aragonese Otranto, made the previous year by Willey Reveley, the delighted Walpole responded: 'I did not even know that there was a castle of Otranto.' As a reminder of the grimness of the past, the *Cappella dei Martiri* in the eleventh-century cathedral includes the skulls and bones of many of those beheaded in 1480 by the Turks when they conquered the city for refusing to convert to Islam. The cathedral also holds a twelfth-century mosaic with a tree of life balancing on the back of two improbable elephants.

A different legacy from the past was mentioned in 1781 by Sir William Hamilton, the British ambassador (and husband of Nelson's later mistress, Emma), who witnessed a survival of the cult of Priapus on a visit to Isernia. Wax votive phalli (penises), dedicated to the local saints by the women of the town, were brought back to London by Hamilton and given to the British Museum. These then formed the illustration for the frontispiece of Richard Payne Knight's *An Account of the Remains of the Worship of Priapus* (1786).

CHAPTER SIXTEEN

The Islands

SICILY

The largest island in the Mediterranean, and an island of great agricultural and commercial potential, Sicily has been more the subject, even victim, of history than its maker. This has had a major impact on its society and culture. Indeed, to a degree, Sicily has been a canvas on which other cultures have been painted. For example, there has been extensive debate as to whether Sicilian is a dialect of Italian (itself an unclear designation) or whether it is a language of its own, as a regional Romance. The former is more politically correct, at least from the perspective of the Italian state, but the latter appears more accurate.

Competed over between Carthage and Greek cities, notably Syracuse, which was founded from Corinth in 734 BCE, Sicily was taken over by Rome, Byzantium, Arabs and Normans, before going to the German House of Hohenstaufen, the Angevins and the Aragonese (Spaniards). After Charles V (Charles I of Spain) visited the island in 1535, the next ruler to do so was Victor Amadeus II of Savoy-Piedmont in 1713. Briefly under the House of Savoy from 1713, Sicily was conquered by Spain in 1718.

Ruler in that brief period, Victor Amadeus sought administrative reform and sent officials from Turin to help his viceroy, Count Annibale Maffei, implement his policy. Information was a key dimension. Victor Amadeus ordered censuses of mulberry and olive trees in Sicily and tried to build up a register of roads and bridges, as well as seeking to limit the bearing of arms. He had scant success and the local élite offered little resistance to the Spanish invasion.

Due to Spain's isolation and defeat in the war of 1718–20, Austria then ruled Sicily from 1720 until it was conquered by the Spanish Bourbons in 1734 and became a major part of the new independent kingdom established in Naples under Charles VII, a son of Philip V of Spain. Seigneurial rights increased under the Bourbons, peasants being forced to use nobles' mills and olive presses, and prevented from competing with them. The flour excise was politically acceptable as it fell most heavily on the poor. The role of the nobles in the assessment and collection of taxes enabled many to minimise their liabilities. Hunting became a prerequisite of the wealthy, their methods – falcons and dogs – being accepted, while those of the poor – netting and traps – were prohibited. Spanish was commonly the language of official documents until the 1760s and in part the language of bureaucracy into the nineteenth century. In 1860, Garibaldi conquered the island from the Neapolitan Bourbons.

Whereas many regions of Italy were divided between a number of independent or semi-independent states for much of their history, this was not the case with Sicily over the last millennium. This created tension within the island, notably the long-standing rivalry between the cities of Palermo and Messina.

As has been made clear repeatedly in this book, Sicily has suffered from misgovernment, and notably so over the last two centuries. To the outside world, it is known most for the Mafia, which is both fair and unfair. Most Sicilians are in no way involved with the Mafia, but all are affected by its abusive corruption and the malaise it has brought or encouraged. This malaise is reflected in illegal, inadequate, delayed or non-existent development, as in the suburbs of Palermo. Protection rackets operate as a tax on the economy, and, if violence is not currently so much to the fore as in the recent past, corruption remains an abiding problem.

To go to Sicily was long an adventure for tourists. Distance ensured that relatively few tourists visited the island, which had a semi-civilised reputation. Messina was the last city in Western Europe to have an outbreak of the plague, in 1747. The impressive Arab-Norman style of medieval Sicily, as in the cathedrals in Palermo and Monreale, and the *Chiesa di Santa Maria dell'Ammiraglio* in Palermo, was not of interest until the nineteenth century, but now is much appreciated.

The island could be reached by sea from Naples or Rome, although Sir James Hall was 'stormstayed' a week in Stromboli on the way there in 1785. Henry, 2nd Viscount Palmerston, however, decided not to go in 1764 as 'I should most likely have lost much of the pleasure by sickness'. Travelling through Sicily in 1788, Thomas Watkins ate a 'cake of bread, whiter than any' he had hitherto come across. He also wrote that the pigeons 'in this country are so much superior to any I have ever eaten, that they seem a different kind of bird. They are as large as grouse, as fat as ortolans, and so agreeable to the taste, that if some of our English epicures were to feed upon them, they would probable eat themselves to death.' He wrote of Syracuse, 'the environs of the city produce thirteen kinds of excellent muscadine wines; all of which we had before us every day'. Some tourists sailed round the island. The most popular destination was Etna and, after that, the Greek temples. The first excavations on the theatre at Syracuse were carried out in 1756, while the temple was restored in 1781, and the dramatic temples of Juno and Concord at Agrigento in 1787–8.

Travelling in Sicily was not easy. In 1792 Charles, Lord Bruce and Thomas Brand found 'great hospitality' at Palermo, but were unimpressed by the quality of Sicilian roads and of accommodation outside the cities: 'There is not a wheel in the whole country, the roads are mere paths for a single mule and the few huts scattered round are as bad as Hottentot kraals.' Brand wrote of the road to Segesta: 'it is rugged and precipice or mud'. Charles Cadogan toured the island and climbed Etna in 1785, reaching the crater at dawn having walked eight miles over the snow.

SARDINIA

Long-inhabited, eventually by the Bronze Age *nuraghic* people, Sardinia was, in part, under Phoenician control from the ninth century BCE, with the Carthaginians taking over, to be followed by the Romans who gained control in 237 BCE after the First Punic War. Independent kingdoms in Sardinia in the Middle Ages resisted Pisa and Genoa, but the Aragonese overcame Sard resistance in the fourteenth century, albeit with considerable difficulty. Spain was then in control until the island was conquered in 1708. Briefly, from 1708, Austrian and then, from 1717, Spanish again, Sardinia was under the House of Savoy from 1720, an unwelcome exchange for Sicily. In 1759–73, the courts and administration of the island were changed in order to integrate it into Savoy-Piedmont. Several feudal jurisdictions were suppressed, the independence of the religious orders was limited, and the curricula of the universities established at Cagliari and Sassari were changed radically in order to educate officials for local administration.

Sardinia never enjoyed the vogue that resistance to French annexation in 1768 briefly brought in Britain to Corsica, and it lacked important Classical sites. British warships had helped in the conquest of Sardinia in 1708, but subsequently it was largely ignored, as well as having a serious problem with malaria. From the 1960s, Sardinia has been a major destination for beach holidays.

Much of its interior richly repays visiting, not least as it offers a different Italy to that of the more frequently visited sites. Alongside the *nuraghe*, which, in the case of the *Nuraghe Su Nuraxi*, provide Sardinia's only World Heritage Site, there are the settlements that were successively Phoenician, Carthaginian and Roman, especially Nora and Tharros. Of the medieval towns, Alghero provides much evidence of its medieval past. It is also typical of Sardinia in drawing together various cultural influences, although the mix is different to those in Sicily. Thus, the Catalan-Gothic style is much in evidence in Alghero.

AEOLIAN ISLANDS

Italy's coastline is scattered with many islands, some famous tourist sites, such as Capri and Murano, and others less well known. Each of those that is inhabited has its history. The cross-currents of the past are particularly apparent in islands, and notably so in the Aeolian Islands north of Sicily. The most important, Lipari, has been settled since the fourth millennium BCE. Its archaeological museum highlights the significance of trade in the Classical world with its display of shipwreck cargoes. Aside from the masses of amphorae, there are also impressive land finds, from the Neolithic period on.

COFFEE CULTURE

Outside Italy, coffee culture is in part authenticated by the Italian example, with Italian chains, baristas and terms of great significance. The espresso, *ristretto*, *lungo*, macchiato, cappuccino and latte all look to Italy. There is a long tradition of coffee in Italy. In part, this is due to its location. The initiative came from further east, from coffee in the Islamic world, and notably its import into the Mediterranean from Yemen and its port of Mocha. Coffee culture, in evidence in Venice in the sixteenth century, was taken further when the quantity of coffee coming into Europe rose in the seventeenth century as a result of new production in the West Indies. Mass production in Brazil followed in the eighteenth century, and coffee became far less expensive. Moreover, Italy did not have a tea culture to match that of Britain. *Espresso* technology began in the nineteenth century, with the commercial machines produced by Gaggia from 1948 making this process more consistent and providing an image of modernity. Italians prefer a different coffee to Americans, taking the course of stronger roasts. In 1943–5, American soldiers diluted espresso with hot water to try to make the coffee to which they were accustomed. Today in Italy there is often less coffee per shot than in British espressos. The cups used and measures provided are smaller than in Britain or the United States.

Conclusion

The list of Italian islands was much longer in the past, but historical weaknesses led to the loss of many islands, including Cyprus (1570–1), Crete (1669), Corsica (1768), the Ionian Islands (1797), Malta (1798) and Rhodes (1943). This serves as a reminder of the lack of fixed boundaries for Italy, a lack that it is easy to overlook. The *Risorgimento* appeared to many to become ridiculous with the seizure of Fiume in 1919. Moreover, it could overlap with an imperialism that saw Italy wish to dominate the Mediterranean, notably the eastern Mediterranean; imperialism directed not only against other imperial powers – Britain and France – but also against Greece, Yugoslavia and the Arab world.

These points have considerable weight, but there is also the role of chance and contingency that makes Trieste and Trent parts of Italy, but not Corsica, Nice or Rhodes. In particular, it is interesting to consider how far Italy would be differently shaped had it remained neutral in the last world war. Spain, as a result, kept the Spanish Sahara until 1976 and keeps Ceuta and Melilla today, while Portugal still has the Cape Verde Islands.

In this, as in much else, there is a reminder of the extent to which Italy's history was not fore-ordained. That, however, is not a conclusion that has suited successive regimes and ideologies. Linked to this dislike has come the use of the past to proclaim visions of inevitability. Such constructed histories, literally constructed in the case of buildings that memorialised both past and present as a prospectus for the future, can be found in all countries. They appear more urgent, however, in the case of Italy because its statehood was long non-existent or precarious, and its people divided. Linked to this has come a lack of clarity over how far the nation and state did, and should, spread. In part, this is a reflection of the desire to develop support for unification, but there was also a carry-over of imperial, indeed universalist, aspirations from Italy's past. Most clearly expressed with imperial Rome and the papacy, there were also strong imperial aspirations on the part of the Liberal governments of unified Italy and their Fascist successor.

Since the overthrow of Mussolini in 1943, Italy has struggled to find a role, one that can provide meaning and overcome its strong divisions. The new government formed in 1943 and the Resistance were dependent on the Allies and divided. Economic growth, the first post-war panacea, morphed into European unity, while many Italians came to put their trust in alternatives that did not rise to the challenge, for example Euro-Communism and, even worse, Berlusconi's *Forza Italia*. Today, there is a measure of political, even national, exhaustion born of broken hopes and the retreat to family and friendship groups. The Italians deserve much better, but there is scant sign that they will get it. The return to pre-Napoleonic small states might be an option, but there is little traction for it, and the process to which it could occur is obscure.

Selected Further Reading

Three categories of book deserve attention: histories of Italy, histories of Europe and the accounts of contemporaries. The most accessible English-language histories of Italy are the Longman series, although D. Carpanetto and G. Ricuperati, *Italy in the Age of Reason, 1685–1789* (1987), needs replacing. There are other more impressive volumes, including Massimo Pallottino, *A History of Earliest Italy* (1991) and Paul Ginsborg, *Italy and its Discontents: Family, Civil Society, State, 1980–2001* (2001). Ciro Paoletti's *A Military History of Italy* (2007) is very useful.

For histories of Europe, the Macmillan series is the best. *Sixteenth-Century Europe* (1993) by Richard Mackenney, an Italy specialist, is particularly good. Roger Collins's *Early Medieval Europe, 300–1000* (1991) is valuable. Outside the series, see in particular Tony Judt, *Postwar: A History of Europe since 1945* (2005). On geography, Brian Blouet, *The EU and Neighbors. A Geography of Europe in the Modern World* (2008). For the accounts of contemporaries, John Stoye, *English Travellers Abroad, 1604–1667* (2nd edn, 1989); Bruce Redford, *Venice and the Grand Tour* (1996); and Jeremy Black, *Italy and the Grand Tour* (2003).

Index